T0098164

# BLAZING AHEAD

Benton MacKaye, Myron Avery, and the
Rivalry That Built the Appalachian Trail

**JEFFREY H. RYAN**

Appalachian Mountain Club Books
Boston, Massachusetts

AMC is a nonprofit organization, and sales of AMC Books fund our mission of protecting the Northeast outdoors. If you appreciate our efforts and would like to become a member or make a donation to AMC, visit outdoors.org, call 800-372-1758, or contact us at Appalachian Mountain Club, 10 City Square, Boston, MA 02129.

outdoors.org/publications/books

Distributed by National Book Network.

Front cover photograph courtesy of the Appalachian Trail Conservancy
Cover design by Jackie Shepherd
Interior design by Eric Edstam

Library of Congress Cataloging-in-Publication Data

Names: Ryan, Jeffrey H., author.
Title: Blazing ahead : Benton MacKaye, Myron Avery, and the rivalry that
   built the Appalachian Trail / Jeffrey H. Ryan.
Description: Boston, Massachusetts : Appalachian Mountain Club Books, [2017]
   | "Distributed by National Book Network"--T.p. verso. | Includes index.
Identifiers: LCCN 2017026463 (print) | LCCN 2017032770 (ebook) | ISBN
   9781628420647 (ePub) | ISBN 9781628420654 (Mobi) | ISBN 9781628420630
   (paperback)
Subjects: LCSH: Appalachian Trail--History. | MacKaye, Benton, 1879-1975. |
   Avery, Myron H. (Myron Haliburton), 1899-1952. | Conservationists--United
   States--Biography.
Classification: LCC F106 (ebook) | LCC F106 .R93 2017 (print) | DDC 974--dc23
LC record available at hhps://lccn.loc.gov/2017026463

The paper used in this publication meets the minimum requirements of the American National Standard for Information Sciences-Permanence of Paper for Printed Library Materials, ANSI Z39.48-1984. ∞

Outdoor recreation activities by their very nature are potentially hazardous. This book is not a substitute for good personal judgment and training in outdoor skills. Due to changes in conditions, use of the information in this book is at the sole risk of the user. The author and the Appalachian Mountain Club assume no liability for accidents happening to, or injuries sustained by, readers who engage in the activities described in this book.

Interior pages contain 30% post-consumer recycled fiber.
Interior pages and cover are printed on responsibly harvested paper stock certified by The Forest Stewardship Council®, an independent auditor of responsible forestry practices.
Printed in the United States of America, using vegetable-based inks.

10 9 8 7 6 5 4 3 2 1     17 18 19 20 21

FSC
www.fsc.org
MIX
Paper from
responsible sources
FSC® C005010

*To Benton and Myron,*
*who both saw the view and invited us up.*

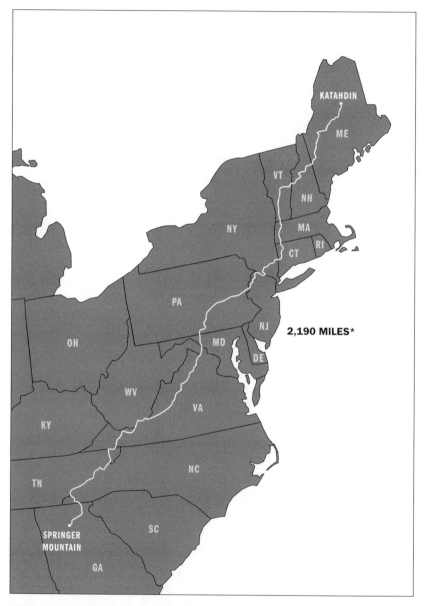

The Appalachian Trail, 2017. Map by Rachel Carter, Puelle Design.
*Appalachian Trail Conservancy, appalachiantrail.org/home/explore-the-trail

# CONTENTS

## Part 3: The Duel and Its Aftermath

# ACKNOWLEDGMENTS

I SUPPOSE MOST WRITERS ARE PRONE TO MONTHS-LONG DEEP DIVES INTO research followed by intense, caffeine-fueled drafting sessions. For this book, I practiced both to the extreme. Between research engagements, I bounced around the country behind the wheel of my 1985 VW Vanagon camper, one of my favorite places to formulate and refine the big ideas that become the building blocks of the final product.

The Papers of the MacKaye Family are housed in the Rauner Special Collections Library on the Dartmouth College campus. The collection is extensive and extremely well organized (a blessing indeed). The days I spent at the library were extremely productive. Thank you to Jay Satterfield, special collections librarian, and your staff for your assistance and encouragement.

I am also indebted to Larry Anderson, who wrote the definitive biography *Benton MacKaye: Conservationist, Planner, and Creator of the Appalachian Trail.* His book goes into greater detail regarding the MacKaye family, Benton MacKaye's non-AT related projects (which were many), and the period between his rift with Myron Avery and MacKaye's death.

For Myron Avery research, the archives of the Maine State Library were indispensable. The Maine Author Collection in Augusta houses virtually all of Avery's correspondence—thousands of letters in all. The letters provide enormous insights into Avery's drive and reach into nearly every facet of building and promoting the Appalachian Trail. A special thank you to research librarian Melanie Mohney of the Maine State Library for her enthusiasm and support for this project.

I cannot express enough thanks to the Appalachian Mountain Club for getting behind this book from the beginning. Special kudos to Becky Fullerton, AMC's archivist, who pointed me to several valuable sources, books project editor Shannon Smith, copyeditor Dayna Isley, and editorial director Jennifer Wehunt, who all offered valuable edits and insights along the way.

Finally, I am indebted to every library I visited in the past year that still offers quiet places to work and to the staff of the Residence Inn of Fort Collins, Colorado, who honored my three-day "do not disturb" request at a critical juncture.

# CAST OF CHARACTERS

*In Order of Appearance*

**James Sturgis Pray**

James Sturgis Pray was president of the American Society of Landscape Architects. In 1908 he succeeded Frederick Law Olmsted Jr. as chairman of the School of Landscape Architecture at Harvard University. Pray's influence on Benton MacKaye was significant. He introduced a then-18-year-old MacKaye to hiking and the art of trail construction. Both would help inform MacKaye's grand idea, the Appalachian Trail (AT).

**Major William Addams Welch**

Major Welch gained prominence as an engineer in the 1890s and early 1900s. In 1912, the newly formed Palisades Interstate Park Commission hired Welch as an assistant engineer. Within two years, he became its chief engineer, overseeing a number of impressive initiatives, including the design and construction of the Storm King Highway along and above the Hudson River. In 1923, Welch designed the famous AT insignia with the interlocking "A" and "T." In 1925, he became the first chairman of the Appalachian Trail Conference (ATC). He would later serve on the Southern Appalachian National Park Commission.

**Raymond H. Torrey**

Raymond H. Torrey was an enormously influential journalist. In the 1920s, he wrote a weekly column in the *New York Post,* "The Long Brown Path," which extolled the benefits of hiking and listed local hikes. Torrey introduced the general public to the AT in 1922. He helped build the first section of the AT. He negotiated easements with property owners and organized volunteer trail-building efforts.

In 1935, Torrey became disillusioned with the direction Myron Avery was taking the ATC (particularly as a result of proposals ATC passed that year). He stepped back from involvement with the AT and died three years later of a heart attack at age 58.

### Arthur "Judge" Perkins

Arthur Perkins, a lawyer and judge from Hartford, Connecticut, was one of the earliest proponents of Benton MacKaye's vision of a 2,000-mile-long, uninterrupted footpath through the Appalachian Mountains. Perkins was chairman of ATC in the 1920s. A leader in the early days of hiking and mountaineering clubs, he often served as unofficial mediator between the irrascible Myron Avery and Arthur C. Comey.

### Arthur Coleman Comey

Arthur C. Comey studied landscape architecture under the tutelage of Frederick Law Olmsted Jr. at Harvard University. Upon his graduation in 1907, Comey worked in park design and then shifted to urban planning as his primary focus. He was among the first urban planners to advocate building-height restrictions as a means of retaining a city's character.

Comey was as committed to hiking as he was to planning. He was an active board member of the Appalachian Mountain Club, serving on a number of committees. He also served as chairman of the New England Trail Conference.

### Robert L.M. Underhill

Robert Underhill left his mark in the varied fields of mountaineering, mathematics, and literature. He was pursuing first ascents in the Alps by age 22 and received a Ph.D. from Harvard by age 27. He taught both mathematics and philosophy at the school. Underhill and his wife, Miriam, were avid mountaineers. Their climbing adventures included expeditions to Europe, the Wind River Range, the Sierras, and Grand Teton. In 1960, Robert and Miriam completed winter climbs of all of the 4,000-footers in the White Mountains. In 1928, Robert Underhill became the editor of *Appalachia*, resurrecting the publication after a hiatus to transform it into the leading mountaineering journal of its day.

## Walter Greene

Walter Greene was one of the most fascinating individuals among the dozens that led to the creation of the Appalachian Trail. Greene was born in Baltimore in 1872. He was a Broadway actor who appeared in seventeen plays between 1901 and 1936. He spent his winters in New York City at The Lambs Club (an organization that hosted actors, songwriters, and others involved in the theatre) and the rest of the year mostly by himself in a cabin on the shores of Sebec Lake, Maine, or tramping around the woods between his cabin and Katahdin. A chance meeting with Myron Avery in the woods led to Greene's involvement in building the AT through Maine.

## Harry Davis

Harry Davis was a Maine fire warden and co-owner of the Eastern Gum Factory, a manufacturer of spruce gum in Monson, Maine. Based on Davis's woodland skills and local knowledge, Myron Avery hired Davis to build a section of the AT from Bald Mountain to Long Pond, Maine. The deal subsequently went sour, and Walter Greene stepped in to take on the task.

## Ronald Gower

Ron Gower was an active member of the Appalachian Mountain Club for many years. He held a number of positions, including heading the Rock Climbing Committee. Gower and Myron Avery initially worked well together, but their relationship soured over time. Gower led a highly publicized AMC trip through Maine's 100-Mile Wilderness, which may have raised Avery's hackles. Over time, Gower took exception to Avery's non-collaborative style, exemplified in internal memoranda Gower sent to the leadership of AMC.

## Dr. John Frank "J.F." Schairer

Trained as a mineralogist and a petrologist (study of the composition and structure of rocks), Frank Schairer's love of the mountains earned him an invitation to the first meeting of what was to become the Potomac Appalachian Trail Club (PATC). He was the organization's first treasurer and then served as its supervisor of trails. Schairer was part of the small work crew that blazed the AT south from near Harpers Ferry, West Virginia. Under

Schairer's supervision, PATC built some 260 miles of the AT between 1928 and 1932.

## Dr. Shailer Philbrick

A graduate of DePauw University and Cornell University (where he received his Ph.D. in geology) and later a faculty member of Johns Hopkins University, Shailer Philbrick played an integral role in mapping the Appalachian Trail in Maine. Philbrick's dissertation on the rock formations in the vicinity of Monson, Maine, required him to prepare his own topographic maps of the region. His maps became the basis for those used in the first *Guide to the Appalachian Trail in Maine*. He also made a number of scouting and trail-blazing trips on behalf of MATC and ATC.

## Helon Taylor

Only Walter Greene and Myron Avery played a larger role in the development of the Appalachian Trail in the Pine Tree State than Maine Game Warden Helon Taylor. A woodsman and explorer by nature, Taylor often took it upon himself to see that the trail was scouted, blazed, and built right the first time. Taylor notably closed the gaps between Bigelow Mountain and Sugarloaf and between Bigelow Mountain and Saddleback. He also scouted and built a 7-mile trail over the Bigelow Range. Taylor would go on to become the supervisor of Baxter State Park, where a trail up Katahdin bears his name.

## Charles W. Blood

Charles Blood was a tireless contributor to the Appalachian Mountain Club. He helped build and maintain a number of trails, including participating in the work crew that scouted and built Webster Cliff Trail between 1912 and 1914. He also wrote a number of articles for AMC's esteemed journal, *Appalachia*. Blood served on a number of AMC committees, including the Guidebook Committee for 1916's *Guide to Paths in the White Mountains and Adjacent Regions*. He became president of AMC in the 1920s. His lukewarm support for Katahdin-region projects, such as a separate trail guide covering the area and the AT's extension into Maine, rankled Myron Avery.

# INTRODUCTION

THE APPALACHIAN TRAIL AND I FIRST MET ON THE SLOPES OF KATAHDIN, Maine's highest mountain, in the early 1970s. I was one of several youngsters taking part in a church group hike. The sight of the white paint marks on the trees and rocks showing I was on the "AT"—the path to the summit and back—are still indelible.

Closing in on 50 years later, I find that the trail is still urging me on. I've hiked all 2,190 miles once (it took me 28 years starting in 1985) and parts of it as many as five times. I've worked as a trail maintainer, helped build a couple of lean-tos on "the Trail," and written two books about it (this being my second). And I'm not done hiking yet.

I never exactly took the Appalachian Trail for granted. But, in the last few years I've begun to hike with a greater appreciation for those who created it.

There are days I look out from a ridge top knowing how lucky I am to be soaking in a panorama with only hawks and clouds above me. Even more often, I feel how fortunate we are to have thousands of miles of trail to explore and to be reasonably sure our great-grandchildren will be able to explore them, too. That's why I set out to write this book.

I had heard that Benton MacKaye and Myron Avery made the Appalachian Trail possible. I even knew a little about each man. But not nearly enough. What I wanted to know is where the idea for the trail came from and just how it got built in such a remarkably short time. For that, I'd have to do a little digging.

What I found was two men driven by completely different motivations.

Benton MacKaye came from a family of big thinkers. Yet, unlike some in his family—notably, his father—Benton's dreams were grounded in observation and measurement. It was MacKaye's need to understand and articulate how natural and human-made systems worked that spawned the idea for the Appalachian Trail—the backbone of a much larger plan designed to encourage people to move back out of America's cities to establish working communities in proximity to the great footpath.

The only part of MacKaye's plan that was adopted was the building of the AT itself. For that, almost all credit is due to Myron Avery—a man who saw a job that needed to be done and took it on with zeal. His extraordinary drive enabled him to expand, build, promote, and publicize the trail largely through his sheer determination and at a time when success never seemed to be assured. Yet, as we see, his great accomplishments also came at great expense.

In the end, the dreamer needed the doer and the doer needed the dreamer. It is hard to fathom that a trail visited by at least 4 million hikers per year would have ever been built otherwise.

## A Note About Avery's Letters

When it comes to the correspondence of Myron Avery, the customary research practice of extracting sentences or phrases isn't so simple. Unlike the writings of Benton MacKaye, where kernels of thought could be extracted while retaining their context, Avery's letters are often (understandably) constructed like lawyerly arguments. Thus, I often found it difficult to extract phrases without losing the context of either his comments or his emotional outbursts. For those reasons, I chose to present selected letters in their entirety. Extracts have been left with their original spelling and underlining to maintain authenticity.

# PROLOGUE

*Mountains of Promise*

THE IDEA TO CREATE THE APPALACHIAN TRAIL DIDN'T COME AS A BOLT of lightning, a eureka moment, or anything of the sort. Like many great ideas, it flared up from the embers of a fire that had been built by those who came before.

To trace the first explorations of the great mountain chain requires a journey back to the settlement of New England. The earliest inhabitants of the White Mountains were the Abenaki, whose presence is most felt today in the names of the region's mountains, rivers, and streams: Passaconaway, Chocorua, and Kancamagus among them. The high peaks' significance to the native people is captured in the lore of Chief Passaconaway himself. According to at least one legend, "He was carried to Mount Washington in a sleigh drawn by wolves, whence he rose toward Heaven in a chariot of fire."[1]

The native people who inhabited the region before contact with outsiders did not summit the mountains, believing the peaks were sacred spaces reserved for gods. There existed in indigenous culture a reverence and, indeed, trepidation of the summits that future European settlers would eventually climb for sport. As Russell M. Lawson writes in his book *Passaconaway's Realm*, "The native peoples—the Penacooks, Sokokis, Ossipees, and Pequawkets of the Saco, Androscoggin, and Pemigewasset rivers—who lived in sight of 'the place of the Great Spirit of the forest,' Agiocochook [Mt. Washington], were in awe of the mountain and its noisy spirits, in awe of Passaconaway; they humbled themselves before his power and refused

---

1   Frederick W. Kilbourne, *Chronicles of the White Mountains* (Boston and New York: Houghton Mifflin Company, 1916), 4.

to ascend the mountain, preferring to live on the bounty that cascaded from above."[2]

The first ascent of Mount Washington is credited to a man who hailed from Exeter, New Hampshire, named Darby Field. In 1642, he made at least one ascent of the mountain—and likely two. Field described a treeless summit plateau where he collected stones he thought were diamonds, "but they were most crystal."[3] These early explorations were followed by a steady progression of visitors, spurred by descriptions of the mountains. Their names also grace the maps of the region: Belknap, Tuckerman, Cutler, Bartlett, Evans—and, in 1816, Dr. Francis Boott, for whom a spur on Mount Washington is named.

While an increasing number of people were intrigued by the prospect of seeing the White Mountains, it wasn't until 1819, when Ethan Allen Crawford and his father built a trail from Crawford Notch to the summit of Mount Washington, that the idea of climbing the Whites really began to take root. The newspapers carried accounts of the new trail, which brought even more visitors to the region, including Henry David Thoreau (who climbed Mount Washington twice and also climbed Mount Lafayette), Ralph Waldo Emerson, and Nathaniel Hawthorne.[4]

The establishment of railroad service—west from Portland, Maine, in 1851 and then much later from Boston—led to a boom in visitors and in the construction of grand hotels and less-grand boarding houses to serve them. As the author Frederick Kilbourne wrote, "By reason of the attractiveness of their location, the excellence of their cuisines, and the general high degree of comfort and convenience provided, [the hotels] have done much to draw visitors to the region and to increase and to spread far and wide that high repute of White Mountain hospitality which the older hotels had created by the excellence of their accommodations." The grandest hotel of all was the Mount Washington Hotel in Bretton Woods. Featuring Tiffany glass windows, electric lighting designed by Thomas Edison, and the handiwork

---

2   Russell M. Lawson, *Passaconaway's Realm: Captain John Evans and the Exploration of Mount Washington* (Hanover and London: University Press of New England, 2002), 2.

3   Kilbourne, *Chronicles of the White Mountains*, 21.

4   Ibid., 77.

of 250 Italian stone masons, it was built in the remarkably short period of thirteen months and opened for business in late July of 1902.[5] (The hotel still stands and is now known as the Omni Mount Washington Resort.)

Most of the trails initially built in the White Mountains were not created with loop hikes in mind. That is to say, the trails led up to a viewpoint or mountain summit and then back down via the same route—in many cases, a route that began on the grounds of a hotel or in proximity to a train station. This began to change with the advent of hiking clubs.

The first organized hiking club in the United States was the White Mountain Club, founded in 1873 in Portland, Maine. Its inaugural excursion turned out to be the club's most arduous. The six-member party, led by the club's president, Edward Elwell, climbed Mount Carrigain between August 29 and 31, 1873. Upon their return, Elwell wrote, "We never heard of it before and hope never to see it again. It is none of your civilized mountains, the resort of tourists, made easy of ascent by foot-path, carriage ways and railroads, like your tame Mt. Washingtons [sic]."[6] According to the Museum of the White Mountains, the White Mountain Club disbanded in 1884.

Three years after the founding of the White Mountain Club, "a little group of earnest men met at the Massachusetts Institute of Technology in Boston, at the call of Edward C. Pickering," who had sent invitations to 50 recipients who might be "interested in mountain exploration."[7]

The purpose and mission of the organization founded that evening in 1876 was set forth in the first issue of its journal, *Appalachia*, that same year: "The Appalachian Mountain Club was organized in 1876 for the advancement of interests of those who visit the mountains of New England and adjacent regions, whether for the purpose of scientific research or summer recreation."[8] In the following decades, the Appalachian Mountain Club would advance the exploration of New England's mountains in word and in deed. The organization envisioned and built trails, backcountry huts,

---

5   Ibid., 331.

6   "Ascent of Mt. Carrigain," *The Portland Transcript*, September 13, 1873.

7   *Appalachia* 14, no. 1 (December 1916): 6.

8   *Appalachia* 1, no. 1, (June 1876): 81.

and shelters that enabled an ever-increasing number of visitors to enjoy the mountains.

One of the club's most influential trail proponents was Sturgis Pray, who, upon graduation from Harvard University in 1898, had gone to work for the Olmsted Brothers landscape architecture firm in Boston and would become the head of Harvard's landscape architecture program.[9] Pray was an old hand at exploring the mountains of New Hampshire. By 1903, he was advocating for the Appalachian Mountain Club to connect the disparate trails in the White Mountains to create one great network of interconnected trails—an idea that was adopted and developed with great success.

Pray's reverence for the mountains and his trail-building acumen gained him a considerable following. One of the most enthusiastic participants in Pray's explorations and trail-building adventures was a man eight years his junior, a fellow Harvard alumnus named Benton MacKaye.

9   Larry Anderson, *Benton MacKaye: Conservationist, Planner, and Creator of the Appalachian Trail* (Baltimore: Johns Hopkins University Press, 2002), 43.

*Part 1*

# THE DREAMER

# CHAPTER 1

## *Family of Optimists*

IN SEPTEMBER 1893, A 15-YEAR-OLD BOY FROM MASSACHUSETTS SPENT THE day touring the Chicago World's Fair. He had traveled there by train with two of his older brothers to visit their father, who had spent the previous year onsite, preparing for the event. The family patriarch, Steele MacKaye (pronounced Mack-eye), had arrived in Chicago in 1892 with a plan so great it could not be contained within the fairgrounds. He proposed and received backing to build the largest auditorium in the world, which he called the Spectatorium.

For two days, the MacKaye clan (father Steele and sons Benton, Percy, and James) explored the spectacular fair designed by the world's greatest building and landscape architects: Daniel Burnham, Frederick Law Olmsted, and John Wellborn Root among them. The fair's promenade, with its gleaming white neoclassic buildings, created a stunning vision of dreams realized.

The three sons took turns pushing their father's wheelchair through the fairgrounds (Steele had been severely affected by the stress of preparing for the exhibition) then paused at the site of the Spectatorium. Steele's dream, the most ambitious theatre project ever attempted, had gone bankrupt. The enormous half-built structure stood silent. In a few days, "The Spectatorium, the large pile of steel and wood at the north end of the World's Fair grounds,"[1] would be torn down to be sold as scrap iron.

Steele blamed the failure of the Spectatorium on "poor weather, labor troubles, a tight money market and an article declaring the project a failure."[2]

---

1   "Tearing Down the Spectatorium," *Chicago Tribune*, October 7, 1893.

2   Ibid.

The backers of the project lost more than $800,000—a staggering sum in late-1800s America.[3]

The next day, the MacKaye brothers went home to Massachusetts. They never saw Steele again. The strain of the Spectatorium's imminent failure took him down. He died in February 1894 at age 51, leaving his wife, Mary, and seven children (including his second-youngest, Benton) to face financial uncertainty.

The Spectatorium hadn't been Steele's only ambitious scheme. It was simply the most spectacular. Steele's career as an actor, dramatist, inventor, innovator, and teacher subjected the family to many changes of fortune. His unconventional ideas were at times capable of making more money than they lost—bringing Buffalo Bill Cody to Broadway being one of his heralded successes. Steele's contributions to the American stage were profound, if not profitable. He dreamed big and set his plans into motion, taking the results as they came. As early as 1883, Steele was touting the need for acting schools, a revelation in its time.

> *If public schools are a benefaction, if medical schools, divinity schools, schools of music, are essential to the progress of mankind, then dramatic schools should have been established long ago, because there is no one factor in civilization that wields a more powerful influence than the art of the theatre.*[4]

As one academic put it, "Even though Steele MacKaye was a financial failure in establishing his acting schools, he was possibly the most important single influence in the establishment of formal actor training in the United States."[5]

Steele and his family had settled in Shirley, Massachusetts, following a burdensome financial decline in 1888, when Steele's father, James, died of a stroke in Paris at the age of 83. James MacKaye had amassed a fortune during

---

3   Ibid.

4   Percy MacKaye, "Steele MacKaye, Dynamic Artist of the American Theatre: An Outline of His Life Work," *The Drama: A Quarterly Review of Dramatic Literature*, no. 4 (November 1911): 138–161.

5   Richard A. Mangrum, "Steele MacKaye: Inventor–Innovator" (master's thesis, University of North Texas, December 1970), 20, digital.library.unt.edu/ark:/67531/metadc131337/.

The MacKaye home in Shirley, Massachusetts, circa the 1940s. Photo: Courtesy of Dartmouth College Library.

his lifetime. He had held several prestigious positions, including sharing a law partnership with Millard Fillmore, the thirteenth president of the United States; co-organizer of American Express Company; secretary of Wells Fargo and Company; and president of American Telegraph Company.[6] Upon his death, James MacKaye's fortune was bequeathed to his son (and Steele's half-brother) William. But the MacKaye family tragedies were not over. William died of a stroke only days after his father. According to William's wishes, his inheritance passed to his wife, Maggie, who also died unexpectedly, just a few weeks after her husband. Upon Maggie's death, James MacKaye's considerable fortune passed into the hands of her relatives. Thus, Steele's side of the family would never receive a penny from his father's estate. [7]

Fortunately, Benton MacKaye's second-oldest sibling, William Payson MacKaye, had made an investment that would put a roof over the family and would serve as a source of stability for decades to come. Will, as he was known to the family, had followed his father's path and become an actor. At

---

6  Larry Anderson, *Benton MacKaye*, 12.

7  Ibid.

Shirley Center School, 1892. Thirteen-year-old Benton MacKaye is on the far right, with his hand on a classmate's shoulder. Photo: Courtesy of Dartmouth College Library.

19 years old, he was already part of a successful troupe and earning enough to make a $100 down payment for the cottage in Shirley, an area the family had visited in 1878. In July 1888, the MacKaye clan downsized out of necessity. With the family inheritance gone, they moved from New York City to Shirley, which would become the most important place in Benton MacKaye's life.

The holiday season of 1888 would be the last the family would spend together. Will died of respiratory failure in January 1889.

For the next few years, the nomadic MacKayes would spend summers in Shirley and winters in Washington, D.C., where sons Harold and James held government jobs with the U.S. Patent and Trademark Office and U.S. Census Bureau, respectively. Steele MacKaye's income was hardly predictable (he was often on the road, trying to cobble together his next money-making scheme), but his sons were able to help financially. Percy MacKaye moved in with his two eldest brothers, while the rest of the family stayed at a rooming house.

The winters in Washington, D.C., had a profound influence on Benton MacKaye's trajectory. In 1890, on his first full day in the nation's capital, 11-year-old Benton's Aunt Sadie took him and two of his brothers to the Smithsonian Institution and the Agricultural Museum. That evening they attended a lecture on South America by the president of the National Geographic Society.[8]

Before long, Benton became a regular visitor to the Smithsonian. The staff let him set up his camp stool in front of exhibits so he could make sketches of birds and other wildlife. Eventually, the staff allowed Benton into the research wings to meet scientists and view parts of the ornithology collection not on display to the general public. He also continued to attend lectures with his family.

Seventy-nine years later, Benton would look back at those exciting days in Washington, D.C., and acknowledge their influence on his life. In 1893, at 14 years old, he began taking "sylvan jaunts" around Shirley, where his aim would be "to conserve game and maintain their generations."[9]

> "Expeditions" I called them. Why this imposing title? Well, I had at one time been in Washington, frequenting the Smithsonian Institution. There I met collectors from distant lands and saw the product of their expeditions. I had laid eyes on illustrious explorers, including [Admiral Robert E.] Peary, starting on his first voyage to the Arctic; and [John Wesley] Powell, recounting his own and the white man's first voyage ever through the Grand Canyon of the Colorado. Then and there I caught the bug. Why shouldn't I, my own self, be an explorer?—up there in my own homeland, containing the "canyons of the Squannacook [River]?"[10]

So much more than woodland walks, Benton's expeditions were thorough explorations of the land within a 4-mile radius of the MacKaye cottage.

---

8   Ibid., 18.

9   Benton MacKaye, *Expedition Nine: A Return to a Region* (Washington, DC: The Wilderness Society, 1969), 1.

10  Ibid., 1.

In the wake of his father's death, which Benton took particularly hard, they also helped him discover nature's restorative qualities.

Sketchbook in hand, Benton mapped everything from the bushes on the banks of Mulpus Brook to the life cycle of the forest. His maps and drawings of plants and animals were exquisite, his powers of observation profound for a young teen. He explained the formation of rivers and hills. He categorized Shirley Center as a planned town: "a direct descendent of the moot-hill, the planned village of A.D. 400."[11]

Benton's favorite expedition, number 9 of 20, was the one that led him to the summit of Shirley's Hunting Hill. The variation in habitat was enough to fill his naturalist's notebook, and the last paragraph of his book *Expedition Nine*, a retrospective of his childhood ramblings, indicates that this exploration, more than any other, filled him with something else: the excitement and possibilities inherent in discovering a life's calling.

> *The view from Hunting Hill yet scans a land fertile for expeditions. For jaunts for would-be explorers and naturalists. We can't all be great explorers, like Peary and Powell, nor great naturalists, like Thoreau and Humboldt. But anyone who prizes the sights and sounds of nature in action, whether robins at the window or muskrat in the stream, or bog born of the ages, such a one is, within his measure, an explorer and naturalist. And his job is cut out for him; to make of his region, as seen from its highest hill, a place for taking expeditions.*[12]

This fascination with geographic features and planned communities would drive Benton MacKaye's private and professional life for more than eight decades. It would lead him to become one of the first and most influential regional planners, and it would spawn the idea that became his greatest plan of all.

---

11   Ibid., 4.

12   Ibid., 45.

# CHAPTER 2

## *Into the Mountains*

THE MACKAYES WERE A FASCINATING LOT. IN WRITING A PIECE FOR A publication called *The International*, famed journalist Walter Lippmann noted the family's assets were vast and accumulated through "a love of the joy of life." "That is the MacKaye inheritance—novels, plays, poems, acting, scientific research, 'fun, fishing and philosophy' for all the world—a creative strain, strikingly like the criminal strain. It is in their blood."[1]

Benton had certainly inherited "the creative strain" of his forebears. Unlike his father or his brothers, Percy the playwright and Will the actor, whose searches for fulfillment were illuminated by the bright lights of center stage, Benton was fueled by exploration, observation, and insights.

Although he studied hard to gain acceptance to Harvard University, staying there presented a consistent challenge. According to the MacKaye biographer Larry Anderson, "He scraped by in French, failed Spanish, and ended his freshman year on probation because of his lackluster academic performance."[2]

Not surprisingly, Benton put most of his undergraduate energy into learning everything having to do with earth sciences. As the new century dawned, great philosophical debates were taking place. The American landscape was being redefined in the wake of the industrial age. Ever-evolving manufacturing capabilities and expanding factories, changing transportation systems (the rapid change from trains to cars was already underway), and the growth of cities were all driving the need for significant social reform. Concepts such as sustainable land use and planned cities that would retain a sense of both

---

1    Walter Lippmann, "All the MacKayes," *The International* 3, no. 2 (January 1911): 29.

2    Larry Anderson, *Benton MacKaye*, 31.

communal scale and economic vitality were subject to vigorous debate. One of Benton's favorite weekly activities was attending a roundtable discussion led by the professors of Harvard's geology department. The spirited debates took concepts out of the classroom, giving them a depth of meaning that appealed to Benton's strengths as an observer of the world around him.

After his freshman year at Harvard, Benton and a couple of classmates spent two weeks exploring the White Mountains of New Hampshire. Climbing the summit of Mount Tremont at dawn after a terrific rainstorm was a moment the then-18-year-old would always remember: "The grandest sight I ever saw was now before me, nothing but a sea of mountains and clouds."[3]

Later in the same trip, Benton and friends would ascend Mount Washington and traverse the Presidential Range to Crawford Notch. Much of their hike was by way of what would become the Appalachian Trail (AT). It's easy to imagine that walking atop those giants of the Northeast directly influenced the grand idea Benton would unveil to the world 24 years hence.

When Benton MacKaye graduated from Harvard in 1900 with a Bachelor of Arts degree[4], he did so with the countenance of someone who was not sure how to apply what he had learned. While camaraderie and adventure were motivating factors for tramping around in the woods and ambling above the treeline, they didn't seem to be pointing him toward a career. Yet Benton was always cataloging his experiences through the eyes of a geologist and naturalist. He would come to find out that by doing what he loved, he was in training all along.

The post-graduation trip he took with his brother Percy and his close friend and Harvard schoolmate Horace Hildreth was the most ambitious of all. In July 1900, the trio set out from Shirley to climb Vermont's major peaks, from south to north. First traveling by train, then on foot—using dirt roads and carriage paths or bushwhacking, when necessary—the young men reached the summits of Haystack Mountain, Stratton Mountain, and Bromley Mountain in the first week. At that point Percy departed, but not before he handed his brother a notebook as a gift. Inside the cover he had written,

---

3   Benton MacKaye, diary, 16 August 1897, Papers of the MacKaye Family, Rauner Special Collections Library, Dartmouth College.

4   Harvard University did not require students to declare "majors" until later in the twentieth century. (Source: Harvard University Archives communication to the author.)

Benton MacKaye on the day of his graduation from Harvard University, June 1900. Photo: Courtesy of Dartmouth College Library.

"Benton—record your details—and Keep a-peggin away." [5] The two Harvard alums thus continued their hiking adventure. Over the next week, the pair climbed three of the four highest peaks in Vermont: Killington, Camel's Hump, and Mount Mansfield.

At a time when the approaches to high peaks, if any, were mostly dirt roads and the young men often counted on the kindness of farmers or their own resourcefulness for food and shelter, it was an ambitious and exhilarating feat. Yet the memory that stuck most with MacKaye was how it felt to stand above the clouds.

---

5    Larry Anderson, "A Classic of the Green Mountains: Benton MacKaye's 1900 Hike Inspires Appalachian Trail," *hut2hut* (blog), October 6, 2015, hut2hut.info/a-classic -of-the-green-mountains/.

Sixty-four years after the expedition, Benton shared a memory of the trip with attendees of the 1964 Appalachian Trail Conference (ATC) held in Stratton, Vermont, through remarks he prepared to be read in his absence.

> We walked up through the trailless woods to the top of Stratton Mountain and climbed trees in order to see the view. It was a clear day with a brisk breeze blowing. North and south sharp peaks etched the horizon. I felt as if atop the world, with a sort of "planetary feeling." I seemed to perceive peaks far southward, hidden by old Earth's curvature. Would a footpath someday reach them from where I was then perched?[6]

Upon his return from the post-graduation trip, Benton was confronted with the need to earn a living. In many ways, the task of finding a vocation emulated his various mountain adventures—lots of ambling on uncertain pathways with glimpses of something better in the distance. Family finances were such that he couldn't philosophize about it for long. Of necessity, he spent two years in New York City as a tutor, admitting to his brother James that the work was strictly for money and not a long-term career. As spring arrived in the city in 1901, he shared his list of job requirements.

> A career which takes me over the country, out of doors, and into all communities and places, is the one for me; it is a scheme to be developed and difficult to be attained, but one toward which I shall "hammer, hammer, hammer."[7]

As it turned out, Benton wouldn't need to look further than his alma mater for a vocational adventure that would last another 75 years.

Since graduation, and probably well before, MacKaye had pondered how he could continue to pursue the subjects he loved—geology, biology, cartography—while making a living from them. He had considered writing but realized the market for his work would be scant or, at least, a long time in development. He enjoyed the few summers he spent as a summer camp

---

6   Ibid.

7   Benton MacKaye to James MacKaye, 7 April 1901, Papers of the MacKaye Family, Rauner Special Collections Library, Dartmouth College.

counselor because it gave him a chance to spend time outdoors , but it was seasonal. "The necessity [of steady employment] is making itself felt more and more as time goes on," he wrote to his brother, James, "And so Forestry has been suggested to me."[8]

The suggestion to pursue forestry as a career had come from a number of people including one of his hiking companions, Sturgis Pray. Benton decided to follow up by looking into the Yale forestry program. When he heard back from the school's director (and future U.S. Forest Service Director) Henry S. Graves, he was surprised to learn that Harvard was starting a forestry school of its own. On Graves's advice, Benton enrolled with his alma mater for the fall 1903 semester.

---

8    Benton MacKaye to James MacKaye, 20 October 1903, Papers of the MacKaye Family, Rauner Special Collections Library, Dartmouth College.

# CHAPTER 3

*Forests and Trails*

IN 1903, THREE YEARS AFTER RECEIVING HIS B.A. FROM THE SCHOOL, Benton MacKaye was the first student to enroll in Harvard University's forestry program. The curriculum had been created within Harvard's Lawrence Scientific School and announced the year before.

This pairing of eager student and evolving curriculum seemed destined. Benton had spent his youth exploring and observing the woods, hills, and mountains of New England. He had seen both vast tracts of uninterrupted wilderness and clear-cut mountainsides left in the wake of lumbering operations. (He and Horace Hildreth had visited a lumber camp during their 1900 Vermont trip, and both the Pemigewasset and Zealand areas of what would become the White Mountain National Forest were heavily logged by 1896, the time of Benton's first visit to the region.)

The forestry school movement in America was just starting. Two of the predecessors to Harvard's program were the Biltmore Forest School, established in 1898 to manage the forest holdings of George W. Vanderbilt's Biltmore Estate in North Carolina, and the Yale Forest School, established in 1900 and later renamed the Yale School of Forestry & Environmental Studies. The two schools had one thing in common: Both traced their origins to Gifford Pinchot.

Pinchot's contribution to forestry is incalculable. That he made such an impact is all the more impressive when one considers how he came to the field. Shortly before Pinchot entered Yale University in 1885, his father asked him, "How would you like to be a forester?" This was a provocative question at a time when there was no clear path to the career. Certainly no universities offered degrees in the field; young Pinchot, however, readily embraced the idea. Years later he would say, "I had no more conception of what it meant to be a forester than the man in the moon. . . . But at least a forester worked in the woods and with the woods—and I loved the woods and everything about them. . . . My Father's suggestion settled the question in favor of forestry."[1]

Upon obtaining his undergraduate degree from Yale in 1889, Pinchot traveled to France and enrolled in the L'Ecole Nationale Forestière. Founded 65 years before, the school was well known for advancing practices that balanced timber harvesting with conservation. Pinchot was so excited to put into practice what he learned that he returned to the United States in 1890, having spent only one year in France. How he viewed America's timber industry at the time is instructive.

> *When I came home not a single acre of Government, state, or private timberland was under systematic forest management anywhere on the most richly timbered of all continents. . . . When the Gay Nineties began, the common word for our forests was "inexhaustible." To waste timber was a virtue and not a crime. There would always be plenty of timber. . . . The lumbermen . . . regarded forest devastation as normal and second growth as a delusion of fools. . . . And as for sustained yield, no such idea had ever entered their heads. The few friends the forest had were spoken of, when they were spoken of at all, as impractical theorists, fanatics, or "denudatics," more or less touched in the head. What talk there was about forest protection was no more to the average American than the buzzing of a mosquito, and just about as irritating.*[2]

Pinchot was anxious to make an impression on his chosen field. He applied for positions in the U.S. Department of Agriculture and the U.S. Department of the Interior, but finding no opportunities there, he went to California to spend a year as a forestry consultant. His first big break came in January 1892, when he was hired to manage the 125,000-acre forest tract on the Biltmore Estate in North Carolina.

---

1   "Gifford Pinchot," *Forest History Society*, foresthistory.org/ASPNET/People/Pinchot/Pinchot.aspx.

2   Gifford Pinchot, *Breaking New Ground* (Washington, DC: Island Press, 1998), 27.

By the late 1800s, the estate had been largely denuded to support farming and timber extraction. In 1889, Vanderbilt had hired the landscape architect Frederick Law Olmsted to begin restoring the grounds. Among Olmsted's recommendations for the estate was incorporating a managed forest that could be used as a model for sustainable forestry practices. Vanderbilt agreed and hired Gifford Pinchot to manage the tract.

Pinchot reveled in the opportunity to put his concepts into action, creating the first managed forest in the United States—one that improved the habitat while allowing the landowner to profit from periodic harvesting. Pinchot's work at Biltmore garnered national attention. He left the estate[3] to become a special forest agent for the federal government in 1897 and, one year later, he became the chief of the Division of Forestry, the predecessor of the U.S. Forest Service. While in that role, Pinchot convinced his parents to endow a two-year forestry program at Yale, established in 1900.

That year, 1898, also marked the fateful first meeting of Gifford Pinchot and Benton MacKaye. MacKaye's freshman year at Harvard was winding down when Pinchot arrived on campus. Realizing forestry was poised for unprecedented growth, Pinchot was keen to attract collegians. He spoke informally to students after giving a brief evening talk titled, "Forestry as a Profession." The *Harvard Crimson* captured some of the speech for posterity.

> *Forestry is in itself purely economic; it has to do with making masses of trees useful to man. Upon its results depends to a great extent the industrial future of the United States; over fifty per cent of our country's area must eventually come under its activities. The great work of the forester will be to plant the treeless West, and to master the economic problems connected with lumbering in its relation to taxes.*
>
> *Three questions naturally asked by a man who contemplates making forestry his life-work are: If he prepares will he find work to do?*

---

3   Two years before he left his post at the Biltmore Estate, Pinchot noted that he needed more help to manage the forest. Vanderbilt then hired Carl A. Schenck to assist Pinchot. When Pinchot left for Washington, Schenk took over the job of managing the forest. As more people came to the estate to learn about sustainable forest practices, Schenk asked Vanderbilt if he would allow a forestry school to operate on his grounds. Vanderbilt agreed, and in 1898, the Biltmore Forest School became the first school of forestry in America. (The New York State College of Forestry at Cornell University opened just a few weeks later.)

*Will it pay? What sort of life is it? As to the first question—there is no fear of lack of work to do for years to come and it is college graduates who are wanted. In New York, New Jersey, Michigan, California, and many other states activity in this field is beginning. In regard to pay, salaries are from $1,000 to $2,500. Just as in college teaching a large part of compensation is in the pleasure of the occupation. Forestry is a science yet to be developed and this constitutes one of its chief fascinations. Although the life is a fine, healthy outdoor one, it is not without its monotony both in the woods and at the desk. Hardiness, cheerfulness, power of observation are necessary qualities. The pay for those who do the summer work is twenty-five dollars a month. For thorough preparation two years at a forestry school and one year abroad are necessary.[4]*

The importance of the meeting was lost on both the chief forester and the student, who hadn't yet glimpsed a career in forestry ahead of him. In future years, MacKaye would confide to Pinchot that he "regretted not signing up with him that night as one of his 'student assistants.'"[5]

After spending a couple of years in New York City as a tutor and a year in Boston as a first-year graduate student, Benton was ready to spend some time outdoors. He secured a position as a camp counselor at a newly opened Camp Moosilauke boys camp in New Hampshire. One of the highlights of his summer was co-leading a ten-day hike over the 4,802-foot Mount Moosilauke to the summit of Mount Washington—again following much of the route of the future Appalachian Trail.

In the aftermath of the hike, MacKaye wrote an article for the camp's newsletter titled, "Our White Mountain Trip: Its Organization and Methods." The piece encapsulated the evolution of Benton's ideas regarding sustainable forestry and the need to set aside parcels of land for recreational use.

---

4   Gifford Pinchot, "Forestry as a Profession: Opportunities for College Graduates in Forestry as a Life Work," *The Crimson*, March 3, 1900, thecrimson.com/article/1900/3/3/forestry-as-a-profession-pmr-gifford/.

5   Benton MacKaye speech (transcript) to Harvard Class of 1900, June 1960, Papers of the MacKaye Family, Rauner Special Collections Library, Dartmouth College.

There was room for both, he concluded, as long as the timber harvester and the recreational visitor respected the land.

> *The simplest rule of conduct for a camper is to leave a place as he would like to find it. . . . There is no other sport or mode of living which so clearly exemplifies the need of each to do his share and the dependence of all upon the resources of nature. If we are to have these resources, whether lumber or other; if things are to be used and not dissipated; if we are to have a camping ground and not a desert, we must work and fight for these ends.[6]*

During his quest for a postgraduate degree, Benton roomed with his brother James, who was a research engineer by day and an author by night. James was consumed by philosophical questions, including how mankind could achieve the highest measure of happiness. His explorations yielded a 500-plus page book titled, *The Economy of Happiness* (Little, Brown & Co., 1906). In it, James argued that: "If men have failed to solve the problem of happiness it is because they do not know how to solve it. It is not because they lack the will, but because they lack the knowledge." James believed pain and pleasure could be quantified much like any commodity: "tons of pig iron, barrels of sugar, bushels of wheat" and the like. The question society needed to address was: "What conditions would allow happiness to be produced with the greatest efficiency?" James concluded that what was needed was a type of socialism he dubbed "pantocracy."[7]

While *The Economy of Happiness* initiated lively discussion among the student body of Harvard, at least one reviewer, Albion W. Small of *The American Journal of Sociology*, thought the principles would be better served with the benefit of more life experience behind them. He called the book "the work of a man who has broken away from dogmatic leading-strings, and is

---

6   Benton MacKaye, "Our White Mountain Trip: Its Organization and Methods," logbook of Camp Moosilauke (Wentworth, NH: 1904).

7   James MacKaye, *The Economy of Happiness* (Boston: Little, Brown & Co., 1906), 183–184.

seeing with his own eyes, but has not yet seen enough to give his observations the weight of authority."[8]

While others saw potential in James's thoughts and writings, Benton saw wisdom already at work. James's philosophies would emerge in Benton's thoughts and writings during the latter's career as a public servant and as a private citizen. As Benton MacKaye biographer Larry Anderson put it:

> Benton nonetheless remained his brother's most faithful disciple. His life's work embodied Jamie's "pantocratic" ideas for a social utopia, a cooperative commonwealth in which the skills and knowledge of scientists and technicians would serve the end of happiness, not simply material accumulation. For Benton, forestry provided the skills to pursue a more ambitious and altruistic end than the mere cultivation of trees.[9]

For forestry in America, 1905 was a pivotal year. In February, Gifford Pinchot consolidated all federal forest administration under the Department of Agriculture's Bureau of Forestry. In July, he renamed the bureau the U.S. Forest Service (USFS). With the full support of President Theodore Roosevelt, Pinchot also began growing the number of acres under USFS control, from 60 forest reserves covering 56 million acres in 1905 to 150 national forests covering 172 million acres in 1910. Pinchot introduced the concept of holistically managing natural resources while also protecting them using the term "conservation," a word many Americans were hearing in that context for the first time.

One immediate task was to staff the USFS with qualified foresters and forest rangers. In 1905, Pinchot presided over a change in hiring practices designed to ensure the best candidates filled the need. The era of employment by political appointment was over. Selections would now be made through "comprehensive field and written civil service examinations. These

---

8    Albion W. Small, review of *The Economy of Happiness*, by James MacKaye. *The American Journal of Sociology* 12, no. 4 (January 1907): 567.

9    Larry Anderson, *Benton MacKaye*, 51.

new standards helped create a workforce that was well qualified, satisfied, and inspired by Pinchot's leadership."[10]

While many found Pinchot's vision for sustainable forests progressive, it did not go far enough for some activists, such as John Muir, who believed national forests should be preserved in their natural state. Once great friends, Pinchot and Muir would have an irreparable falling out over the construction of a reservoir in the Hetch Hetchy Valley of Yosemite National Park. As Pinchot testified to Congress:

> *I have never been able to agree with [Muir] in his attitude toward the Sierras for the reason that my point of view has never appealed to him at all. When I became Forester and denied the right to exclude sheep and cows from the Sierras, Mr. Muir thought I had made a great mistake, because I allowed the use by an acquired right of a large number of people to interfere with what would have been the utmost beauty of the forest. In this case I think he has unduly given away to beauty as against use.*[11]

Pinchot steadfastly saw the role of the USFS as balancing the needs of miners, loggers, and other industries with the need to sustain resources for future generations. To ensure forest officers in the field adhered to best practices, Pinchot and nine rangers and supervisors from across the country formed a committee to review and revise existing USFS regulations. The resulting book, *The Use of the National Forest Reserves* (commonly known as the "Use Book"), published in 1905, succinctly stated the objectives of the USFS.

> *In the administration of the forest reserves it must be clearly borne in mind that all land is to be devoted to its most productive use for the permanent good of the whole people, and not for the temporary benefit of individuals or companies. All the resources of the forest reserves are for use, and this use must be brought about in a thoroughly prompt*

---

10  Gerald W. Williams, Ph.D., *The USDA Forest Service—The First Century* (Washington, DC: U.S. Department of Agriculture, 2005), 17, 14.

11  *Hetch Hetchy Dam Site: Hearings on H.R. 6281, Day 1, Before the Committee on the Public Lands, House of Representatives*, 63rd Cong. 1 (25–28 June 1913; 7 July 1913) (statement of Gifford Pinchot).

*and businesslike manner, under such restrictions only as will insure the permanence of these resources.*[12]

Just ten weeks after the publication of the "Use Book," Benton MacKaye received his own copy. Forestry degree in hand, he was hired to join the USFS as a forest assistant and told to report to Washington, D.C., for duty on September 1, 1905.

---

12    Gifford Pinchot, *The Use of the National Forest Reserves: Regulations and Instructions* (Washington, DC: U.S. Department of Agriculture, Forest Service, 1905), 10.

# CHAPTER 4

## *Fits and Starts*

BENTON MACKAYE'S CAREER WITH THE USFS WAS A BIT LIKE HIKING with a pebble in your boot. The initial fit seemed perfect, but the path to becoming a professional forester was filled with stops and starts.

MacKaye never made it to Washington in September 1905. On his train ride to the capital, he received a telegram advising him to report to Keene, New Hampshire. He was to study the forests there and offer expertise to lumber companies and private woodlot owners seeking to learn about sustainable forestry.

After a year in southern New Hampshire (where he worked closely with one of the future giants of American forestry, Raphael Zon), MacKaye was hired by Harvard to teach forestry for one semester. Gifford Pinchot had personally recommended him for the job. MacKaye taught graduate and undergraduate courses in the principles of forestry and forest measurement before resuming his duties as a USFS advisor to private woodlot owners throughout New Hampshire, Massachusetts, eastern New York, and western Maine.[1]

As he was marking trees in New England forests, MacKaye was on the threshold of one of his most important friendships. In Boston, the oldest and best-known outdoor organization in the country, the Appalachian Mountain Club (AMC), needed to develop a forestry plan for a 300-acre tract of land in Fitzwilliam, New Hampshire. The land had been donated to the organization under the condition that rhododendron grove and pine forest "be held

---

1   Benton MacKaye, reports on eight forest tracts, August–September 1907, Papers of the MacKaye Family, Rauner Special Collections Library, Dartmouth College.

as a reservation property protected and open to the public . . . forever."[2] The president of AMC, Allen Chamberlain, reached out to the USFS for help in meeting the required conditions and was told to contact MacKaye.[3]

When the two met to assess the Fitzwilliam property in April 1907, they immediately hit it off. At the time of their meeting, Chamberlain's impact and insights into the need for conservation had already been felt both within AMC and by the general public. A prolific journalist, he boldly lobbied for the protection of wild lands in the pages of the *Boston Herald, Boston Post, Boston Transcript,* and *Appalachia.* His efforts within AMC were exemplified by his 1900 move to change the name of the organization's Department of Exploration to the Department of Exploration and Forestry, better positioning AMC in its effort to protect the White Mountains from clear-cutting. In the coming decades, Chamberlain's passion for protecting forests would help ensure the passage of landmark legislation, such as the Weeks Act in 1911 and the creation of national forests in the White Mountains and the Southern Appalachians.[4]

After surveying the Fitzwilliam tract, MacKaye and Chamberlain celebrated by hiking up nearby Mount Monadnock. As they stood on the summit once visited by luminaries such as Thoreau and Emerson, they could not yet know that in fourteen years they would both help ensure the creation of the longest hiking-only footpath in the world.

That fall, MacKaye reported back to Harvard to teach. As part of his duties, he was asked to prepare a statement in support of the creation of eastern national forests for his boss, Richard T. Fisher, to deliver to the House Committee on Agriculture in January 1908. For a few months that year, MacKaye's forestry duties took him to the forests of eastern Kentucky. It was his first experience in the Southern Appalachians and added fodder to what was slowly becoming his grand plan.

---

2   "Rhododendron State Park," last modified April 19, 2011, newhampshire.com/apps/pbcs .dll/article?AID=/99999999/NEWHAMPSHIRE0304/110419946.

3   Allen Chamberlain, "Reports of the Councilors for the Autumn of 1907: Exploration and Forestry," *Appalachia* 12, ( July 1909): 81–85.

4   "AMC and the Weeks Act," last modified February 9, 2011, outdoors.org/articles/ amc-outdoors/allen-chamberlain-weeks-act/.

While Benton was in Kentucky, Harvard was busy bolstering its fledgling forestry program. For the few years the program had been operating, students had done their field work on other people's woodlots. The university didn't have a forest of its own. That changed when Harvard received a gift from a former student: 2,000 acres located in the central Massachusetts town of Petersham. A booklet written in honor of Richard T. Fisher (Harvard's first instructor of forestry and Benton MacKaye's superior) highlighted the importance of the Harvard Forest to the school.

> [Fisher's] truly constructive period began as soon as the Petersham tract was given to Harvard. The Forest immediately became several things in one—an indispensable aid to instruction, a field laboratory in which investigations could be carried on and observations could be accumulated without interruption, and a place where new methods of silviculture could be demonstrated.[5]

In order for the site to become a well-functioning field laboratory, Fisher needed someone to develop a forestry plan. He summoned MacKaye for the task. Back from Kentucky, MacKaye spent the autumn of 1908 on location at the newly named Harvard Forest, where he taught classes from a farmhouse on the property. When the weather got cold, he shifted his classes back to the school's campus in Cambridge.

When he got there, instructor MacKaye also became an active social reformer. In the past few years, progressives had successfully pushed for sweeping reforms such as trust-busting, labor reform, and government regulation. (Just two years before, the outcry surrounding Upton Sinclair's book, *The Jungle*, chronicling the horrid work conditions present in the meat packing industry, led to the adoption of new food and drug regulations.) Nowhere were the questions of the day being debated more vigorously than on college campuses. Corporate corruption, political corruption, civil rights, women's suffrage, prohibition, worker's rights, government reform and economic equality were all fodder for passionate, ongoing debates.

---

5   Harvard University Alumni, *The Harvard Forest 1907–1934: A Memorial to its First Director Richard Thornton Fisher* (Cornwall, NY: The Cornwall Press, Inc., 1935), 3.

Twenty-nine-year-old MacKaye was exhilarated by the progressive discourse. In fact, his room at 21 Stoughton Hall became a hub of political activity. Here, he held nightly discussions on how to implement social reform and hosted meetings of the Harvard Socialist Club. MacKaye's brother James often held court on campus as well, including as a lecturer in a series orchestrated by the journalist and celebrated muckraker Lincoln Steffens, who attempted to "excite a searching interest in the common problems of politics and government, discover that those problems had to go to economics for their solution, then develop an intelligent, practical interest in economics as an unborn science."[6]

Other than a summer stint for the USFS in the Adirondacks in 1909, MacKaye's professional life revolved around the university: his campus activism, his work on the Harvard Forest, his teaching load. He even began drafting a forestry textbook in his spare time. So it came as a major blow when Fisher sent a note stating MacKaye would not be offered a teaching position for fall 1910. Whether MacKaye's prominence as a reformer motivated his dismissal is open to conjecture, but the effect was seismic. For the next ten years, MacKaye would be an itinerant worker, never able to find solid footing within the realm of federal agencies. His upbringing, training (both formal and informal), and temperament made him ill-suited for bureaucratic work. He was happiest studying in the field and developing far-reaching plans, yet his proposals were often too progressive and too complex to gain enthusiastic support. Only when he became a private citizen would he find himself positioned to make the greatest contribution of his life.

---

6   Lincoln Steffens, *Autobiography of Lincoln Steffens* (New York: Harcourt, Brace and Company, 1931), 645–646.

# CHAPTER 5

## *Controversy Hits Home*

IN 1910 BENTON MACKAYE LOST HIS JOB. IN 1911 HE WOULD LOSE his fiancée.

MacKaye's engagement to Mabel Foster Abbott, whom everyone called Lucy, was generally a surprise. Only the closest members of his family knew the two were an item. Born in Plymouth, Ohio, 80 miles southwest of Cleveland, in 1888, Lucy graduated with honors in English in 1909 from Radcliffe College, where she held the prestigious title of president of the English club.[1] Lucy met MacKaye through his sister Hazel, who briefly attended Radcliffe as well.[2]

The relationship faced two difficult challenges from the start: MacKaye's need to secure work after his sudden dismissal by Harvard and Lucy's simultaneous rise to fame. MacKaye's quest for employment would, at least for the short term, require the engaged couple to live apart. His first opportunity to secure a job came from his sister Hazel, who had befriended a well-to-do couple in Peterborough, New Hampshire. When Hazel found out the couple was seeking someone to plan the grounds of their estate, she recommended her brother. His new job managing the woodlot brought in enough money to get by but ended as soon as the snow fell.

Throughout his life, MacKaye experienced depression and other health-related problems, such as debilitating digestive issues, following times of disappointment and loss. One manifestation of his condition was isolation.

---

1   John William Leonard, ed. *Woman's Who's Who of America: A Biographical Dictionary of Contemporary Women of the United States and Canada 1914–1915* (New York: The American Commonwealth Company, 1914), 34.

2   Larry Anderson, *Benton MacKaye*, 61.

Percy (left) and Benton MacKaye, circa 1900. Photo: Courtesy of Dartmouth College Library.

As far back as the days after his father's death, MacKaye would embrace long walks as a means of escape. When his woodlot job ended, instead of returning home to live with his fiancée, MacKaye initiated yet another form of isolation: He hunkered down in his brother Percy's house in Concord, New Hampshire, to draft a comprehensive forestry textbook. MacKaye was certain his opus would impress USFS officials sufficiently to earn him full-time employment. In February 1911 he shared the results of his winter's work—a compendium of all he had learned as a forester and educator, complete with statistical charts—to James and Hazel, who were both mightily impressed.[3]

As MacKaye holed up writing and drawing for days at a time, James worried about his brother's mental state. Benton was putting enormous pressure on himself to present material that would secure his place in the USFS ranks and provide steady income for him and his bride-to-be. James urged Benton to look to other influences, such as Thoreau, to jog his younger brother's mind away from the textbook from time to time.[4] Soon after Benton

3   Benton MacKaye to Mary MacKaye, 14 March 1894, Papers of the MacKaye Family, Rauner Special Collections Library, Dartmouth College.

4   Hazel MacKaye as told to Mary MacKaye, 27 February 1911, Papers of the MacKaye Family, Rauner Special Collections Library, Dartmouth College.

completed his book, he wrote to his mother to report that, while drafting his book, he had spent too much time in his "meditative mind," preoccupied with his own thoughts, and realized it had been unhealthy to do so.[5] The family may have been relieved to hear Benton acknowledge that his isolation and obsession were excessive; however, the pressure on Benton and his fiancée would only increase, as the name Mabel "Lucy" Abbott would soon become associated with a political scandal.

## The Ballinger–Pinchot Controversy

In 1906, Congress passed a law to protect Alaskan land from commercial exploitation. The provisions of the law stated that no more Alaskan land would be given away, but that legitimate claims filed before 1906 would be honored.

A man named Clarence Cunningham had filed 33 Alaskan land claims in the name of various parties prior to 1906. In the summer of 1907, Cunningham illegally sold a 50 percent interest in the claims to the Morgan–Guggenheim syndicate (also known as the "Alaska Syndicate," which had been formed by J.P. Morgan and Simon Guggenheim to dominate the transportation and mining facilities in Alaska[6]). If discovered, the sale would be declared illegal and most likely invalidated due to the passage of the aforementioned legislation.

Louis R. Glavis, chief of the Portland (Oregon) Field Division of the Government Land Office (GLO), heard rumors of the illegal sale and urged his boss, the GLO commissioner Richard A. Ballinger, to investigate. Shortly thereafter, Miles C. Moore, a Washington State politician, visited Ballinger. Moore was a friend of the GLO commissioner and also one of the Cunningham claimants. Ballinger subsequently ordered the 33 claims to be "clear listed," the first step toward granting deed to the tracts. Glavis intervened and talked Ballinger into rescinding the order. Soon thereafter, Ballinger resigned

5  Benton MacKaye to Mary MacKaye, 29 April 1911, Papers of the MacKaye Family, Rauner Special Collections Library, Dartmouth College.

6  Rachel White Scheuering, *Shapers of the Great Debate on Conservation: A Biographical Dictionary*, vol. 4, *Shapers of the Great American Debates*, ed. Peter B. Levy (Westport, CT: Greenwood Press, 2004), 21.

from his federal post and moved back to Seattle to practice law—in part as counsel to the Cunningham claimants.[7]

When William Howard Taft became president on March 4, 1909, he immediately fired the secretary of the interior, James R. Garfield, the son of the former president James A. Garfield, and named the former GLO Commissioner Richard Ballinger as Garfield's replacement. Conservationists' fears that Theodore Roosevelt's public land policies would be weakened were confirmed a few weeks later, when Ballinger restored 3 million acres of formerly designated federal land for private use.[8]

When the Cunningham case entered the spotlight again in the spring and summer of 1909, Ballinger claimed to pass the matter to the first assistant secretary, Frank Pierce. Ballinger then pressed for hearings to begin right away. When Glavis said he couldn't possibly finish investigating the case before the hearings began, Ballinger replaced him with a far less experienced lawyer.

Glavis appealed to Gifford Pinchot for help. Pinchot advised Glavis to make the case to President Taft that Ballinger was negligent and endangering public lands. Glavis presented a 50-page report to Taft, in person, at Taft's summer retreat. Ballinger responded by giving Taft a 730-page report in defense of his actions. One week later, after discussing the case with the attorney general, Taft fired Glavis for insubordination. When Pinchot subsequently protested the firing of Glavis and raised questions about the president's honesty, Taft fired him as well.

The story became a nationwide sensation with a cover article in the November 13, 1909 issue of *Collier's Weekly* titled, "The White-Washing of Ballinger" and written by the recently discharged Glavis himself. In it, the author stated he was dismissed for attempting to point out an injustice to the president: the loss of some of the most valuable lands in the United States.

Inspired by the state of the conservation movement, in general, and the provocative Ballinger–Pinchot affair, in particular, MacKaye's fiancée, Lucy, an aspiring reporter, began some investigative reporting of her own.

---

7   "Synopsis of the Ballinger–Pinchot Affair," Louis D. Brandeis School of Law Library, louisville.edu/law/library/special-collections/the-louis-d.-brandeis-collection/ synopsis-of-the-ballinger-pinchot-affair.

8   John T. Ganoe, "Some Constitutional and Political Aspects of the Ballinger–Pinchot Controversy," *The Pacific Historical Review* 3, no. 3 (September 1934): 323.

From November 1909 to July 1911, her five-part series "A Brief History of the Conservation Movement" ran in the publication *Conservation News*. On the strength of that series, she became an editorial writer for *Collier's Weekly*, the same magazine that had run the Glavis article, bringing the influence of the Morgan–Guggenheim syndicate into question.[9]

While an article about the struggle over the control of Maine's hydroelectric resources in the March 1911 issue of *Collier's* gained Lucy a measure of notoriety, her article in the May issue, "The Latest in Alaska," sparked an outright controversy. In the article, she charged that the improprieties in Alaska land use didn't end with the Ballinger–Pinchot affair and that the Morgan–Guggenheim syndicate was acting illegally yet again. Citing an executive order signed by President Taft to remove acreage from Chugach National Forest, allegedly on behalf of Richard Ryan, an agent for the Morgan–Guggenheim syndicate, Lucy raised questions of whether the president himself had engaged in illegal activities. "Why in this case did the President use the executive order and not the usual public form of proclamation? Why did practically no one even in the Forest Service know about the executive order? Who is Richard Ryan at whose insistence the President took this step?"[10]

The story became even more of a sensation thanks to her subsequent research. Searching through files of correspondence in newly appointed Secretary of the Interior Walter Fisher's office, Lucy reported finding a letter from Richard Ryan to (then) Secretary of the Interior Richard Ballinger implicating the president's brother, Charlie Taft, in what became known as the Controller Bay Scheme.

An article published July 3, 1911, in the *Portland Journal* (Oregon) written by Lucy hinted that the postscript in Ryan's letter implicated the president in the scandal. Four days later, she provided more detail. On July 7, 1911, a follow-up story ran in Scripps–McRae syndicated newspapers. In the article, Lucy reported the alleged postscript read: "Dear Dick: I went to see the President the other day. He asked me who it was I represented. I told him, according to our agreement, that I represented myself. But this didn't seem

---

9    John William Leonard, *Woman's Who's Who of America*, 34.

10   M.F. Abbott, "The Latest in Alaska: Controller Bay and Its Control of the Alaska Situation," *Collier's Weekly*, May 6, 1911, 19.

to satisfy him. So I sent for Charlie Taft and asked him to tell his brother, the President, who it was I really represented. The President made no further objection to my claim. Yours, Dick."[11]

According to the Congressional Record, "The publication of the story with this added feature [citation of the famous postscript, which became known as the 'Dick to Dick letter'], caused it to be seized upon by the sensational press of the country, and it was headlined 'The Controller Bay scandal' and widely published in the newspapers, and especially in those that are characterized as 'muckraking' journals."[12]

On July 6, the day before Lucy's article ran containing the details of the postscript, the U.S. House of Representatives introduced House Resolution 237, acknowledging the scandal. This action initiated a fact-finding mission. Appearing before the committee, Secretary of the Interior Fisher stated he would completely support the investigation and that he had been unable to find the "Dick to Dick" letter among any department files. He did note that several employees had left the department, a fact that could explain how the file might have disappeared, if it ever existed at all.[13]

If Secretary Fisher was unsure about the veracity of Lucy's story, President Taft was anything but. In a lengthy defense of his integrity, Taft stated the existence of the postscript was completely fabricated. "[Charlie Taft] never wrote or spoke to me in reference to Richard S. Ryan or the subject of Controller Bay or the granting of any privileges or the making of any orders in respect to Alaska. He has no interest in Alaska, never had, and knows nothing of the circumstances connected with this transaction. . . . Ballinger never saw the letter of July 13, 1910, to which this postscript is said to be attached."[14]

Taft went on to explain that Mr. Carr, Ballinger's private secretary, forwarded the letter in question directly to the president, that neither of them recalled a postscript appearing on the letter, and that the president turned over the letter and all other related files to the Interior Department on

11  John William Leonard, *Woman's Who's Who of America*, 34.

12  *House Reports, vol. 6129, Report 178, 62nd Cong., 2d sess., December 4, 1911–August 26, 1912,* (Washington, DC: Government Printing Office, 1912), 2.

13  Ibid., 3.

14  Ibid., 6–7.

April 22, 1911. President Taft then concluded his statement, calling the character of Mabel "Lucy" Abbott into question by stating that she was "seeking to create a sensation."[15]

Taft said Lucy's request to review the Controller Bay files had been approved by the president—the inference being that if the president had anything to hide, he would not have granted her access to the files. Second, Lucy reviewed the files in the presence of Fisher's private secretary, Mr. Brown, who "states that there was no such postscript in the papers when he showed them to the correspondent and that he never saw such a postscript."[16]

In the aftermath of the inquiry, the Interior Department promised to revise its policies regarding Alaskan development. Richard Ryan, reportedly under pressure from the Interior Department though never compelled to testify or to submit a statement, withdrew his claims to Controller Bay.

Lucy continued to pursue progressive journalism, covering subjects such as child labor and women's suffrage, but she would never again rise to national prominence.[17] Her relationship with Benton MacKaye also would never be the same. By December 1911, the couple decided to call off their engagement. By 1912, Lucy would be living in New York City while MacKaye toiled in Washington, D.C., or in the field. Did the attention created by the Controller Bay scandal contribute to the couple's split? There are no known pieces of correspondence indicating so, but the timing makes it a possibility, at least.

## The Establishment of Eastern National Forests

As Lucy alternately struggled and thrived in the public spotlight, MacKaye was quietly forging his own path forward. Although his textbook was never published, it was likely instrumental in securing him a new job, in 1912 as forest examiner. He was offered the position by the head of the Forest Service himself, Henry Graves, who had reviewed an early manuscript of the now

---

15   President William Howard Taft, *Chugach National Forest Lands in Alaska: Message from the President of the United States Transmitting in Response to a Senate Resolution of June 27, 1911, All Papers and Information Relating to the Elimination from the Chugach National Forest of Certain Lands Fronting Upon Controller Bay in Alaska*, 62nd Cong., 1d Sess., S. Doc. No. 77, (Washington, DC: U.S. Senate, July 26, 1911), 14.

16   Ibid., 46.

17   John William Leonard, *Woman's Who's Who of America*, 34.

32-year-old's book.[18] The timing of the job put MacKaye on the fringes of legislation whose legacy, over time, would far outshine the Ballinger–Pinchot controversy.

On July 23, 1909, Rep. John W. Weeks (R-Mass.) introduced bill H.R. 11798 to the U.S. House of Representatives. The bill, which would become known as the Weeks Act, had two stated objectives. The first was: "To enable any state to cooperate with ally other state or states, or with the United States for the protection of the watersheds of navigable streams, and to appoint a commission for the acquisition of lands for the purpose of conserving the navigability of navigable rivers." The second was to help prevent wildfires in proximity to those watersheds.[19]

After several months of wrangling, the Weeks Act passed, and on March 1, 1911, President Taft signed it into law. While the law's official purpose was to protect the navigability of rivers, proponents fought to ensure it would establish and protect tracts of forest in the eastern United States, as well. The Weeks Act was also known as the "Appalachian bill."

Within days of the bill's passage, the American Forestry Association ran an editorial offering its perspective.

> *The passage by the Senate on Wednesday of the bill commonly known as the Weeks, or Appalachian, bill ends the first stage of a long struggle for national forests in the eastern mountains, a struggle that began in 1899. The bill now enacted bears little resemblance to those that preceded it up to the time of the Sixtieth Congress, although its purpose bas been well understood to be the same, that is, the perpetuation of forests upon the great watersheds of the Appalachian ridge. It is a general law, providing for no particular locality, but there can hardly be a question raised as to its intent or as to the regions which are in present need of action by the nation.*[20]

---

18  Larry Anderson, *Benton MacKaye*, 69.

19  *The American Forestry Bulletin—No. 3, The Weeks Bill*, H.R. 11798, 61st Cong., 1d Sess., (July 23, 1909), 2–3.

20  "The Passage of the Appalachian Bill," *American Forestry* 17 (March 1911): 164–170.

The USFS made its own announcement concerning the Weeks Act, issued as a circular on March 27, 1911. After reciting the many benefits of the legislation (protecting purity and regularity of stream flow, preventing erosion, preserving timber supply, and providing recreational opportunities), the agency listed areas where "proposals for sale are invited." The areas deemed worthy of joining the national forest system in the east included the White Mountain Area (New Hampshire and Maine), Natural Bridge Area (Tennessee and Virginia), the Mount Mitchell Area (North Carolina), the Smoky Mountain Area (North Carolina and Tennessee), the Pisgah Area (North Carolina), and the Nantahala Area (North Carolina and Tennessee). Each area would eventually become federal land and, even later, would be traversed by the Appalachian Trail.[21]

While the passage of the Weeks Act was a personal victory for activists such as AMC's president, Allen Chamberlain, who had worked so diligently to get it passed, not a single new national forest could be created unless two hurdles were cleared. One was indifference. The American Forestry Association warned: "It is a weakness of the American people to develop great enthusiasms, embody them in law and then forget them, to become absorbed in their daily vocations and in fresh interests. . . . In the face of public indifference [this new forest law] will become a useless instrument. Forcefully and intelligently sustained, it may be the beginning of greater good to the people of the whole country than even its most ardent friends have claimed."[22]

The other, more concrete hurdle to achieving national forest designation was a precondition "that the control of such lands will promote or protect the navigation of streams on whose watersheds they lie." Lands that did not significantly impact watersheds could not be become national forests. In addition, one of the concessions to enacting the bill was that, although the USFS could identify desirable areas, as it had in its circular, the U.S. Geological Survey (USGS) would be charged with obtaining the proof.[23]

---

21  "The Appalachian Forests Putting the New Law Into Operation," *American Forestry* 17, (March 1911): 290–293.

22  Ibid., 164–170.

23  Ibid.

The task of measuring the stream flow at various points within ten river basins in the White Mountains seemed the perfect fit for one Benton MacKaye, and he was reassigned to the USGS for the task. MacKaye spent the summer and fall of 1912 taking measurements in New Hampshire and the winter in Washington, D.C., drafting the report that would help ensure the creation of the White Mountain National Forest. Getting the chance to explore and work in the region he loved—and earn a living at it—was a highlight of his career as an employee of the U.S. government.

# CHAPTER 6

## *A Man of Ideas*

THE DECADE FROM 1911–21 WAS ONE OF UNCEASING TURBULENCE FOR Benton MacKaye. Some of his mentors and advocates (notably, Gifford Pinchot, who had been fired in the Ballinger–Pinchot fallout and would later become governor of Pennsylvania) were now out of the picture. In addition, MacKaye's social views often didn't align—or align closely enough—with those of his employers, which meant he had a hard time building the kinds of lasting relationships that could keep him working in any one agency over time.

After a few years in Washington, D.C., with the USFS, MacKaye was sent by the agency to Wisconsin, Minnesota, and Michigan in the summer of 1914 to study the effects of clear-cutting. The job was far different from his previous agency fieldwork, wandering in the relatively pristine woods of New Hampshire's soon-to-be national forest. In the upper Midwest, the timber industry had "cut and run," leaving behind "an economically and environmentally devastated landscape."[1] MacKaye weighed in on the situation saying: "The region had been the scene of giant first-growth pine trees whose stumps were equally gigantic. The game was to sell all these lands to the prospective settler, omitting to advertise the stumps. I reported to one of the outfits the large number I counted on one of his acres. His response was swift and pungent, 'For God's sake, don't tell anybody!'"[2]

Before departing for his summer in the field, MacKaye had fallen in love with a lecturer and social activist, Jessie Hardy Stubbs, who went by the name

---

[1]  Larry Anderson, *Benton MacKaye*, 81.

[2]  Benton MacKaye, "Powell as Unsung Lawgiver," Papers of the MacKaye Family, Rauner Special Collections Library, Dartmouth College.

Betty. They were married in June 1915, having known each other only a year and having been apart for much of it. Nonetheless, the couple were intellectual soul mates, their political and social views sparking and sustaining their mutual attraction. When MacKaye went back to the Midwest to resume his fieldwork in the autumn of 1915, Betty went with him.

The effects of the USFS's policies on the forests of the upper Midwest disappointed MacKaye. Seeing the results of cut-and-run forestry firsthand, he concluded the agency was under too much industry influence. MacKaye felt the timber companies weren't managing the forests so much as decimating them. As a forester, he believed it was his duty to advocate for more sustainable practices. In his reading on the subject, MacKaye found something that interested him in a 1915 report by the U.S. Department of Labor. In the report, the department called for the federal government to take a more active role in creating jobs, on both publicly and privately held lands. Inspired, MacKaye pitched the Department of Labor on a formal joint study with the USFS, but it didn't win approval. Instead, with the permission of his superiors, he developed a new proposal with the assistant secretary of labor, Louis F. Post.

MacKaye's plan called for the development of communities on public lands supported by lumbering, cattle grazing, farming, and mining. He proposed that a national colonization board composed of the secretaries of labor, interior, and agriculture would run the enterprise. The land involved would not be owned by the companies nor the employees who worked on it but by the public. The federal government would hold permanent title.[3]

Two themes here are worth noting for their recurrence in MacKaye's life. One is that the plan was too far-reaching to be enacted. The second, the "government holding title" provision, would show up again as a never-implemented part of MacKaye's Appalachian Trail proposal.

Although the proposal didn't pass, a project approved by Post called for studying the potential for "joint land colonization" between the Department of Labor and the Department of Agriculture in the Pacific Northwest. Although MacKaye worked for neither department, he was sent to survey the

---

3   Larry Anderson, *Benton MacKaye*, 90–92.

area in the autumn of 1916.[4] Meanwhile, Betty stayed in Washington, D.C., where she remained active in the women's suffrage movement and worked on the behalf of several antiwar organizations.

MacKaye spent years working on the colonization project for the Department of Labor. By the time his 144-page report, *Employment and Natural Resources,* was published in 1919, the federal appetite for broad projects, particularly social projects, was low. Even so, the report was a blank canvas on which MacKaye could develop and articulate his ideas for offering stable employment and building strong communities—a response to the plight of transient timber workers and over-harvested lands he had observed on the job.

As was the case with his forestry textbook, Benton's MacKaye's intense focus and dedication resulted in a piece of work that was impressive but struggled to find a receptive audience. As a result, the end of his days as a federal employee were in sight. The political climate had changed. Progressive social programs, such as those championed by MacKaye and his reform-minded colleagues, were out of favor and could barely muster support. By July 1919 he was no longer employed by the USFS. Louis Post was able to help MacKaye get a six-month assignment with the U.S. Postal Service, studying whether the postal delivery system could bring farm products to market. It would be MacKaye's last job as a federal employee.[5]

Once in the private sector, MacKaye decided to try his hand as a newspaper columnist. In the fall of 1920, the columnist Herbert Brougham invited MacKaye and Betty to move to Milwaukee, where MacKaye would write the daily editorial for the *Milwaukee Leader.* Within five months, the job ended in a whirlwind of controversy. In early December, Betty, head of the newly organized Milwaukee branch of the Women's Peace Society, made a speech calling for women to refuse to have children in the name of preventing war. The fallout was swift. The owner of the *Leader,* Elizabeth Thomas, refused to run either an article by Brougham or an editorial by MacKaye about the incident. Within two weeks, both MacKaye and Brougham had resigned from the *Leader,* and the MacKayes were headed back east.[6]

---

4    Ibid., 103.

5    Ibid., 125.

6    Ibid., 135.

Like MacKaye, Betty had experienced several debilitating incidents related to depression. Back in 1918, she had had a nervous breakdown, followed by almost two months of "sleepless nights and mental disturbance."[7] She was subsequently nursed back to health by a close friend, Mabel Irwin, at Irwin's home in Croton-on-Hudson, New York, away from the bustling city. On April 15, 1921, while visiting a friend in Quebec on a recuperative journey of his own, MacKaye received a telegram from Kathryn Lincoln, a woman he had arranged to stay with Betty while he was away. Betty was having another breakdown.[8]

MacKaye hurried back to New York and made arrangements for Betty to once again stay with Mabel Irwin. On April 19, 1921, as MacKaye and Betty made their way toward Irwin's house, accompanied by a nurse, Betty disappeared. The story was carried in *The New York Times* under the headline, "MRS. MACKAYE GONE, THREATENED SUICIDE."

The article describes the circumstances in lurid detail. While her husband was buying train tickets, "She had eluded an elderly woman, her nurse for the last week, in one of the station's retiring rooms." Betty reportedly told her nurse, "I'm going to end it all," before she ran from the room and disappeared into the crowd. "She was last seen walking rapidly in East Forty-Second Street near Lexington Avenue. . . . Benton MacKaye denied that his wife said she was about to commit suicide."[9]

"I recall that as we were going to the station in a taxicab she said she would prefer to go to a hospital rather than into the country for rest and treatment," [MacKaye] said. He also told the police that "his wife often said she intended to end her life by jumping into the Hudson or East River."[10]

That afternoon, a woman's body was recovered from the East River. When MacKaye was informed, he chose not to go to the undertaker. He still held out hope that Betty had checked herself into a hospital. Irwin and a friend of MacKaye's, Charles Whitaker, went to the funeral home the next morning to identify the body. Betty MacKaye was dead.

---

7   Ibid.

8   Ibid., 138–139.

9   "Mrs. MacKaye Gone, Threatened Suicide," *The New York Times*, April 19, 1921.

10   Ibid.

# CHAPTER 7

## *A Bold, New Plan*

IN THE AFTERMATH OF THE UNEXPECTED LOSS OF HIS WIFE, BENTON MacKaye moved in with his brother Hal and Hal's family in Yonkers. Soon thereafter, Benton received an invitation from his close friend and the editor of the *Journal of the American Institute of Architects*, Charles Harris Whitaker, to recuperate at Whitaker's farmstead in Mount Olive, New Jersey.[1] Whitaker had consistently come to Benton's aid through the harrowing days immediately following the loss of Betty. He had helped identify her body at the funeral home and received her cremated remains on Benton's behalf.

MacKaye moved to Whitaker's farmstead in June 1921. Without a partner or any immediate job prospects, he spent his days developing and refining an idea that was taking root in his mind and coming to life on the pages of his diary and notebook. From his early teens, MacKaye had displayed a unique gift for viewing the landscape holistically. In the beginning, he carefully catalogued what he saw on his expeditions in the countryside. In his twenties, his climbs to mountain summits widened his perspective. He witnessed and pondered the interactions of man and nature playing out around him. His forestry training added a critical dimension to his understanding of sustainable practices and the need to establish dedicated recreational lands. His exposure to progressive economic and political ideas, through formal and informal education, brought philosophical thought into the equation. His time with Whitaker added another dimension.

In the early 1920s, progressive urban planners and architects—such as MacKaye's host, Charles Whitaker, and Whitaker's friend Clarence Stein—worked exclusively on community-scale projects. Their work would lead to

---

1    Larry Anderson, *Benton MacKaye*, 143.

the development of planned communities, such as the town of Radburn, New Jersey, which would influence urban planning for generations to come.

But MacKaye's vision encompassed far more than that of a single community. His was a bold, new plan for the entire Appalachian Range: a recreational and economic plan that evolved around a footpath extending "the full length of the Appalachian skyline—from the highest peak in the north to the highest peak in the south—from Mt. Washington to Mount Mitchell."[2]

Whitaker saw the potential for MacKaye's idea and set up a meeting with Stein, who headed the American Institute of Architects' Committee on Community Planning, to discuss next steps. On July 10, 1921, MacKaye, Whitaker, and Stein met at Hudson Guild Farm, a facility then operated as a recreational retreat, in Netcong, New Jersey. All three men were enthusiastic about the plan—so much so that Whitaker offered to run an article in the *Journal of the American Institute of Architects*, and Stein agreed to promote the plan through his committee.

Hudson Guild Farm, where MacKaye, Whitaker, and Stein met to launch the Appalachian Trail. Photo: Courtesy of Hudson Farm Club.

---

2    Benton MacKaye, "Memorandum on Regional Planning," (1921), 19–25. Papers of the MacKaye Family, Rauner Special Collections Library, Dartmouth College.

MacKaye may not have known just how famous his grand plan would become, but immediately gaining the support of influential backers had to be a refreshing change. Now he could get busy preparing his article for October publication. The finished piece, "An Appalachian Trail: A Project in Regional Planning," was, and is, a tour de force. (The full article can be found in Appendix A.) MacKaye began by making a well-considered case for more recreational land in the eastern United States:

> It fortunately happens that we have throughout the most densely populated portions of the United States a fairly continuous belt of under-developed lands. These are contained in the several ranges which form the Appalachian chain of mountains. Several National Forests have been purchased in this belt. These mountains, in several ways rivaling the western scenery, are within a day's ride from centers containing more than half the population of the United States. . . . The skyline along the top of the main divides and ridges of the Appalachians would overlook a mighty part of the nation's activities. The rugged lands of this skyline would form a camping base strategic in the country's work and play.[3]

MacKaye then evoked the image of a "giant standing high on the skyline along these mountain ridges, his head just scraping the floating clouds," to establish the lay of the land in the reader's eye. Beginning on Mount Washington, MacKaye conducted an aerial tour of the region and illustrated how the mountains and surrounding lands could offer us "opportunities for recreation . . . possibilities for health and recuperation . . . 25 acres of grazing and agricultural land," as well as opportunities to practice sustainable forestry.[4]

> First there would be the "oxygen" that makes for a sensible optimism. Two weeks spent in the real open—right now, this year and next—would be a little real living for thousands of people which they would be sure of getting before they died. They would get a little fun as they went along regardless of problems being "solved."

---

3 Benton MacKaye, "An Appalachian Trail: A Project in Regional Planning," *Journal of the American Institute of Architects* 9, no. 10 (October 1921): 326.

4 Ibid., 326–327.

*Next there would be perspective. Life for two weeks on the moun-*
*tain top would show up many things about life during the other fifty*
*weeks down below. The latter could be viewed as a whole—away from*
*its heat, and sweat, and irritations.... Industry would come to be seen*
*in its true perspective—as a means in life and not as an end in itself.*[5]

MacKaye's plan included four components:

1. **The Trail:** "The beginnings of an Appalachian trail already exist,"
   MacKaye wrote, citing the "good work in trail building" by the Appalachian Mountain Club in New Hampshire and the Green Mountain
   Club in Vermont. Regarding management, MacKaye proposed that
   "the trail should be divided into sections, each consisting preferably
   of the portion lying in a given State, or subdivision thereof. Each section should be in the immediate charge of a local group of people."[6]

2. **Shelter Camps:** Modeled on the lean-tos, or open-sided shelters of
   the Northeast, MacKaye suggested building enough of them "to allow
   a comfortable day's walk between each." He also stipulated that "as
   far as possible the blazing and constructing of the trail and building
   of camps should be done by volunteer workers. . . . The enterprise
   should, of course, be conducted without profit. The trail must be well
   guarded—against the yegg-man [burglar] and against the profiteer."[7]

3. **Community Groups:** MacKaye proposed establishing "little communities" near the trail where people could live in private domiciles
   that were communally owned. "Each camp should be a self-owning
   community and not a real-estate venture. The use of the separate
   domiciles, like all other features of the project, should be available
   without profit." MacKaye envisioned these communities could be
   used to host "summer schools or seasonal field courses" or "scientific
   travel courses . . . along the trail."[8]

---

5   Ibid., 327.

6   Ibid., 328.

7   Ibid.

8   Ibid.

# AN APPALACHIAN TRAIL

by a labor group in New York City. They have erected a sawmill on their tract of 2000 acres and have built the bungalows of their community from their own timber.

Farm camps might ultimately be supplemented by permanent forest camps through the acquisition (or lease) of wood and timber tracts. These of course should be handled under a system of forestry so as to have a continuously growing crop of material. The object sought might be accomplished through long term timber sale contracts with the Federal Government on some of the Appalachian National Forests. Here would be another opportunity for permanent, steady, healthy employment in the open.

## Elements of Dramatic Appeal

The results achievable in the camp and

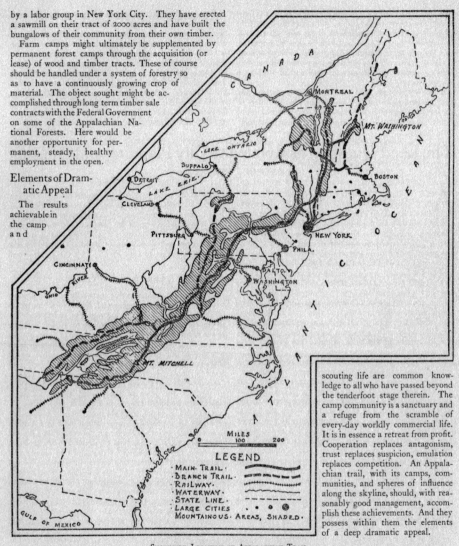

scouting life are common knowledge to all who have passed beyond the tenderfoot stage therein. The camp community is a sanctuary and a refuge from the scramble of every-day worldly commercial life. It is in essence a retreat from profit. Cooperation replaces antagonism, trust replaces suspicion, emulation replaces competition. An Appalachian trail, with its camps, communities, and spheres of influence along the skyline, should, with reasonably good management, accomplish these achievements. And they possess within them the elements of a deep dramatic appeal.

SUGGESTED LOCATION OF APPALACHIAN TRAIL

Main line from Mt. Washington to Mt. Mitchell. Large cities are tapped through branch lines and certain railways. Area shown contains more than half the population of the United States and over one third the population of Canada. Cities shown comprise all metropolitan centers over 100,000, relative population being indicated by size of dot. Thirty six of these centers, including a third of the area's population, are from one to eight hours ride from the trail system. Centers named are those of more than 400,000.

Benton MacKaye's map of the Appalachian Trail, as it appeared in his article "An Appalachian Trail: A Project in Regional Planning," published in *Journal of the American Institute of Architects* in October 1921. Courtesy of the American Institute of Architects Archives, Washington, D.C.

4. **Food and Farm Camps:** MacKaye felt the development of food and farm camps along the trail "could provide tangible opportunity for working out by actual experiment a fundamental matter in the problem of living" and "provide one definite avenue of experiment in getting 'back to the land.' It would provide an opportunity for those anxious to settle down in the country: it would open up a possible source for new, and needed, employment."[9]

The last two facets of MacKaye's regional plan would never come to fruition. Most Americans were not ready to embrace communal living or farming. But, as Whitaker and Stein predicted, the hiking community and the general public were ready to get behind the idea of MacKaye's "super trail."

Two months after the Appalachian article appeared, MacKaye presented his plan to the annual meeting of the New England Trail Conference (NETC), a consortium of outdoor clubs and other organizations interested in creating and connecting New England trails. (MacKaye's friend and AMC president Allen Chamberlain had co-founded NETC five years earlier.) The NETC meeting energized those in attendance, including a highly regarded city planner from Boston named Arthur Comey, who would come to play an integral role in the development of the Appalachian Trail (AT). It is likely that word of the AT spread quickly within the represented groups.

MacKaye spent the winter of 1921–22 in Shirley, where he began working on a manual for "those who would actually 'scout' the trail on the ground." The project soon included more than determining the placement of the footpath; it became an exercise in determining the "industrial potential" of various locations along the Appalachian Range.[10]

By the spring of 1922, Benton resolved to get more energy behind the AT project. Between March and June, he reconnected with old friends and made new ones in the interest of promoting his new trail. In Boston, Allen Chamberlain arranged another meeting with hiking advocates and foresters. MacKaye also spent a month in New York, where he met Raymond Torrey, an avid hiker, guidebook writer and editor, club organizer, hiking activist, and columnist for the *New York Evening Post*. Torrey arranged an April meeting

---

9   Ibid.

10   Larry Anderson, *Benton MacKaye*, 157–158.

between MacKaye and influential members of the New York hiking scene. The next day, Torrey's article in the *New York Evening Post* ran under the headline, "A Great Trail from Maine to Georgia!" and treated the general public to its first map of the AT.[11]

MacKaye then headed to Washington, D.C., to meet with a number of old friends from his USFS years, as well as Robert Sterling Yard, the president of the National Parks Association, and Arno Cammerer, the assistant director of the National Park Service. Both men would resurface as part of a drama involving the AT a dozen years hence.

By early summer, Benton MacKaye was back in the familiar territory of Shirley Center. His finances were also in familiar territory: He was broke. He spent the summer and fall poking away at his trail-scouting guide and pouring most of his energy into his next great work, a book that he called *The New Exploration*.[12] As a result, his AT idea began losing momentum.

At this critical stage, Clarence Stein helped MacKaye refocus. During Thanksgiving of 1922, Stein visited Shirley Center, and the pair formulated a new four-point plan that would support both the creation of the AT and the social initiatives that were part of MacKaye's vision.[13] The most important trail-related initiative was to create a consortium of thirteen regional hiking groups (including NETC and the recently formed New York–New Jersey Trail Conference) to formally adopt and build the trail. The implications of this act were significant and would come to impact the building, maintenance, and philosophy behind the AT. The creation of the federation would take the burdensome task of managing the siting and building of the trail out of MacKaye's hands. Perhaps Stein appealed to MacKaye to give it up so that MacKaye could dedicate his time to the socially progressive aspects of the trail project. Perhaps he pointed out that managing wasn't MacKaye's forte; ideas were. Maybe MacKaye came to the conclusion himself. In any case, MacKaye would continue to be recognized as the visionary behind the Appalachian Trail movement and would continue to provide the grand overview and guidance the project needed in this stage of development.

---

11   Ibid., 159.

12   Ibid.

13   Ibid., 164.

Another initiative was to seek assistance from state governments to help build the trail. Pennsylvania and New York were deemed likely candidates due to existing connections. The last two action items produced by the "Thanksgiving summit" were to find funding for a new MacKaye initiative (studying ways to increase manufacturers' industrial efficiency along the Appalachian Range so workers would have more time to enjoy the trail), and finding a publisher for *The New Exploration*.[14]

At the January 1923 NETC meeting, MacKaye inspired the attendees by reiterating the reasons he first conceived of the trail.

> *This is not to cut a path and then say—"Ain't it beautiful!" Our job is to open up a realm. This realm is something more than a geographical location—it is an environment. It is the environment, not of road and hotel, but of trail and camp. It is human access to the sources of life.*[15]

From 1923–25, MacKaye's energy was pulled in three directions: promoting the AT; writing his new manuscript, *The New Exploration*; and carrying out regional planning jobs through a new organization called the Regional Planning Association of America (RPAA). Launched in April 1923, the RPAA membership boasted America's leading practitioners of architecture, transportation design, and community development. Three of the most active members were MacKaye, Clarence Stein, and the prolific journalist Lewis Mumford. The three would remain collaborators and friends for decades. Stein helped put MacKaye's theories into an actionable framework. Mumford helped explain them. And they all challenged each other with spirited intellectual debate.

The RPAA agreed to take on the "regional planning features" of MacKaye's AT project. MacKaye spent the summer working on the plan, which included surveying parts of the trail in New Jersey.[16]

---

14  Ibid.

15  Benton MacKaye. "The Job Ahead," from New England Trail Conference speech (January 1923). Papers of the MacKaye Family, Rauner Special Collections Library, Dartmouth College.

16  Larry Anderson, *Benton MacKaye*, 182.

To maintain momentum on the trail-building aspect of the plan, MacKaye, Stein, Major Welch (the chief engineer of New York's Palisades Interstate Park Commission), and Raymond Torrey (the *New York Evening Post* columnist) organized a late October 1923 conference at the Bear Mountain Inn in Rockland County, New York. The three-day meeting offered the chance to update attendees on the status of the trail and to make plans for its continuation. Welch also presented his design for the AT trail marker, the famous combination of letters that forms the now-familiar logo.

In the wake of the conference, movement was incremental and diffuse. First, MacKaye was commissioned by *Survey Graphic* magazine to write an article in which he "calculated, in horsepower, the units of potential energy available through coal and water resources along the Appalachian spine."[17] In 1924, he drafted an extensive report for the RPAA, made an appearance on behalf of the organization and the AT project in Washington, D.C., and spent his summer on a paid regional planning project that involved travel throughout New York.[18]

Meanwhile, by late 1924, having made little progress in surveying and procuring new sections of trail, the RPAA realized that, in order for the Appalachian Trail to come to fruition, the hiking community needed to be recruited to build it. The first step was to formally organize the federation of hiking clubs posed by Stein and MacKaye two years before. In December, a number of trail-community luminaries, including Allen Chamberlain, Major Welch, and MacKaye, attended the National Conference on Outdoor Recreation in Washington, D.C. While there, they discussed meeting in early 1925 to create the new trail planning and oversight entity.

On March 2, 1925, the first Appalachian Trail Conference (ATC) convened in Washington, D.C., at the Hotel Raleigh. The array of speakers included MacKaye, Stein, and the country's current, and first, director of the National Park Service, Stephen Mather, "who commended the activities of

17  Keller Easterling, *Organization Space: Landscapes, Highways, and Houses in America* (Cambridge, MA: MIT Press, 1999), 30.

18  Clarence S. Stein, *Report of the Commission of Housing and Regional Planning to Governor Alfred E. Smith and to the Legislature of the State of New York* (Albany, NY: J. B. Lyon Company Printers, 1925).

volunteer trail-blazers and mentioned 'the possibilities of developing a Trail service' to further trail developments throughout the country."[19]

The most important organizational decision made at the conference was the election of officers. Major Welch was named chairman; Verne Rhodes of the USFS became vice-chairman; and Harlean James was named secretary; Clarence Stein, Raymond Torrey, Frank Place (one of the founders of the New York–New Jersey Trail Conference), and Arthur Comey (who had earlier given a riveting presentation on "going light" as a backpacking technique[20]) were among those named to the board who had been with the project from almost the beginning.

Most curious was that MacKaye wasn't elected to the board, although he was appointed a position: field organizer. Whether MacKaye was offered a position on the board and declined or whether it was an oversight is not known. But the election of officers at the first Appalachian Trail Conference would impact MacKaye's relationship with the ATC, as well as his influence within the organization and the trail community at large over time.

With the trail work now in the hands of the ATC, MacKaye poured more energy into regional planning. He became interested in the concept of "commodity flow," or the global movement of natural resources, commodities, and people initiated by industry, and wrote a three-part series on the subject for the magazine *The Nation*. He also created a report on open spaces for the Commonwealth of Massachusetts and continued his work on *The New Exploration*, which was published by Harcourt, Brace and Company in fall of 1928. The work sustained him emotionally, if barely financially. The RPAA was able to pay him a small stipend for project work on occasion, and articles and commissioned studies provided sporadic income.

Following the 1925 ATC, the AT project continued bumping along, mostly due to the efforts of individual clubs. The NY–NJ Trail Conference was among the most active, blazing new trail through its territories. In the

---

19  "Brief Proceedings of the Appalachian Trail Conference Called by the Federate Societies on Planning and Parks" (Washington, DC, March 1925). Papers of the MacKaye Family, Rauner Special Collections Library, Dartmouth College.

20  While hiking with ultralight gear is currently a focus of backpackers and manufacturers, it is interesting to note that Arthur Comey was a staunch proponent of the idea more than 90 years ago. You can read his "Going Light" pamphlet online at outdoors.org/articles/amc-outdoors/the-dawn-of-ultralight-backpacking/.

Northeast, members of AMC were scouting routes to link existing trails. But the ATC was not coordinating efforts. One reason could be that its chairman, Major Welch, was busy serving on the Southern Appalachian National Park Commission, an assignment that required significant meeting and travel time.

When the New England Trail Conference convened in January 1927, MacKaye met with Major Welch and Arthur "Judge" Perkins to discuss the ATC's status. Judge Perkins was a retired Connecticut lawyer who had acquired an intense interest in hiking and trail work in his 50s. Perkins had the time and inclination to take the reins of the ATC, and the trio quickly decided it should be so.[21]

Perkins was perfectly suited for the job. He had already made a name for himself in the trail community as president of AMC's Connecticut Chapter and chairman of the NETC's committee of through-trails. No armchair adventurer, Perkins was so inspired by the AT project that he spent the summer of 1927 scouting a possible route for the AT from the summit of Katahdin to Moosehead Lake, in Maine, and then along the Connecticut–New York border. He also started scouting around for clubs and individuals south of New England to help build out those sections of trail.[22]

The most important of those recruits would approach him first: a 28-year-old named Myron Avery.

---

21  Larry Anderson, *Benton MacKaye*, 212.

22  Robert A. Rubin, "The Short, Brilliant Life of Myron Avery," special issue, *Appalachian Trailway News, Trail Years: A History of the Appalachian Trail Conference* (July 2000): 27.

*Part 2*

---

# THE DOER

# CHAPTER 8

## *An Irrepressible Force*

IN MAY 1926, HARRIE B. COE, THE MANAGER OF THE MAINE PUBLICITY Bureau, penned a letter to Maine's governor, Ralph O. Brewster, and the Honorable Willis E. Parsons that began:

> *I have been very much interested in reading some articles on Mt. Katahdin, which I have received from Mr. Myron H. Avery, an attorney in Hartford, Connecticut, with whom I have been in correspondence during the last two or three years on the subject of Katahdin.*[1]

The governor may not have been familiar yet with the name Myron Avery, but the young man would come to leave a lasting impression on the state of Maine and indeed, the hiking world.

Myron Halliburton Avery was born on November 3, 1899, in the coastal town of Lubec, Maine, a place located as far "downeast"—or up the Maine coast, toward Canada—as you can get. It was, and remains to this day, a hardworking town where generations of locals made and lost everything based solely on the health of the fishing industry. Myron's father, Halliburton Avery, was the manager of the North Lubec Canning Company, a sardine processing plant owned by a Lubec family whose sons were too young to yet take over the day-to-day operations.[2]

Growing up in an environment where getting and staying ahead was an ongoing challenge inspired Myron Avery to study hard and to focus on a career outside of the fishing industry. His classmates certainly took notice.

---

1   Harrie B. Coe to Ralph O. Brewster and the Honorable Willis E. Parsons, 25 May 1926, Avery Collection, Maine State Library Special Collections.

2   Robert A. Rubin, "The Short, Brilliant Life of Myron Avery," 23.

North Lubec, Maine, Grammar School, circa 1911. Myron Avery is in the front row, third from left. He would leave this coastal village to make his mark in the mountains. Photo: Courtesy of Lubec Historical Society.

In 1916, the inaugural Lubec High School yearbook, the *Quoddy Light*, predicted that the class president and valedictorian would become a judge who "evidently followed the profession of his heart."[3]

Avery went straight from high school to Bowdoin College in Brunswick, Maine. In another competitive environment where he could test himself, he became a member of Phi Beta Kappa, ran cross-country, and managed the track team. In those years, every Bowdoin student was asked to create a scrapbook to be filed in the school archives as a record of his time on campus. Avery filled his with programs from various track meets and a few playbills from Boston stage productions. Both extracurricular activities excited the young man from Lubec, where there were not as many opportunities. Even so, he regretted not having the means for more fun. In one letter to his

3   Ronald Pasha, "Myron Avery, Lubec, and the Appalachian Trail," *Lubec Historical Society*, lubec.mainememory.net/page/1197/display.html.

mother, Avery poignantly said, "I wish I had even a little money, so I could do more with my friends."[4]

After graduating from Bowdoin in 1920, Avery attended Harvard Law School, where he graduated with an LL.B. (bachelor of laws) degree in 1923. After serving a short stint as a law clerk, he practiced maritime law for the United States government. His law career was one of two arenas in which Avery applied his remarkable drive. The other was in—and on behalf of—the mountains and trails of the eastern United States.

If Harrie Coe of the Maine Publicity Bureau was already impressed with Avery's work in 1926, there was a lot more to come.

Myron Avery's approach to researching historic explorations of Katahdin was comprehensive, impressive, and, some might say, obsessive. The project consumed most of his non-working hours from 1923–28. How did a young man who grew up in a coastal Maine town become so enamored of the state's highest mountain and the regions surrounding it? Nobody knows for certain. His son Hal once remarked that in the summer, when "everyone in town worked in the fish-processing business," Myron blazed a different path, working inland with the companies that managed Maine's timber industry.[5] As one researcher noted, "It was sometime during this period that Avery first encountered Katahdin, a mountain he would study for the rest of his life and about which he would write volumes."[6]

Throughout the Katahdin project, Avery's prodigious output of correspondence, attention to detail, and unwillingness to back down from convictions established a pattern he would repeat for the remainder of his life: producing awe-inspiring work while openly voicing contempt for those who didn't fully embrace his views. In fact, Avery's relentless drive, obsession to detail, and need to prove himself right ultimately cost him important spheres of support and assuredly contributed to his early death.

One measure of Avery's thorough study of the early explorers of Katahdin and the trails they blazed to its basins and summit ridges is the volume of

---

4   Myron Avery to Myra Bather Avery, 1918, George J. Mitchell Department of Special Collections & Archives, Bowdoin College.

5   Robert A. Rubin, "The Short, Brilliant Life of Myron Avery," 23.

6   Ibid., 24.

letters he wrote to various experts on the subject. After reading every account of explorations he could get his hands on, dating back to 1836, Avery wrote to a number of area foresters, paper company officials, family members of the explorers, and state of Maine officials in quest of materials that would corroborate the history of events he assembled. Avery was particularly interested in pinning down the precise routes the early explorers took, where possible, and determining whether trails described as having been cut by subsequent hikers were actually new routes or simply the old routes being opened again due to the need to keep vegetation at bay.

In addition to tracing the routes of the different hiking parties, Avery was a perfectionist when it came to place names. He spent countless hours drafting inquiries on the origin of geographic names to people he felt were in positions to know. And when he saw an opportunity to honor the early visitors to Katahdin by naming physical features after them, he lobbied hard.

Avery also lobbied a number of publishers to get paid for his efforts. In 1926, he partnered with Edward S.C. Smith, head of the Union College Geology Department. According to the onetime Maine state librarian, Henry Dunnack, Smith was "the best living authority on the famous mountain and its characteristics."[7]

Avery described his working relationship with Smith in a letter to Harrie Coe:

> Ever since our interest in Katahdin commenced, Professor Smith and I have worked in a sort of partnership—sharing the labor and making the finds common property. This arrangement continues and I trust will continue.[8]

Yet even as Avery recorded that sentiment, he was putting his signature on a contract dissolving the partnership. The stated reason for the dissolution was that Avery was "desirous of concluding his work on a certain Bibliography of Mt. Katahdin and of recouping certain expenses incurred therein." Avery sent the bibliography to Smith, who paid Avery $25, plus "typewriter

---

7   "State Library to Publish Pamphlet on Mt. Katahdin," *Bangor Daily Commercial* (Bangor, ME), August 20, 1926.

8   Myron Avery to Harrie Coe, 20 November 1926, Avery Collection, Maine State Library Special Collections.

costs incurred during the copying of said Bibliography." In addition, Avery was free to submit the bibliography to AMC's journal, *Appalachia,* or to any other publication, starting May 1, 1927. Any profit generated by the publication would be split with Smith on a 50–50 basis.[9]

At the same time, Smith wanted to be free to explore the publication of a "treatise on Katahdin." Thus, the contract stipulated that if Avery's bibliography was incorporated into such a treatise, Avery would receive one-half of the profits. An additional provision stated that, if Smith sent Avery "such portions of said work or treatise sufficient to establish in the fair judgment of M.H. Avery the fact of a bona fide preparation of such treatise concerning Katahdin," the date of Avery's permission to send his bibliography for publication would change to November 15, 1927.

The contract was signed and dated by Avery on November 23, 1926, and by Smith on November 29, 1926.[10]

Avery felt the prospect of Smith ever writing a treatise were slim. Avery wasn't going to wait until May 1, 1927, to see if he could generate income from his hard work on the history of the Katahdin region. In the process of assembling his bibliography of Katahdin-area explorations, he assembled a number of firsthand accounts he felt should be published verbatim.

Avery pitched the idea of running reports of George H. Witherle's explorations of Katahdin to *Appalachia,* but was rejected. (Witherle had climbed the mountain at least nine times, beginning in the 1880s.[11]) In a letter dated November 26, 1926, William P. Dickey, the journal's editor, wrote to Avery, "At present our space is so limited by financial considerations that we cannot undertake its publication," and suggested the Maine Historical Society as an alternative publisher.

Four days later, Avery wrote to Harrie Coe at the Maine Publicity Bureau:

> *I have two Katahdin original unprinted manuscripts which I think ought to be printed. Both are long. One is a surveyor's account*

---

9   Myron Avery to E.S.C. Smith, 23 November 1926, Avery Collection, Maine State Library Special Collections.

10   Ibid.

11   Aislinn Sarnacki, *Family Friendly Hikes in Maine* (Camden, ME: Down East Books, 2017), 110.

*of Katahdin in 1825—the second oldest account. The other deals with explorations on the 1880s of that little known region north of Mt. Katahdin—the Klondike, etc. Both accounts are of intense interest and in my opinion worth preserving.*

*They are too long for Appalachia. I am writing to ask if you would tell me what Maine publications I should approach on this matter.*[12]

On the same day, Avery sent a letter to the Maine Department of Inland Fisheries and Game, asking if the department knew whether *Sprague's Journal of Maine History* was going to be continued as a publication. If so, he assured the department the transcripts of early Katahdin explorations would be of interest, noting both manuscripts were "original Witherle journals."

In a letter dated December 3, 1926, Coe wrote back to Avery, suggesting the latter contact the editors at *Sun-Up,* a magazine based in Portland, Maine, to gauge their interest in Avery's piece about Katahdin. On the same day, Avery heard from the Maine Department of Inland Fisheries and Game that "representatives of Mr. Sprague's estate have decided to discontinue the *Journal of Maine History*" and that perhaps [Avery] should contact a magazine called *Sun-Up.*[13]

Avery took the advice of both sources and reached out to *Sun-Up.* He also contacted Great Northern Pulp & Paper Company, the publisher of a small-circulation magazine called *The Northern.* In addition to making the case for how interesting readers would find the manuscripts, he threw in a healthy dose of flattery: "For a number of years you have kindly carried my name on the mailing list of *The Northern.* I have often wished that I could show my appreciation other than in words."[14] What transpired thereafter provides insight into both Avery's persistent drive and unwillingness to yield—traits that would define his legacy.

12  Myron Avery to Harrie Coe, 30 November 1926, Avery Collection, Maine State Library Special Collections.

13  Harrie Coe to Myron Avery, 3 December 1926, Avery Collection, Maine State Library Special Collections.

14  Myron Avery to editor, *The Northern,* 8 December 1926, Avery Collection, Maine State Library Special Collections.

## The *Sun-Up* Magazine Saga

In a letter dated December 16, 1926, the editor of *Sun-Up*, Virginia Gates, responded to Avery's inquiry, stating that if his manuscript was accepted, the magazine would pay half a cent per word. He immediately sent his manuscript for review.

It is unclear if any correspondence between Avery and Gates took place between December and the following July. If any letters were exchanged, they apparently were not retained. What we do know is that Avery wrote two letters to Virginia Gates dated July 11 and 22, 1927. On July 29, Gates responded with a letter citing Avery's aversion to cutting any of his article, a theme we see consistently repeated. Gates's response is included here in its entirety, as it paints a clear picture of what Avery expected of the magazine.

> My dear Mr. Avery:
>
> I hope you will forgive me when you realize that even editors are out of town upon occasions. I have been away for two weeks, therefore your letters of July 11 and 22 are just coming to my attention.
>
> I am really at a loss to know what to say concerning your splendid article. It is just the kind of thing I should love to use in SUN*UP, but it is so terrifically long that I do not know how I can possibly do it if, as you say, it can not possibly be cut down and must be used intact. In one issue we absolutely can not use an article any longer than 2 or 3000 words and even that is a terrific stretch. The map, the photograph, and the article are so interesting that it seems a shame to have a Maine magazine be forced to turn it down, but unless you have suggestions to make as to length, I am at a loss to know what else to do about it.
>
> The words have not been counted in this article but I can judge sufficiently to realize it is a great deal longer than our usual length. Of course the article could be continued from one issue to the next, but I do not think that is a very wise plan with this type of article. If we should in any way be able to use it, I assure you that any instructions to cut, etc. will be followed out. I am sorry that in the past we have not been sufficiently attentive to your requests. I do not recall the incidence.
>
> I very much appreciate your willingness to even submit so splendid an article to us. You mention that you would want 20 or 30 copies. We always supply our authors with two or three if they desire them and

*any above them we supply at the reduced rate of 10 cents a copy. You speak of prospects for financially recouping to make up with us for the larger issue which this article would article [sic]. I fear that the selling of single copies would not do this as our price of 15 cents is literally a loss to us. It does not begin to pay for the printing costs. It would cost us several hundred dollars to add sixteen pages to our magazine, which we would have to do in order to run your article as it is poor economy to run four or eight extra pages. The sum, I fear, would be hard to make up by the selling of copies.*

*I appreciate your suggestion, however and would, of course, attempt to circulate it as widely as possible. We feel that the article would be a good feature and for that reason would like to use it.*

*I note in your letter you had another possible outlet for your story. I fear that they would pay you so much more than we could that perhaps you will not care to have us use it after all. Our rates as you may know, are ½ cent a word.*

*Thank you once more, and I assure you I am awaiting with interest your opinion on these various matters.*

*Most sincerely yours,*

*Virginia L. Gates, Editor*[15]

Avery's response, just days later, was equally telling. He was clearly frustrated with the lack of progress and editorial inability to accommodate his demands. After conceding he could probably "eliminate four or five of my pages," he continued,

*clearly the article can't be reduced to magazine limits. . . . You say that running four or five extra pages is poor economy. I take it that at least this would be needed. I fear that after all it is a question of your willingness to extend the magazine and how much you are willing to do it. I shall be, of course, glad to cooperate in every way which preserves the value of my labors. I appreciate full your problem. I leave for the Maine Woods for a month on August 10th. I should like to have the*

15   Virginia Gates to Myron Avery, 29 July 1927, Avery Collection, Maine State Library Special Collections.

*matter settled before that time. There is a bare possibility that I should be in Portland from 6 to 9 P.M., Friday, August 12th. If so we might be able to go over the matter and make some reduction.*[16]

That Avery and Gates did meet in Portland is made clear in a letter she sent him on November 29, 1927. During the meeting, the two agreed that *Sun-Up* magazine would publish an abridged version of Avery's manuscript, one that was shorter than the draft Avery originally submitted and longer than what the magazine would normally publish. They also established that *Sun-Up* would receive the revised manuscript from Avery in time to run in either the October or November issue of the magazine.

None of this happened, however. Instead, Avery sent an entirely different piece to the publication, which was exceedingly long. Gates responded in exasperation.

*I don't know how to make you understand that it is absolutely impossible for us to accept such a long article. . . . I did say we would make the exception in the one article which we discussed at length this summer, but I also told you that in order to do that I should have to have it for the October or November issue, but it has apparently never come.*

*I would judge this new article you sent me is several thousand words long. It is a splendid article and I should love to use it, but mechanical requirements and financial situations make it impossible to use an article of this length. 1500 is usually our limit as I told you this summer. But to run this article, pay you half a cent, make four or five large cuts, and print extra pages to accommodate the story, extra postage to send out the magazine would cost us several hundred dollars and you must realize that we cannot put that much into one article, no matter how good it is.*

---

16   Myron Avery to Virginia Gates, 3 August 1927, Avery Collection, Maine State Library Special Collections.

> *I appreciate your interest and I do know you have given me some*
> *very splendid material, but I do not know what I can do about it. May*
> *I hear from you relative to this matter?*[17]

Hear from him she did. Avery responded with equal aggravation. After admonishing Gates for not recognizing his latest submission, "The Monument Line," as a completely different article than the one he originally submitted months ago, his exasperation pours out on the page.

> *I appreciate that I don't know your game but I do have a feeling*
> *your length limitation shuts out anything other than slap and dash*
> *stuff. Your issues should contain material of real value in Maine history*
> *and development. Fifty years from now that should be worth looking*
> *into as a matter of record.*
>
> *Under the circumstances I guess you will have to send it all back*
> *to me and I will run it in* Appalachia.[18]

These correspondences illustrate the great paradox of Myron Avery. He was a man who lived in a world of absolutes. He was convinced that if he just kept pushing, he would get his way. Most often, he was accurate in his assessment. And because of that, he got a tremendous amount of work done. But he did not seem to consider the consequences of his irrepressible drive.

When it came to *Sun-Up*, his efforts produced two unpublished articles and the sore feelings left in his wake.

Given Avery's reluctance to compromise, the *Sun-Up* saga lasted a surprisingly long time. Sixteen months after Avery first contacted the magazine, he received a letter from Stanton Woodman, the publication's business manager. In it, Woodman explained that Gates had been in New York for several months, was going to visit Portland, Maine, for a week or so, and that after her brief visit, "we rather assume that she will not be connected with *Sun-Up* in the future."

Woodman went on to write:

---

17  Virginia Gates to Myron Avery, 29 November 1927, Avery Collection, Maine State Library Special Collections.

18  Myron Avery to Virginia Gates, 30 November 1927, Avery Collection, Maine State Library Special Collections.

*We are awfully sorry about the whole business but we here in the office are absolutely at a loss as to what to tell you, because frankly, we don't know just what it is all about. You will yourself admit that the whole thing has become rather complicated on account of the many changes that have taken place since Miss Gates first talked to you about the manuscript.*

*We would be very glad to have you send us the details of your manuscript, telling us just how long the story is and how many cuts would be required, etc. and we will be only too glad to definitely decide just how to settle the matter once and for all.*[19]

On April 7, 1928, Avery responded to Woodman, explaining he had made the necessary cuts to the article when he visited with Gates and that he had been waiting for map revisions from an associate, Henry Buck, which Avery did not receive until December. In a rare moment of contrition, Avery adds, "and for this delay I am responsible."

He continues by making an impassioned pitch for the article:

*Katahdin has been a hobby of mine. Appalachia has twice printed a bibliography which Professor Smith and I compiled. I have an article on Katahdin in this next issue and The Maine Woods carried our story of this year's trip. I am not so much interested in compensation for the article as I am in making available what I hope will be a valuable history of a section on this region. I hope we can work out something.*[20]

On May 12, 1928, Woodman again wrote to Avery. This time, Woodman left no uncertainty, stating, "We regret exceedingly that we are obliged to write you in this way, but we feel your article is far too long for publication in our magazine." Woodman then offered to share the manuscript with the editor of the *Portland Sunday Telegram*.[21]

---

19  Stanton Woodman to Myron Avery, 2 April 1928, Avery Collection, Maine State Library Special Collections.

20  Myron Avery to Stanton Woodman, 7 April 1928, Avery Collection, Maine State Library Special Collections.

21  Stanton Woodman to Myron Avery, 12 May 1928, Avery Collection, Maine State Library Special Collections.

On July 3, 1928, Lillian Draper wrote to Avery on behalf of *Sun-Up* to report that Woodman had personally delivered Avery's manuscript to Mr. Goodwin, the editor of the *Portland Sunday Telegram*.[22]

On August 6, 1928, *Sun-Up* contacted Avery again to report that his manuscript had been rejected by both the *Portland Sunday Telegram* and the *Evening News* because it was too long.[23]

Avery and *Sun-Up* never corresponded again.

### The Katahdin Nomenclature Dustup

The *Sun-Up* saga provides a glimpse into Avery's persistence and ability to turn acerbic, but it pales to what transpired between him and the AMC Nomenclature Committee and its chair, Arthur Comey.

The Katahdin bibliography project was the first in which Avery's irascible behavior took on a vindictive note. While the tone of his letter to Gates of *Sun-Up* was harsh, he never took issue with her character. Instead, he questioned the judgment of *Sun-Up* in not running the work he had spent so much time creating. With AMC, however, Avery's approach would turn personal and even vindictive.

Avery's dismay with Arthur Comey evolved through their correspondence in 1927 and 1928. At the time, Comey was the chair of the AMC Guidebook Committee and was in his third year of teaching at Harvard University, where he was also lecturing in the School of Landscape Architecture and in the School of City Planning. (Prior to that, Comey had received an AB from Harvard in 1907, where he had studied landscape architecture under Frederick Law Olmsted Jr., who, like his father, became an internationally famous landscape architect.)[24]

Comey had gained notoriety as a city planner, having submitted plans for the city of Houston's parks in 1912–13 as well as for a number of New England municipalities. He was well regarded by his professional colleagues

---

22  Lillian Draper to Myron Avery, 3 July 1928, Avery Collection, Maine State Library Special Collections.

23  *Sun-Up* Magazine to Myron Avery, 6 August 1928, Avery Collection, Maine State Library Special Collections.

24  "Arthur Coleman Comey," *The Cultural Landscape Foundation*, tclf.org/pioneer/arthur-coleman-comey.

and his fellow AMC board members. As chair of both the Guidebook and the Nomenclature committees, Comey communicated club decisions to Avery regarding Avery's Katahdin guidebook and its ever-evolving accompaniment of maps.

Avery had spent several years performing an exhaustive study of the Katahdin region and its place names. This included inquiries to historians, locals (camp owners, avid hunters, and fishers), corporations that did business in the area (such as paper companies), and state entities to discern how natural features in the Katahdin area got their names and whether those names were still being used.

In addition to making sure existing places were *correctly* named on maps and in print, Avery wanted to add place names he felt were overlooked. He lobbied AMC's Nomenclature and Guidebook committees chair Comey for two places, Witherle Ravine and Keep Path, to be formally named and for other places, such as Mullen Mountain, that had been formerly unrecognized to be demarcated on the new map.

The back-and-forth communications with the Guidebook Committee and the Nomenclature Committee, both with Comey as the prime communicator, clearly frustrated Avery. In Avery's mind, he had spent years doing due diligence on the veracity of place names and had the evidence to back it up. Conversely, he felt the decisions of the committees were arbitrary and piecemeal. The relationship between Avery and Comey had deteriorated so completely by autumn 1927 that Judge Perkins, who recently had taken over for MacKaye as the active chair of the ATC and also was an AMC member, stepped into the fray as the arbitrator. Perkins crafted a letter to Avery in October 1927 that began with a paragraph likely designed to assuage Avery's concerns:

> My dear Avery,
> Arthur Comey is apparently tremendously pleased with the material that you prepared for the Katahdin Guide Book, which I sent him some days ago. I also sent him some further material which we had collected . . . it is a splendid addition to the Guide Book and I hope you will be pleased with that.[25]

---

25   Arthur Perkins to Myron Avery, 19 October 1927, Avery Collection, Maine State Library Special Collections.

How badly Avery's relationship with Comey had crumbled was further emphasized by the second paragraph of the letter.

> *I had a letter from him yesterday in which he asked me fourteen questions, on one of which, with reference to the geographical names, he wants your advice. I am enclosing you, therefore, a copy of his letter, and if there are any of his questions you can answer, will you please write me a letter, giving such answers as you can, so that I can forward it to him with other memoranda from Buck, Williamson, and myself.*[26]

Perkins attempted to inject some humor into the letter's final paragraph. After asserting that he did "not approve of names of individuals, and especially contemporary individuals, for any of the natural features around the mountain," he added, "I did not notice your reference to 'Comey Ridge' in the material you sent me, but for the above reason I do not think I should be enthusiastic about it."[27]

If Perkins, and the AMC committees, hoped to navigate through the Avery/Comey minefield with minimal damage, his efforts were for naught. Five days later, Avery crafted a highly incendiary response and even went so far as to send a copy to Comey.

Avery began his letter by thanking Perkins for going into detail about the AT. It is clear that Perkins had asked Avery to spearhead the formation of a hiking club in the Washington, D.C., area and that Avery had done some legwork. Avery reported learning that MacKaye had talked to an informal organization in D.C. two years prior that had "promised to do some work on the link in this region." Avery proposed that informal group become the working nucleus for the formation of a larger organization. (In fact, that group would later become the Potomac Appalachian Trail Club, with Myron Avery as its first chair.)

Avery then turned his discussion to Comey and the AMC Nomenclature Committee. He pulled no punches:

---

26  Ibid.

27  Ibid.

*There is another matter which I shall write of quite frankly—I do this in the hope that the result will be a better spirit of cooperation and confidence on the part of those of us who wish to help. I was very glad to take time to compile data for the Guidebook for whatever use—if any—Mr. Comey cares to make of it. It is for the common good. For this reason I answer his question 7 by saying that the present wheel road (now in use) comes in from Katahdin Lake (down over a sharp pitch), roughly ¼ mile below Depot Camps. My knowledge as to Avalanche Brook was based entirely on the map and (as I have no map here and traveled alone) I can only repeat my impression that I crossed Avalanche Brook between Depot Camps and Basin Ponds. Unless by "Old Sandy Stream Road" Mr. Comey has in mind the G.N.P. [Great Northern Paper] Road from Millinocket to Basin Ponds, I do not understand him.*

*But I do not, so whole heartedly, fall in with Mr. Comey's article 13. I take this to be a direct invitation to me to send on to him any suggestions which I may have as to Katahdin nomenclature. As I read his suggestion, if my proposals meet with his approval—and I am to support my recommendation with "outside authorities"—he will place them before the Nomenclature Committee. If he disapproves, the proposals are buried—dead. If I were planning to lay such proposals before the Nomenclature Committee, I should prefer one less hurdle in my way. And my reason is this. I am not sure of the standards of judging such proposals. I have formed the impression that such proposals have been and would be measured by the yardstick of personal opinion and of the individual reaction. I feel that this is an intolerance and rough overriding of suggestions which have had a respectable support. Now, if some of the innovations (and, for example I do not mean Governor's Spring which is so officially fixed that no unbiased mind could question it) have not originated with Mr. Comey they have—as the changes of the May Bulletin—circulated as the personal reactions of a small group. Yet in his list he ignores the proposals for Witherle Ravine signed by some thirty odd A.M.C. members. Mr. Comey and his friends change and initiate to fit their personal reactions. In the last A.M.C. map not only was the term Witherle Ravine of Mr. Buck's map dropped but the contours drawn to disguise the physical fact of the existence of a ravine. Of this there can be no question. Such a thing—almost the fabrication of a map—creates a feeling of the existence of the intolerance and state of mind of the churchmen who immersed Galileo in the well.*

But Avery was just getting warmed up.

*Mr. Comey "hates" Mullen Mt. Why? Not so pretty a word? Personal reaction? Why not inquire into the meaning of Mullen and the peculiar fitness of that name. And he calls it the highest Peak of Wassataquoik. I see that it is hard to yield the opinion that the "sharp, white-tipped cone" (Mullen) is Wassataquoik. Surely it is, if Doubletop, The Brother, Coe, Mullen and Wassataquoik are peaks of one mountain.*

After a few more pointed barbs at Comey, Avery returned to what he believed was the larger issue.

*I only ask for a feeling of fair play in these matters. A willingness to permit others to give names as we do ourselves. Witherle Ravine, Keep Ridge, Harvey Ridge—have a real significance—we endeavored to inform the Committee. These terms have received publicity within the last two months in Maine newspapers under the Governor's sanction. Isn't it a trifle irritating or flaunting to come back to those that sanctioned this, overlook the carefully reasoned and supported petition and asked to have all other suggestions referred to this personal arbitration.*

*I wish I could see evidence of a genuine consideration of the right of others to initiate also. I can judge only from experience. From this I feel that the only yardstick is personal reaction and whim. (Chamberlain Lake is quite all right but not Parsons Trail.) Historical connections or peculiar fitness seem ignored. Attempts to rationalize lead one through a labyrinth of conflicting mental processes. I do not relish this situation enough to abandon and turn over Mr. Comey's disposal matters which you know from Buck are under consideration.*

*I have written quite fully and frankly. I have pointed out certain facts not to arouse controversy but to bring home conditions. I am sending a copy of this letter to Messrs. Comey, Buck, and Smith.*[28]

If Avery truly wished to avoid arousing controversy, his pointed, personal criticism of Comey and the process for placing names on maps failed spectacularly.

The first to respond was Henry Buck, whose letter dated October 31, 1927, certainly warrants reading in full.

*Dear Avery—*

*How hard it is to be consistent! You seem to think it's impossible, so why try! You condemn Comey for being tactless, then you out-comb Comey by sending him a copy of that letter to J.P [Judge Perkins]. For heaven sake, what good do you think that can do?*

*I agree with you on most everything in it as I believe Smith and Judge Perkins would too—so far the letter is all right and serves to make clear a certain point of view, but when you send it to Comey I don't see what you accomplish except to hurt his feelings.*

*I don't think he wants to be arbitrary or tactless any more than the rest of us do and when you tell him he is you simply arouse the resentment that never need have existed, I believe, if you two really knew and understood each other. It would naturally die out in time if you would let each other alone unless or until you have the chance to get acquainted face to face.*

*I've met Comey many times and like him immensely. I admire a lot what I see in him and so do many of the other members of the A.M.C. He is a mighty able fellow and is doing more real work for the Club than any member I know of outside of perhaps the half-dozen wheel horses like the President, Secretary, Treasurer, Dr. Larrabee, etc.*

*I have owned an Airedale dog and liked him immensely too. I do not expect him to be a lap dog and do not treat him like one. You two remind me of two Airedales who are splendid by yourselves but for*

28 Myron Avery to Arthur Perkins and Arthur Comey, 24 October 1927, Avery Collection, Maine State Library Special Collections.

*some unknown reason seem to bristle at sight of each other. For heaven*
*sake keep away from him and give him a chance to cool off.*

*I had the enclosed all blocked out before I read yours and am send-*
*ing them along although I fear you have spilled the beans so badly that*
*no one else can pick them up. However, do let us try.*

*And believe me, that in spite of your useless prickles, I love you still.*
*Very sincerely yours,*
*Henry R. Buck*[29]

Avery responded to Buck straightaway. He admitted, "You are quite right
and I merit all that you say. This bear-baiting of Comey is unnecessary and
productive of no good results. I am almost ready to give you a bond to keep
the peace as far as he is concerned." Avery went on to reiterate his concern
that Witherle Ravine would not earn its place on the Katahdin map. Then
he wrote something that presaged his future:

*My only consolation is contained in the last sentence of your letter.*
*If Judge Perkins can be similarly tolerant I can repay him by doing*
*some good work here [in Washington, D.C.] on his Appalachian Trail.*
*If he cast me from favor I can do the work just the same.*[30]

Next to weigh in was Perkins, who was much keener on discussing the
AT than Avery's concerns about Katahdin nomenclature and the process for
getting names approved. As for that subject, Perkins's only comment in his
letter read: "I thank you for your views in regard to Katahdin matters, which
take up the rest of your letter. As you sent a copy of it to Mr. Comey, I will
not have to do so."

Perkins also indicated that he had "been appointed a member of the general committee on the Appalachian Trail" and that "as the Appalachian Trail
plans get more developed, we ought to have committees in different localities to help build it and keep it open, and they might as well be called trail
conferences as anything else." He noted the existence of the NY–NJ Trail

29  Henry R. Buck to Myron Avery, 31 October 1927, Avery Collection, Maine State Library
    Special Collections.

30  Myron Avery to Henry R. Buck, 3 November 1927, Avery Collection, Maine State Library
    Special Collections.

Conference and that a similar group was taking shape in Pennsylvania. The groundwork had been prepared for Avery to step into a more active role in the D.C. area.[31]

As might be predicted, Comey's response confronted Avery's claims and insinuations head-on. Comey's November 4, 1927, letter stated:

> Dear Mr. Avery–
> Thank you for sending me a copy of your letter of Oct. 24th to Mr. Perkins, for the valuable information on Katahdin contained therein, though mixed with the sort of scurrilous remarks without which so far as I have been able to observe you are unable to write any letter at all. I will overlook the venom in these remarks and address myself to the other contents so as not to show you up (to yourself, I hope) on every count that you make. I would not <u>do</u> this in retaliation, but because your contributions <u>are</u> valuable and we must continue to work on the same and similar matters; and the only basis on which I can work is above board and, to use your own expression "quite frankly." Believe me, if you really do harbor these thoughts and feelings that you express I would far prefer you to express them and I'll do the same; then perhaps we can keep within reasonable reach of some common understanding.[32]

Comey went on to make a point-by-point case against each of Avery's allegations, including the admission that, "as for Mullen Mt. I do hate it. That <u>is</u> my personal reaction, and valuable just to that degree, and no more." Comey patiently walked through the rationale for each decision, indicating that none of them was made by only one person, and all of them were informed by vigorous input and discussion. Regarding the charge that the map's contours had been changed, Comey stated:

> I don't know whether <u>you</u> would falsify contours, or anything else, but if not, it seems a little discourteous and uncalled for to imply that

---

31  Arthur Perkins to Myron Avery, 4 November 1927, Avery Collection, Maine State Library Special Collections.

32  Arthur Comey to Myron Avery, 4 November 1927, Avery Collection, Maine State Library Special Collections.

*I would, even if I had the nefarious purposes you impute. Perhaps you will have to find out from others whether I would. I am glad to have even this back-handed correction for the map, and would appreciate your sending me an accurate revision of this portion.*[33]

One place where Comey backed down was on the question of Witherle Ravine. He agreed to place it on the map, something Avery truly wanted and had felt was a lost cause.

Comey signed off with, "Finally, may I quote from your letter: Attempts to rationalize lead one through a labyrinth of conflicting mental processes."[34]

In early November, Perkins wrote a letter to Avery attempting to put the nomenclature matter to rest and to smooth things out with Comey. After going over a number of AT-related matters, Perkins finished his letter with the following two paragraphs:

*I have received this morning from Arthur Comey a copy of the letter he wrote to you on November 4th, and am very sorry he saw fit to make the remarks he did in it, especially in the first paragraph. In my opinion no good can come from such a handling of a matter in which we are all interested, and as I said above, I regret it very much, for both of you are very important, and I wish you could work together in harmony.*

*When I wrote to Comey after receiving your letter of the 24th I begged him not to answer at all, for I thought it would only make matters worse if he did, and now I am writing to renew my request to you, not to answer this one, but to let the controversy die out. If any more correspondence is necessary between you two fellows, why don't you write to me as an intermediary, as I am able to get along all right with both of you.*[35]

Correspondence between Comey and Avery ceased, but some discourse continued behind the scenes. Notably, Buck wrote to Comey on November

---

33 Ibid.

34 Ibid.

35 Arthur Perkins to Myron Avery, November 8 1927, Avery Collection, Maine State Library Special Collections.

8, 1927, stating he believed Avery's underlying intention in copying Comey on his letter to Perkins was that Avery "didn't want to say anything behind your back that he wouldn't say to your face" and that "if you can continue to take advantage of each other's knowledge and overlook each other's prickles ... I am sure the Guide Book and map will benefit, which of course is the thing you and all of us are really after."[36]

Avery then wrote to Buck, saying: "You will have received a copy of Comey's letter showing me up ... and to others as well. I really think that after all my letter may have done some good. I call his announcement that he will not oppose Witherle Ravine the greatest conversion since Paul of Tarsus. In compliance with my promise to keep the peace I shall not reply to his letter unless you think some specific matter should be dealt with."[37]

The great Katahdin nomenclature dustup was over, but the sore feelings lingered in its aftermath. That episode, and others like it, would damage Avery's relationship with various members of the AMC board for the rest of his life.

Such pointed accusations and the obsessive need to prove himself right were Avery's hallmarks. What fueled his contempt? It is hard to find many certainties within the letters written between Avery and the recipients of his criticisms, but one absolute is that Avery felt his own well-considered view to be the only one worth entertaining. His "my way or the highway" thinking would be mentioned in the same breath as his prodigious accomplishments until the day he died—and for generations beyond.

When AMC announced its roster of committees for 1929, Comey was no longer assigned a seat on the Nomenclature Committee. There is no record of whether this was Comey's decision or not, but his new role on the Huts and Trails Committee was sure to afford him fewer occasions to work with Avery.

Avery and Comey reestablished correspondence over time, because their professional duties necessitated it. At first the letters almost exclusively conveyed actions taken by the Nomenclature Committee or other business matters. But over time, personal observations and barbs began to show up again.

---

36  Henry Buck to Arthur Comey (copy sent to Myron Avery), November 8 1927, Maine State Library Special Collections.

37  Myron Avery to Henry Buck, November 9 1927, Avery Collection, Maine State Library Special Collections.

In January 1929, Comey warned Avery about badmouthing others publicly. He especially took delight when Avery was named as a new member of the Nomenclature Committee, the group he had so recently maligned. "You should not rap the Nomenc. Com. in print. Now that you are to be on it, you may feel so."[38]

Interestingly, Avery's relationship with Comey was one of the few in his life that survived the stinging accusations Avery was known to bring forth. Perhaps the reason was, in addition to serving on AMC's board, Comey would assume several executive committee seats on the New England Trail Conference (NETC) as the years progressed. NETC was a consortium of trail clubs, associations (such as the Society for Protection of New Hampshire Forests), and state and federal agencies (such as the USFS and the Maine Forest Service) formed to coordinate and preside over the building of the AT in New England. Because NETC was a source of funding and influence, Avery undoubtedly concluded it was best to work in cooperation with the organization. In a future twist of fate, Comey would hold the position of chair of NETC in 1933, when tensions between Avery and AMC would reach new levels.

## Published at Last

In early 1928, Avery sent two large envelope's worth of manuscripts to Robert L.M. Underhill, editor of the Appalachian Mountain Club's then-quarterly journal, *Appalachia*.* Avery made the case for having the Katahdin bibliography published by AMC as a separate book, noting that a similar White Mountain bibliography had been published separately and sold by AMC.

Underhill's response to Avery was evidently quite detailed. What is absolutely known from Avery's subsequent follow-up letter is that Underhill provisionally accepted Avery's article, "The Monument Line," for inclusion in *Appalachia*, under the condition that the article be completely overhauled. In his February letter accompanying the rewrite, Avery thanks Underhill, saying:

---

\* Appalachia is currently a biannual publication.

38 Arthur Comey to Myron Avery, January 1929, Avery Collection, Maine State Library Special Collections.

*You have made a great deal of work for me. But you, too, have also spent considerable time in typing and this attitude of a critic makes one quite willing to do further work. You did a rare thing, Mr. Underhill. I quite appreciate your very great experience along this line and value your suggestions.*[39]

It was one of the few times Avery would accept criticism so graciously.

Interestingly, in the same letter, Avery took a swipe at Arthur Comey. (This was during the period when the Nomenclature Committee was turning down many of Avery's requests.) In questioning the motive behind one of AMC's nomenclature decisions, Avery wrote to Underhill that, "As to the objection to using the term Lake Cowles, I fear that I see here the ... hand of Mr. Comey." Avery then went on to complain to Underhill about his current pet peeve, how Nomenclature Committee decisions were made. He clearly saw no issue with sharing his dismay for Comey with the leadership of AMC, even those who had nothing to do with either the Guidebook Committee or the Nomenclature Committee—again raising questions about Avery's judgment as it related to team dynamics.[40]

In March 1928, Underhill reported back to Avery with decisions regarding the Katahdin bibliography and other submitted manuscripts. This time, the news wasn't nearly as promising.

First, Underhill wrote that the Katahdin bibliography was too lengthy for inclusion in the pages of *Appalachia,* and while it could be published separately and would likely have "a very slow, tho sure, sale," there was "no chance of doing so this year," as the organization's budget had already been allocated. He suggested bringing the topic up again at a later date.[41]

Regarding Avery's article on "the Keep Path, etc.," Underhill maintained that although it represented "a tremendous amount of research on your part,"

39  Myron Avery to Robert L.M. Underhill, 4 February 1928, Avery Collection, Maine State Library Special Collections.

40  Ibid.

41  Robert L.M. Underhill to Myron Avery, 10 March 1928, Avery Collection, Maine State Library Special Collections.

Robert Underhill, right, was an avid outdoorsman, an active member of the Appalachian Mountain Club, and the editor of *Appalachia* from 1928–1934. In this 1960s photo, he takes a break on a trail in Randolph, New Hampshire, with his wife, Miriam. Photo: Courtesy of AMC Library & Archives.

it also was too long for *Appalachia*, even if it were published in two or three installments.[42]

Underhill's letter did, however, end on an upbeat note. He wrote that if Avery could provide a 200-word description on the trail work completed on the Potomac section of the AT, Underhill would try to include it in an upcoming issue of the journal.[43]

Avery's response, only two days later, was important, because it showed that his resolve was hardly shaken. In it, he asked the Guidebook Committee to take a definitive stand on the bibliography and provide money for it in the next budget. He then offered to shorten "The Keep Path and Its Successors" and asked when he should have his 200-word article about the trail work ready.[44]

Underhill responded that he didn't want to assume responsibility for the bibliography and that Avery could send it for budgetary reconsideration in November or December. Further, Underhill reiterated that the committee's opinion was averse to running "The Keep Path and Its Successors," as "it deals chiefly with approaches to the mountain, rather than the mountain itself," and was thus less appropriate for *Appalachia*. Underhill then established an April 1 deadline for the 200-word article.[45]

Underhill soon wrote again. He offered a glimmer of hope that the Katahdin bibliography and "The Keep Path and Its Successors" might find a home. He told Avery that a skeleton committee "is engaged in a new experiment with *Appalachia*" and that the committee would be enlarged to include a new special editor position. He suggested that Avery resubmit his Katahdin bibliography when the committee was at full strength the coming summer and that Avery submit the Keep Path article to the new special editor when that position was filled.[46]

---

42  Ibid.

43  Ibid.

44  Myron Avery to Robert L.M. Underhill, 12 March 1928, Avery Collection, Maine State Library Special Collections.

45  Robert L.M. Underhill to Myron Avery, 17 March, 1928, Avery Collection, Maine State Library Special Collections.

46  Robert L.M. Underhill to Myron Avery, 18 March, 1928, Avery Collection, Maine State Library Special Collections.

In his reply to Underhill, Avery offered a clue toward what might have fueled at least some of the latter's insatiable drive. Avery's letter began with a request that Underhill provide 25 reprints of "The Monument Line Surveyors on Katahdin," an article Avery had written for the June 1928 issue of *Appalachia*, "in addition to the 25 to which I am entitled."[47]

Could it be that Avery yearned to be validated, if not as a writer, at least for his contribution to history? This question rises again in regard to a letter Avery sent three months later to Nathaniel Goodrich, a librarian at Dartmouth College and the newly appointed special editor of historical articles for *Appalachia*:

> *I have spent four years gathering data on this [Katahdin history] and have been at extreme pains to be absolutely correct in the narrative. I claim no literary value for this article but hope that it will appeal to you, as a historian, as a valuable collection of source materials which if not preserved, will be lost. Some day the Katahdin book will be presented by some enthusiast and I should like to have available to the writer this data to the preparation of which I have devoted so much time.[48]*

While submitting the bibliography as a historical article for inclusion in the AMC archives may have brought Avery some relief that his hard work would be officially retained, he was not ready to give up on his goal of getting the work published as a standalone volume. Avery concluded his letter to Goodrich by stating, "In the fall I am to take up with the Publishing Committee the matter of having printed as a separate volume (as the White Mountain Bibliography) our Katahdin Bibliography, which has been greatly expanded since the 1924 issue."[49]

By autumn Avery was expressing disappointment that, of all the materials he had submitted to various outlets, only "The Monument Line Surveyors

---

47   Myron Avery to Robert L.M. Underhill, 20 April 1928, Avery Collection, Maine State Library Special Collections.

48   Myron Avery to Nathaniel Goodrich, August 1928, Avery Collection, Maine State Library Special Collections.

49   Ibid.

on Katahdin" had been published. In late September, Avery's colleague and friend Henry Buck wrote a letter to AMC's then-president, Dean Peabody, informing Peabody of Avery's recent and impressive circumnavigation hike of Katahdin and suggesting that a condensed write-up of the trip be included in an upcoming issue of *Appalachia*.[50] Buck apparently sent a copy of the letter to Avery, as well, for on September 24, Avery wrote to Buck, "Your letter to Peabody is just another instance of the many kind things you have done and are doing for me." Avery's letter was a rare glimpse into his softer side and one that indicated his loyalty to those he believed were loyal to him.[51]

Avery also used the opportunity to ask that Buck "put in a favorable word for [the Keep Path article] in the near future with the right people" for having it published in *Appalachia*. Avery lamented the fact that, two years before, "I had favorable word from the Publishing Committee but I withdrew it to revise it," and that Underhill "was not at all encouraging" for the prospects of having it appear in the magazine.[52]

The next day, Avery received a letter from Goodrich bearing the news that Goodrich had sent "The Keep Path and Its Successors" to Underhill, "with a strong recommendation that it be printed in *Appalachia*." At long last, Avery's doggedness looked as if it would pay dividends.[53]

Underhill informed Avery that "The Keep Path and Its Successors" would run in two installments, in the June and December issues of *Appalachia*. Avery pushed back, hoping the first installment could appear in the December 1928 issue of the magazine. Avery's intention was clear: He had been burned once before with promises of future publication. He wanted to get the first installment published as soon as practicable. His request was ignored.[54]

---

50  Henry Buck to Dean Peabody, 21 September 1928, Avery Collection, Maine State Library Special Collections.

51  Myron Avery to Henry Buck, 24 September 1928, Avery Collection, Maine State Library Special Collections.

52  Ibid.

53  Nathaniel Goodrich to Myron Avery, 22 September 1928, Avery Collection, Maine State Library Special Collections.

54  Myron Avery to Nathaniel Goodrich, 24 September 1928, Avery Collection, Maine State Library Special Collections.

Buck cheered Avery from the sidelines, saying, "Hurrah for *Appalachia*! It looks as if you were going to get the material published in good shape, and I congratulate you on doing a good piece of work."[55]

It was a long path for Avery to achieve publication and, ultimately, recognition for his work. But that recognition came at a cost only to be fully assessed later. He had deservedly been feted for his determination and thoroughness, but he also had gained a reputation for his accusatory tone and unwillingness to accept decisions made by the committees and individuals with the authority to make them (Underhill's editing suggestions being the notable exception). His damn-the-torpedoes approach made even longtime friends, such as Henry Buck, question Avery's motives and lack of tact. The concerns raised did little to affect Avery's behavior, however. His relentless drive was in charge and would be for the rest of his life.

55  Henry Buck to Myron Avery, 23 October 1928, Avery Collection, Maine State Library Special Collections.

# CHAPTER 9

## *From Word Slinger to Trail Builder*

AFTER YEARS OF POURING HIS ENERGY INTO THE EXPLORATION AND documentation of the Katahdin region, Myron Avery was ready to turn the page and began directing his considerable energy and planning capabilities toward other areas.

Back in October 1927, Avery had received a letter from Judge Perkins, who, in his retirement, had become active with both AMC and NETC, the consortium of New England hiking clubs. The letter suggested that Avery either become involved with an existing hiking club in the Washington, D.C., area or start a new one with the intentions of creating awareness for the AT and building trail sections in proximity to the D.C. area.[1] Local inquiries led Avery to discover that two existing clubs had been approached by Benton MacKaye, but MacKaye's attempts to interest them in building sections of the trail had not yielded results.

By November, Avery was among the eight men who convened to form what they agreed to call the Potomac Appalachian Trail Club (PATC). Avery was elected the organization's first president. True to form, Avery had done his homework before the club was officially established. A few weeks before, he had taken part in a scouting trip to assess how difficult it would be to cut an AT route through northern Virginia. Between 1928 and 1932, with assistance from the Civilian Conservation Corps, the Potomac Appalachian Trail Club scouted, constructed, and marked more than 250 miles of trail, from the Susquehanna River to Rockfish Gap in Shenandoah National Park in Virginia.

---

1    Arthur Perkins to Myron Avery, 19 October 1927, Avery Collection, Maine State Library Special Collections.

Judge Perkins, left, Ben Flanagan, and Doc Spaulding scout a potential location for the Maine AT next to Little Niagara Falls, just south of Katahdin, in 1925. Photo: Courtesy of Avery Collection, Maine State Library.

Leading a new organization with a mandate to build hundreds of miles of trails while holding down a full-time position as a maritime lawyer seems enough to keep one man occupied. But that wasn't the case with Myron Avery. In the 1930s, he led efforts to scout, build, and mark more than 200 miles of the AT in Maine. This project reintroduced conflict between Avery and other AMC leaders, most notably his old nemesis, Arthur Comey.

From the time when the idea of the Appalachian Trail was first presented to AMC, the organization had advocated the practice of establishing regional clubs that, in turn, would take on the responsibility for locating and maintaining the AT in each club's given jurisdiction. This approach had successfully built the existing sections of the trail to date, and the expectation was that sections yet to be built could be completed the same way.

Comey had been mapping a route for the AT through Maine as far back as 1925, when he participated in a scouting party that covered the western part of the state, from Grafton Notch to Old Blue, a mountain just west of the Height of Land, in Rangeley. In August 1929, Comey, writing as the chair of NETC, issued a report to Judge Perkins regarding a second, just-completed scouting trip from Old Blue to one-half mile north of The Forks, located at the convergence of the Kennebec River and Dead River. From there, Comey

Myron Avery spent countless weekends scouting, building, and marking the AT, as captured on this 1930 work trip. Photo: Courtesy of Lubec Historical Society.

believed, it would be relatively easy to patch together a series of existing and proposed trail sections to reach Katahdin.[2]

> *The above [description] relates solely to the best route for the Appalachian Trail through Maine IF opened. The problem of the IF is another matter. There is no local interest, and there are many interests in Maine against such a trail, notably the wild land owners, who dictate much of the state's policy.[3]*

Later in the same letter, Comey urges no further action until Maine citizens take up the cause.

> *It is my opinion that no lasting progress can be made in Maine except through local Maine action. When they come to believe that a through trail will help them, they will open it. At present there would be so infinitesimally few through hikers that the opening of the trail for outsiders would be too previous.[4]*

Comey would not have to look far to find a contrarian's opinion on the subject. His old nemesis, the native Mainer Myron Avery, stepped back into the fray.

Avery pointedly argued that Comey's approach wasn't sensible for the Maine portion of the AT, citing that the state was too sparsely populated to expect clubs to organize anytime soon. Instead, Avery insisted NETC and other supporting organizations adopt a "build it first" approach in the Pine Tree State. If the trail was established, Avery insisted, Maine people who recognized its value would create the organizations to support it.

This radical idea ruffled feathers, but Avery didn't wait for permission. He reached out to a number of people who were in positions to get the trail through Maine scouted and built as quickly as possible.

---

2    Arthur Comey to Myron Avery, 27 August 1929, Avery Collection, Maine State Library Special Collections.

3    Ibid.

4    Ibid.

# The State of Maine

To understand what a significant accomplishment it was to build a footpath through Maine in the early 1930s warrants a brief look back in time.

In 1930, the population of Maine was about 800,000. More than half of the state's residents lived in rural communities, where farming and timber were the primary sources of income.[5] When the Great Depression hit, rural Mainers, who were used to living off the land, were less severely impacted than those in more industrial states. (In 1930, unemployment in Maine rose to 15 percent, half of the national average at the time.) While many people could feed themselves, the market for the goods they typically would sell largely evaporated. This, in turn, sent prices tumbling. As just one example, the selling price for potatoes dropped from a high of $2 per bushel in 1925 to just 21 cents per bushel by 1931.[6] In order to get by, most Maine farm families continued doing what they had always done: raising their own food and working whatever jobs they could get on the side.[7]

Proposing to build a footpath through more than 200 miles of the state in this economic environment probably seemed crazy to most observers. But where others saw a fool's errand, Avery saw opportunity. First, Avery was a native, having been born in rural Lubec and a graduate of Bowdoin College. He mentioned his birthplace frequently in his correspondence, when he felt he needed to establish a connection as a fellow Mainer. This can be seen in the numerous letters he wrote to landowners, local historians, hunters, anglers, and businesses while compiling his Katahdin bibliography.

Second, Avery's work on the bibliography had created a network he could tap into to help establish the AT in Maine. He didn't hesitate to ask anyone if they could help him contact the right people or organizations to get assistance.

Finally, and perhaps most important, Avery knew how to take advantage of the economic climate to get the trail built. He reached out to the owners of fishing and hunting camps—often one and the same—to ask their advice on where to place the trail and to make a simultaneous economic pitch for

---

5   *Maine Data Book* (1930), Portland Room at Portland Public Library, Maine.

6   Ibid.

7   Ibid.

having the trail cross their property. Avery told camp owners the trail would provide an added source of income for them—that hikers would come off the trail to gain food and lodging, most often in the slow summer months, after the best fishing ceased and before the hunting season began. To camp owners facing a general downturn in business, the idea of extra income was compelling indeed.

While Avery's actions were critical to laying the foundation for getting the trail established in Maine, there was one significant disadvantage: He was based in Washington, D.C. Even though his correspondence capabilities were unrivaled, scouting and routing a trail from afar was impossible. Traveling the route in person was the only way to ensure the trail was sited and built properly. Fortunately, his previous work researching the history of the Katahdin region had provided enough familiarity to enable him to direct the mapping and building of trail in that part of the state, but it was a fraction of the work that needed to be done.

Meanwhile, if Avery had any free time, he needed to spend it on scouting the route through Virginia, another area demanding his immediate attention due to his position as head of the Potomac Appalachian Trail Club. Clearly, he needed to find a solution for building the Maine section of AT that did not require him to be there. For one of the few times in his life, he would need to trust someone else to help him and actually grant them the autonomy to get the job done.

The man he found was Walter Greene.

Greene was one of the most fascinating and important individuals among the dozens who led to the creation of the AT. Yet, other than the scores of letters he wrote to Avery, relatively little is known about the man. Greene was born in Baltimore in 1872. He was a Broadway actor who appeared in seventeen plays between 1901 and 1936.[8] He spent his winters in New York City at The Lambs Club (a social destination for actors, songwriters, and others involved in the theatre) and the rest of the year mostly by himself in a cabin on the shores of Sebec Lake, Maine, or tramping around the woods between his cabin and Katahdin. He was also a registered Maine Guide.

---

8   Andrew Riley, "Timber, Shotgun, Boot, and Ski: Traditional Meets Modern at Gorman Chairback Lodge and Cabins," *Appalachia* 62, no. 2 (Summer/Fall, 2012): 56–71.

Walter Greene, pictured here on a 1933 Maine trail-building trip with Shailer Philbrick, came closest to matching Myron Avery's incredible drive. He scouted and built many miles of the AT in Maine and served as Avery's trusted man in the field, the only person to earn this distinction. Photo: Courtesy of Avery Collection, Maine State Library.

During Prohibition, Greene also possessed a still for distilling alcoholic beverages, located in the woods behind his cabin. A letter from Avery's friend and Maine geology expert Dr. Shailer Philbrick recapping a 1933 trail work trip mentions going "to Walter's for dinner last night" and "getting around to some of his remarkable beverage," which seems to corroborate the rumor.[9]

Appropriately, Greene met Avery in the vast woodlands north of Katahdin. The two happened upon each other when they were independently exploring the region. Greene described the event and their subsequent partnership in a letter he wrote in 1935.

> *Several years ago, I by chance, met Mr. Avery in the Wissatacook Valley, just north of Katahdin. This chance meeting led to a lasting friendship which I value very deeply. Some time I hope you may meet him. You will find him a fine type of Maine character, brainy, efficient, with an immense amount of quiet drive and initiative and a logical, clear-thinking mind.[10]*

The partnership was interesting from the outset. Greene revered the wilderness. His letters often alluded to the importance of woodland sojourns and periods of solitude to his well-being. In one of his earliest letters to Avery, in February 1929, he wrote:

> *Once in a while here, you hear an owl not too far away. It always has a spell for me. Something that carries the spell of the wild to me more than any other sound. . . . I wander the woods a bit every day. . . . It was good to get away from here [to scout potential trail routes]. When I first came [to Sebec] it was a primitive wilderness. The years and the auto and the kicker [a train's air brakes] have changed it. Too many people. Too much noise.[11]*

9  Shailer Philbrick to "Jack," 17 September 1933, Avery Collection, Maine State Library Special Collections.

10  Walter Greene to H.E. Sweet, 15 February 1935, Avery Collection, Maine State Library Special Collections.

11  Walter Greene to Myron Avery, 8 February 1929, Avery Collection, Maine State Library Special Collections.

Greene sent lengthy handwritten, highly descriptive, and frustratingly illegible letters to Avery through the years that were often met with doses of both praise and scorn. If it were up to Avery, Greene would leave the personal stuff out of his missives and simply provide a list of accomplishments and action items. He often implored the actor to do just that, although Greene rarely adapted his style.

Avery was particularly vexed by Greene's cursive, which made for tough reading to begin with but got progressively worse as its wielder's pencil dulled. "My praise was premature," bemoans Avery to Greene in a letter from 1932. "I struggled as of old with your last letter. I wish sometimes that I didn't know that there would be so much of interest in your letters to keep me struggling for the gems. That gray paper makes it worse."[12]

Unlike Greene's letters to Avery, in which he poured out his soul, Avery's letters back were almost always exclusively about the AT and ancillary subjects. In the hundreds of pages written between the two, Avery mentions his home life only once. In the previously cited letter, Avery writes the following paragraph before getting back to business.

> You ask about myself. We have another trail cutter in the family now—Halliburton Avery. Everything going well. In other ways things are still chaotic. As unsettled as ever. It looks as if vacation would consist of the twelve furlough payless days. No chance to do much.[13]

Although Avery seldom discussed personal matters with Greene, his admiration was undisputable. Avery knew he never could have pulled off the feat of getting the AT through Maine without Greene. Avery made a special point to highlight Greene's contributions publicly and in letters shared with member clubs and the growing number of trail enthusiasts. In a press release Avery issued following the 120-mile trail-blazing achievement of 1933, he wrote:

> Too much credit cannot be given Walter Greene for the completion of the first link in Maine. He worked out the route and made several

---

12  Myron Avery to Walter Greene, 29 June 1932, Avery Collection, Maine State Library Special Collections.

13  Ibid.

*solo scouting trips—by canoe and trail—to work out dubious spots
in it. His single-handed cutting of 39 miles of trail from Blanchard to
Pleasant River is an unequalled feat. With an artist's instinct for the
spectacular views and a woodsman's sense of the route, Greene's trail
seems to us to be the very best part of the route—excepting always, of
course, Katahdin.[14]*

Deeper aspects of the friendship between Avery and Greene would emerge. Greene was always effusive in his praise for Avery, his letters often citing Avery's resolve and dedication to getting the trail built. And Greene ultimately would get more than Avery's chastisements for poor handwriting and ramblings in return.

In 1933, Greene was suffering professionally and, as a direct result, financially. He shared with Avery that, due to the Depression, theatre work had become nonexistent, and he was barely scraping by, living in his cabin. The days of solitude were causing him to dwell on his finances, creating a spiral of despair. Greene was physically exhausted, as well, having blazed 39 miles of trail by himself. Avery had originally hired a Maine fire warden and the warden's son to do the job, but they had pulled out after accepting $75 in pay. Greene took issue with only being paid $20 for the considerable work he had done on the trail, and he let Avery know it.[15] By this time, Greene had been privy to both the $75 payment for work undone and a $45 payment to Dr. Shailer Philbrick for blazing a 50-mile section from Blanchard to Bigelow.

In response, Myron Avery sent a 15-page handwritten letter to Greene. "I don't want to have such a personal matter typed," he wrote in the first paragraph, an indication that he wanted to prevent his staff from reading it.[16] After telling Greene he would rather not have to write the letter at all, Avery expressed concern for Greene's mental state and the underlying resentment

---

14  Myron Avery to Harrie B. Coe, press release, 6 September 1933, Avery Collection, Maine State Library Special Collections.

15  Avery wrote a letter to the NETC in early September 1933 requesting approval of funds from the treasury to pay $20 to Walter Greene to build the relocation and $40 for Shailer Philbrick to blaze 50 new miles of trail from Blanchard to Bigelow. The funds were approved.

16  Myron Avery to Walter Greene, 1 October 1933, Avery Collection, Maine State Library Special Collections.

that arose after Greene pushed so hard to complete his solo trail-blazing effort on Barren–Chairback and the trip from Katahdin to Blanchard.

> *You caught hell. If only it hadn't gotten to you mentally. The physical labor is a benefit. But the toll on the other side has given me endless concern. I am loath to write at all lest you accuse me of a lack of appreciation—of you or conditions. You can't do that. But this resentment is a gnawing thing that must be sorted out of our association.*[17]

Avery then turned the conversation to friendship and finances. He told Greene there would be no additional money forthcoming for the work Greene performed and that Greene would have to buck up like all of the volunteers had had to do. He also appealed to Greene's need for public recognition.

> *If I lose your friendship or esteem, this trail isn't worth it. Far better that it never have been opened. But far more practical is our problem. We can't drop this work now. We can't let go. You are a much publicized man. Your reputation is involved. It grows with each article. For a few years, we have got to keep it open, you and I. It will be judicious use of funds through dependable people on the bad sections. I will have little time there, but expect to spend my vacations on the trail country. I will plan and arrange to get the limited funds.*
> *Remember this always. For it explains the background of our problem. All trail work is voluntary. The workers pay their own expenses, etc. Now you don't have to tell me why Maine is different. Haven't I been hammering away on this theme and getting money for Maine work?*[18]

Avery then counseled Greene against complaining to others about not being paid enough—especially in writing, which creates a lasting record. He also told Greene how to properly present an invoice for the services he had already rendered so that NETC could square its books and issue payment to Greene.

---

17   Ibid.

18   Ibid.

"Now look, this business of putting your accounts in a letter is terrible," said Avery. "How is the Treasurer going to use it as a voucher to support his payments to you? Make out a proper bill on the form like the enclosed." The next two pages contain detailed instructions about how to draft and present an invoice. Although Avery was often quick to judge and criticize the actions of others, in this case, he took the time to advise a friend.[19]

Avery concluded by revisiting the theme of Greene's anguish and where he felt the actor and renowned trail builder should properly assign credit and blame.

> *You will have many occasions to talk of the trail and your work. But do yourself justice by eliminating the resentment that somebody— you don't know who—limited your finances, whereby you suffered much mental and physical hardship. The last is true but no one owes us, you or the trail any obligations. Your talk with us and Philbrick savored of this. It belittles you. Talk of limited finances, if you wish. But that was a condition and [an] unavoidable one. There is no one to blame. In some way you blame the A.M.C. They had* nothing at all *to do with it. Therefore, it made me cross when you kept painting those [signs saying] "Appalachian Mountain Club side trail to x". I had explained the set-up to you. That club has as much* and no more *to do with it than the Georgia or Carolina Mountain Club. When you go to these places, change it to "Appalachian Trail Conference Side-Trail." You have placed the* blame *and* credit *in the wrong place. It has colored your attitude, thoughts and speech. You must force out this idea that anybody owes us anything and didn't come through.[20]*

While Avery's letter contained plenty of his trademark admonishments, he also reminded Greene that the foundation of their association was a genuine friendship. Myron Avery rarely revealed his feelings about anything other than where to place a trail, how to organize a plan, or how well someone was or wasn't doing his job. Yet he was able to communicate to Greene his

---

19  Myron Avery to Walter Greene, 1 October 1933, Avery Collection, Maine State Library Special Collections.

20  Ibid.

concern about Greene's mental and physical health and how Greene was perceived in the public eye.

Years later, Avery would reveal his admiration and respect for Greene once more. But in October 1933, Avery turned his focus back to his own punishing professional schedule, one that would take him from New York to New Orleans to California and back again.

# CHAPTER 10

## *Undaunted and Unraveling*

BY 1933, MYRON AVERY'S RELATIONSHIP WITH THE APPALACHIAN
Mountain Club (AMC) was strained and soon would become irreparable.

Building the Maine section of the AT was taxing Avery's patience. His
ability to solicit input from various state and private entities regarding where
the trail could and should ultimately be placed, deciphering Walter Greene's
letters and assuaging the actor's many concerns and insecurities, presiding
over the trail's construction, writing the trail guide, and shepherding the
maps to completion were considerable accomplishments—particularly
when viewed in light of Avery's full-time job as a maritime lawyer, his efforts
to establish other sections of trail, and his leadership duties as chairman of
ATC and president of the Potomac Appalachian Trail Club (PATC).

The year got off to a poor start. The first letter Avery received in 1933 bore
potentially embarrassing news. Maine Fire Warden Harry Davis sent news
from Monson that his son, Lyman, had not been able to cut any of the trail
in 1932 as originally planned. He also informed Avery that to move forward
with the project, his son and crew would need to make more money than the
$75 originally proposed by Avery in a letter sent six months prior and initially
agreed upon as a fair wage.[1] (According to the U.S. Bureau of Labor Statistics,
the wage proposed by Avery would be the 2017 equivalent of $1,411.85.[2])

---

[1]   Harry Davis to Myron Avery, 2 January 1933, Avery Collection, Maine State Library Special Collections.

[2]   "CPI Inflation Calculator," *U.S. Bureau of Labor Statistics*, data.bls.gov/cgi-bin/cpicalc.pl?cost1=75.00&year1=193301&year2=201701.

Avery was understandably upset at this turn of events and replied, "I know Mr. Greene will be also."[3] Greene had reported to Avery that he had seen Lyman Davis the previous August. Lyman had told Greene in person that, after wrapping up some orchard work in September, Lyman would "work on the trail from time to time and that some of it might even last over until spring."[4]

Avery needed this rugged, nearly 40-mile section of trail (located in an area so remote it would come to be known as the Hundred Mile Wilderness) built to show the AMC board—in particular, Arthur Comey—that they were wrong and that the trail could be built through Maine without having to wait for clubs to form first. Avery wrote to Harry Davis again, reminding Davis that his son struck a deal and should honor it.

> This leaves the project in a most unfortunate state. . . . It was only after considerable difficulty that I received a contribution of $50 from the New England Trail Conference for this work. The Maine Development Commission matched this sum when it learned that you were interested in the project, and because of your reputation with the Forestry Department. This is all of the money and there isn't any more.
>
> I said then that we could raise $75 and, if Lyman wanted to go ahead and try to put the job through under the conditions of my letter, we should like to have him do so. We thought that his situation and interest in the work would perhaps lead him to undertake a project in which (like the rest of us) he couldn't get an equivalent dollar and cent return. The proposition was accepted and he was given what money he wanted for supplies.[5]

Having restated the financial terms of the agreement, Avery moved on to describe the impact of the work not getting done, which predictably focused on how the fallout would affect him.

---

3    Myron Avery to Harry Davis, 6 January 1933, Avery Collection, Maine State Library Special Collections.

4    Ibid.

5    Ibid.

*I can't quite tell from your letter whether he [Lyman] has thrown up the task completely. . . . If so, it is an awful jolt. It hits the entire project hard. I may say that securing these funds was a personal matter and the failure to carry through the project will so impair my standing that my usefulness on such projects in the future is ended. I am going to find it difficult to explain to these people why the project has failed. With the publicity the project has received, such failure will end it for all time.[6]*

Avery also made it clear that getting half of the work completed would be considered a failure. Accomplishing less was unacceptable because it would result in halting the project and returning the money to the sponsors, "with an explanation to the Forestry Department why the project has been abandoned." Because the Forestry Department was Davis's employer, Avery certainly mentioned the entity by name to imply that an incomplete project could negatively affect Davis's professional standing.

Avery wraps up his letter by asking Davis "what can be promised for the unexpected balance of $85?"[7]

Davis responded by explaining his son's situation.

*Being out of money and a young fellow with even a few College debts still remaining to pay off, he was rather discouraged but did a good lot on this trail until the latter part of September when he was offered this position with Dr. Matthews on the orchard work at a fair wage . . . $3.00 per day right through until the snow came . . . Now Mr. Avery, we are in a depression and I hardly think you could ask a man to give up a position in these times that paid very well to work on the trail. This work should be done when there is no pay jobs waiting.[8]*

Davis then pointed out that if the Forestry Department or a lumber company were to cut the trail, the cost would be about $400. In the end, however,

---

6   Ibid.

7   Ibid.

8   Harry Davis to Myron Avery, 10 January 1933, Avery Collection, Maine State Library Special Collections.

Harry Davis still offered to supervise the completion of the trail from York's Camps to Chairback Mountain for the sum of $85.[9]

Avery accepted Davis's proposal, conditional on learning in writing when both of the two phases of work (trail cutting and marking) would be done. Avery pointed out that both steps required when blazing trees (peeling a small section of bark and then applying paint to mark the trail) could not effectively be done at the same time. (The running sap from the fresh cut would prevent the paint from effectively adhering.) Avery demanded specifics.[10]

Davis responded by saying that, as a part-time forester, the only way he could get all of the work done would be to poke away at it over the ensuing spring through fall of 1933.[11] To a results-oriented person like Avery, this answer wouldn't do. Fearing his reputation and the AT project in Maine were both on the line, he took up the matter with Walter Greene. One can imagine it took only a short discussion to decide to cut ties with Harry and Lyman Davis. Poking away at sections was not a suitable plan to either Avery or Greene. Their mission was to get the trail cut, blazed, and publicized as quickly and as affordably as possible. Greene offered to take the lead on the project, and Avery dispatched a letter to Davis notable for its sarcastic tone.

> As you say, it is useless to do anything until spring and until the snow goes . . . we can see how things are at that time . . . I appreciate that other than your public interest, the thing means nothing to you but a lot of labor and we may be able to develop the matter in such a way as to avoid unnecessarily burdening you. But under any circumstances, your advice and knowledge of the country will be indispensable.[12]

In the same letter, Avery mentioned he had been to New York, where he spoke with Greene. It is likely Greene told Avery he would be willing to

---

9   Ibid.

10  Myron Avery to Harry Davis, 18 January 1933, Avery Collection, Maine State Library Special Collections.

11  Harry Davis to Myron Avery, 4 February 1933, Avery Collection, Maine State Library Special Collections.

12  Myron Avery to Harry Davis, 11 February 1933, Avery Collection, Maine State Library Special Collections.

blaze the trail over the Barren–Chairback Range and that there was no need to have Harry Davis involved with trail-building efforts.[13]

Three days later, Avery sent a follow-up letter to Davis, explaining that the trail markers in Davis's possession needed to be sent to Washington, D.C., so they could be treated "with two coats of Bakelite varnish." This terminated Davis's involvement with the project. The communications between Davis and Avery were emblematic of many Myron Avery relationships. The only difference was the relative speed with which communications fell apart: less than one year.

On April 9, 1933, the geologist Shailer Philbrick sent Greene a letter and map detailing completed sections of the AT in Maine and the work left to be completed, from the Boxfish School to West Chairback Mountain, northeast of the town of Monson. With Greene officially given the task, Avery could turn his attention to other brush fires.

Nearly one year after the request to send back the trail markers, Davis wrote to Avery to thank him for sending him "Appalachian Trail Pub No 5" and to express his disappointment "that neither my son Lyman or myself was mentioned in the lay-out of the trail across Maine. . . . To Lyman this might be of value to him but as to myself, personally, it matters but little as I am an old timer case-hardened in the matter of service without appreciation."[14]

Whether omitting Davis and his son from the credits was an oversight or a slight will never be known. There is no record of further correspondence between the two men.

## Tensions with AMC Mount

Avery's frustrations with AMC dated back to his spats with Arthur Comey and the Nomenclature Committee, further fueled by the rejection of numerous articles he had submitted to the organization's quarterly journal, *Appalachia*. Those frustrations would continue to escalate in the latter part of 1933. But a schism also developed on another front.

To promote the existence of the new section of trail in Maine, Avery suggested AMC sponsor a hike of the Maine Appalachian Trail in 1934. At the

---

13   Ibid.

14   Harry Davis to Myron Avery, 3 February 1934, Avery Collection, Maine State Library Special Collections.

AMC president Dean Peabody, pictured here in 1926, favored having AMC's Ron Gower lead a well-publicized 1934 hike on a newly opened section of the Appalachian Trail in Maine. Photo: Courtesy of AMC Library & Archives.

time he suggested the trip, he also recommended that Shailer Philbrick—then a geology doctoral candidate from Johns Hopkins University who had done his thesis on Maine's Barren–Chairback Range, over which Walter Greene had blazed the trail—should lead the excursion.

AMC's president, Dean Peabody, rejected Avery's suggestion of Philbrick as leader, lighting the fuse for yet another row between Myron Avery and AMC. Instead of Philbrick, Peabody appointed the recently inducted board member Ronald Gower, of AMC's Rock Climbing Committee, to organize and lead the trip. Uncharacteristically, in the wake of Peabody's rejection, Avery offered to help Gower put the trip together by lending advice on trip duration, lodging, and other necessary aspects of planning.

The relationship between Gower and Avery began cordially enough. Gower no doubt ingratiated himself with Avery in an early exchange concerning a meeting with Arthur Comey. In a letter written in February 1933, Gower reported that "the guide book [to the AT in Maine] is coming along apace and I hope to have a conference (private name for a fight) with Comey this week, so we can get it to the printers soon."

After speaking of various issues regarding place names in the guide, Gower recounted a recent meeting with Comey, in which they discussed the Traveler, a mountain north of Katahdin.

> *Mr. Comey thinks the name 'The Traveler" is N.G. [no good?]—he favors "Traveller Mt." I quoted all the discussions and precedents from 1837 on, at which he became enraged, suggested that the matter was already closed by a recent ruling of the Nomenclature Committee, and darkly hinted that you were at the bottom of it. Whereupon I rallied to your defense and said you had nothing to do with it. I have given ground for the moment, but, with my eyes already on the 1938 edition of the Guide, I am seeking more precedents and shall most assuredly bring up the matter again.*[15]

Gower concluded the subject for the moment by stating he had found an 1878 article from *Scribner's Magazine* written by a traveling companion

---

15  Ronald Gower to Myron Avery, February 1933, Avery Collection, Maine State Library Special Collections.

of the artist Frederic Church. In the article, he had found two references to a mountain called "The Traveler," which he hoped to use to bolster his case with Comey in the future. Ultimately, he confided to Avery, "I wish the U.S. Geographic Board could be induced to adopt 'The Traveler!' That would rather spike Mr. Comey's guns!"[16]

In a follow-up letter to Avery the same month, Gower further explained his rationale for giving up the fight over "The Traveler" for the time being.

> I think I will keep my fingers out of the Traveler "pie" until perhaps I may have attained a more prominent role in the Club. In the meantime, I'm making a collection of reasons why it should be changed. Mr. Comey has, of course, done a good deal of work in connection with Katahdin, not as much as you have to be sure, but still enough to have his opinions treated with respect by a newcomer like myself. I believe the change can be accomplished just as surely, but perhaps less spectacularly, by biding my time; and with a lot less friction and hard feeling. I rather like Arthur despite his queer, jumpy and ferocious ways; which, I suspect, mask a sensitiveness that few will believe exists.
>
> Our "conference" took place at his home, where after dinner, we sat down in his study and went through the [guide] book. I was amazed at his mildness and readiness with which he joined in with me on a number of things including the change from "lunkasso" to "lunksoos." [This is a point Comey had previously been unwilling to yield on, which rankled Avery to no end.][17]

Interestingly, Gower then shared his perspective on the state of the AMC board. He reported that Underhill was interested in the Katahdin region, particularly as a rock climbing destination, and that Underhill had shared with Gower his opinion that "Mr. Blood and his associates are the ones primarily responsible for the cold reception given Katahdin projects." Even if Avery already knew or suspected this, it must have been a shock to receive in a letter from a relative newcomer to the organization.[18] (At the time of Gower's

---

16   Ibid.

17   Ibid.

18   Ibid.

letter, the club's then-treasurer and former president, Charles W. Blood, held significant sway within the organization. Blood had helped build and maintain a number of trails in the White Mountains, where his allegiance was understandably strong.)

Gower went on to write:

> *Mr. Blood, in addition to being the Treasurer, is chairman of the influential Huts & Trails Extension Committee. The above gentleman has been the prevailing object of my thoughts in this direction for some time. It looks like a tough nut to crack at this distance, however time will tell.*
>
> *I would very much like to see Underhill the next president. . . . He is interested in a number of things which some of the older members will not admit exist—such as Katahdin.[19]*

These two letters from Gower are extraordinary on a number of levels. First, we see that Avery wasn't the only one to witness Comey's irascible attitude. We also see that Avery had gotten under Comey's skin: When Gower brought up the spelling of "The Traveler," Comey went off the rails and concluded that Gower had been put up to it by Avery.

Second, we see that Comey was more likely to collaborate in person and that maybe Avery could have gotten his way more often if he had taken Comey up on the latter's many offers to meet privately in Boston and sort out their differences.

Third, it is fascinating to read Gower's case for choosing his battles judiciously and his assertion that perhaps he could achieve his desired results in the long term by giving in for the moment and then slowly building cases for change. One can't help wonder what Avery's reaction was or whether he could have benefited from adopting Gower's suggestions himself.

Finally comes the revelation that Comey was not Avery's nemesis with regard to Katahdin. It was Charles Blood. We soon find out Avery suspected this all along. In his response to Gower, Avery writes:

---

19  Ibid.

*I am very much interested in what you say about your sessions with Comey. Difficult as it may seem to reconcile things, I like him too and have a high regard for his ability and accomplishments but I do not suppose I have ever battled, or more joyously in the past and probably in the future with any other person.*[20]

Avery then closed the letter by sharing his views on the subject of Blood and the AMC leadership.

*I have long thought, with perhaps inadequate knowledge, that Blood had perpetuated his control over the A.M.C. through his Trail and Hits [sic] Extension Committee and as far as my particular interests are concerned he constitutes the real barrier. I would like to see you go to work on him. I think he is the mortmain of the Club. With his son-in-law as the Trails Committee Chairman his control is intensified. I very much share your sentiment with respect to Underhill. I have always been impressed with the liberality of his attitude. As a New Englander, I know the sanctimonious righteousness of thought, principle and deed that permeates the A.M.C. old guard.*[21]

In a follow-up letter, Gower weighed in with a Comey update:

*Arthur Comey has been assailing me with post-cards of late. After having read my most recent Katahdin MS, he writes, "Why do you ignore the fact that the first winter visit to the NW Basin was made by J. Ashton Allis and A.C. Comey in 1926, see* Appalachia *etc." To which I replied that "my tale was not designed to be a history of the various visitations to the Basin, and that Draper had been there with a crew in 1910–14." The post-card barrage having ceased, he must be either satisfied or else too furious to write!*[22]

---

20 Ibid.

21 Ibid.

22 Ronald Gower to Myron Avery, February 1933, Avery Collection, Maine State Library Special Collections.

Ron Gower, left, and a fellow excursion member install a northern terminus sign on the summit of Katahdin during the AMC-sponsored hike on Maine's AT in 1934. Photo: Courtesy of AMC Library & Archives.

Although Gower and Avery found much to commiserate about from the outset, the relationship would eventually sour, largely due to Avery's increasingly acerbic attitude toward the AMC board. Initially Gower had believed he could serve as peacemaker. Ultimately he came to believe that Avery's sense of entitlement and treatment of others were unconscionable—and that Gower's own allegiance belonged with AMC.

## The Katahdin Supplement

Because the Maine section of the AT was taking shape so quickly, keeping guidebooks up-to-date became a concern. When AMC published an updated *Katahdin Guide* in April 1933, Avery was incensed by the number of errors it contained. He sent a list of corrections and recommendations to

Ralph C. Larrabee, the chair of the AMC Guidebook Committee, and copied Arthur Comey and Ron Gower.[23]

One week later, Avery sent a copy of the map that accompanied the new *Katahdin Guide,* marked up with corrections by Walter Greene, to the same trio. Avery's letter listed Greene's sixteen corrections and included the comment, "Perhaps at another time, you may think it worth your while to give me an opportunity to look over the proof for I should have made the same comments before the final copy was approved."[24]

The fact that Avery, the most knowledgeable person on every aspect of the route of the AT through Maine, never received a copy to proof before it was sent to the printer is, at the least, interesting. In a letter dated May 12, 1933, Gower wrote to Avery that he "understood that Comey had sent a marked up copy of the old book to you for your corrections, else I would have sent a proof to you myself."[25]

The matter escalated over the next two weeks as a frustrated Avery commented to Gower that, when it came to his receiving guidebooks and maps for review, "everybody seems to say that it is up to the other fellow to do it and between them all, unless I keep after it, I will not have the book or the map."[26]

Questions surrounding guidebook production and reviews would continue to be an issue for the existing and emergent AT clubs. The fact that Maine didn't yet have a governing club, and wouldn't for two more years, meant the ever-evolving Maine trail didn't have an official publishing entity—as did, for example, the Potomac Appalachian Trail Club [PATC] with its *Guide to Paths in the Blue Ridge.*

For the time being, NETC stepped into the breach. In 1933, the organization published the *Guide to the Appalachian Trail in New England,* an overview of the AT route from the New York–Connecticut border to Maine.

---

23  Myron Avery to Ralph C. Larrabee, 28 April 1933, Avery Collection, Maine State Library Special Collections.

24  Myron Avery to Ralph C. Larrabee, 4 May 1933, Avery Collection, Maine State Library Special Collections.

25  Ronald Gower to Myron Avery, 12 May 1933, Avery Collection, Maine State Library Special Collections.

26  Myron Avery to Ronald Gower, 17 May 1933, Avery Collection, Maine State Library Special Collections.

A trail-blazing crew looks out from the summit of Katahdin in 1933. Myron Avery's ever-present measuring wheel is visible at lower right. Photo: Courtesy of Avery Collection, Maine State Library.

Avery was thrilled with the result, which largely reflected his own and Comey's efforts. Avery wrote to him:

> Many thanks for your thoughtfulness in forwarding me the copy of the Guidebook which I received Friday morning. It is a fine piece of work and one which, I think will reflect much credit on the [New England Trail] Conference. You are particularly to be commended for the selection of type. This is the clearest and best for its size which I have ever seen."[27]

Avery then pointed out a few minor errors for future reference, including one he took responsibility for causing.

> I suppose I must be entirely responsible for the discrepancies in the Katahdin-Blanchard distance, namely, 117 miles in the text and 120 miles in the outline. I just can't recall or explain it but I must have slipped badly in checking [the] proof. I should have caught it and it must be my fault.[28]

Even when Avery made an error, he had difficulty cutting himself slack. Yet it is refreshing to see that Avery held Comey in high enough regard to compliment the latter on a job well done.

But Avery was still incensed about the number of errors in the recently published *Katahdin Guide*. Further, Avery believed a comprehensive guide to the AT in Maine, which currently stretched from Katahdin to Bigelow, needed to be written, and he sought to produce a supplement to AMC's *Katahdin Guide*. As always, finding the funds to publish the supplement was an issue. During September 1933, he solicited printing bids and asked the Maine Publicity Bureau if it could provide the funds to print the guide.[29]

Meanwhile, Comey weighed in to express his concern with Avery's guidebook publication efforts. "I think you should avoid what could not help

---

27  Myron Avery to Arthur Comey, 13 June 1933, Avery Collection, Maine State Library Special Collections.

28  Ibid.

29  Myron Avery to Harrie A. Coe, 1 November 1933, Avery Collection, Maine State Library Special Collections.

being considered an unfriendly act to the A.M.C. and refrain from duplicating the A.M.C. Katahdin Guide in the proposed AT Supplement," Comey warned in a September letter.[30] He then reminded Avery that any reduction in the sales of the current guide "makes it just that much harder a job for the A.M.C.," which was "the most active permanent group in the New England Trail Conference," and that as such, it "finances almost 50% of the N.E.T.C. as well as at present contributing to the A.T.C."[31]

Avery responded that Comey was way off the mark in his assessments, including the latter's assertions that the existing *Katahdin Guide* was "compact, inexpensive, and kept up to date."

"Perhaps if you had seen the last data sent, your reaction to the sufficiency of the Katahdin Guide might have been different," Avery wrote. "To say that the Katahdin material in the Supplement is an unfriendly act is silly in the extreme."[32]

Avery went on to explain that the *Katahdin Guide* omitted key information due to trail relocations and errors of omission. To emphasize his point, he asked two friends imminently familiar with the trails of Katahdin, Shailer Philbrick and Albert Jackman, to review the publication themselves. Avery reported their findings back to Comey.

> *The critics here—Shailer and Jackman—found much fault with the passages I lifted [from the Katahdin Guide]. They say they are deficient in construction and grammar. My horror at the possibility of fault in an A.M.C. product didn't stay them. . . . I believe that the data re history and approaches—which you say will probably [be edited] out—adds life to the book. It keeps it from being a list of distances.*[33]

---

30  Arthur Comey to Myron Avery, 22 September 1933, Avery Collection, Maine State Library Special Collections.

31  Ibid.

32  Myron Avery to Arthur Comey, 29 September 1933, Avery Collection, Maine State Library Special Collections.

33  Ibid.

By the end of September 1933, when Avery sent the preceding letter, he cared little about the opinions of AMC leadership or the potential negative impact of his actions on the organization. He was in the midst of several simmering feuds with AMC, and each one was about to boil over.

# CHAPTER 11

## *Another Editor Dismissed*

MYRON AVERY WORKED TIRELESSLY TO PROMOTE THE HIKING TRAILS of Maine and beyond. He had spent years researching and writing his bibliography of Katahdin and articles on the history of the region's trails, and he was frustrated with the results. It had seemed for many months that *Sun-Up* magazine was on the verge of publishing his work. He also believed that *Appalachia,* AMC's quarterly digest, would run his Katahdin articles in their entirety. He begrudgingly accepted that cuts proposed by Robert Underhill, *Appalachia*'s editor, were necessary for "The Keep Path and Its Successors" to achieve a sufficient length for publication. Throughout the considerable back-and-forth between the two men over the years, Avery maintained respect for Underhill's editing prowess, once even acknowledging that Underhill's input had made Avery's work better.

In February 1933, Avery shared with Ron Gower that he admired Underhill and agreed with Gower's assessment that Underhill would make a great next president of the AMC. But by October of that same year, Avery and Underhill were heading down an irreconcilable path.

On October 4, 1933, Underhill wrote to Avery, telling him that he was killing two articles that had been planned for the upcoming issue of *Appalachia*: one by Myron Avery about Mount Guyot and another originally to have been written by Shailer Philbrick, who declined the assignment, and then by Albert Jackman, who hadn't delivered a manuscript. Underhill offered that, if Jackman delivered something "good and interesting," it would not be published until the following June. He also advised Avery: "All we have time for now is your brief note (500 words) on the bare accomplishments of your [Katahdin] trip."[1]

This news initiated rounds of correspondence of increasing fury and accusations.

Avery began his response to Underhill by taking ownership of the map snafu that resulted in the need to kill the Guyot story. He then moved on to the subject of the Katahdin article. Avery wanted the publicity that a lengthy article about his group's work trip through Maine would provide. That he couldn't get it was a sore point, and he let Underhill know it.

> *I must say that foreclosing this opportunity, without warning to me, seems most strange. You are busy and rushed I know, but very little time elapsed since our return from the Katahdin trip. Under the circumstances I felt you could have given us more support in our efforts to obtain early publicity for the Maine Trail. Philbrick had a most unusual trip on his 55 miles from Blanchard to Bigelow. I hoped we could cover this in June.*[2]

Avery then reminded Underhill that the latter had a copy of another Avery article (originally written for a publication called *In the Maine Woods*) that Underhill might repurpose in time to meet the deadline for the December issue of *Appalachia*.[3]

When Underhill responded six days later, he began by explaining that, when Shailer Philbrick turned down the chance to write an article and Avery said nothing about the possibility of submitting a substitute piece, "I assumed the whole thing was off." Underhill admonished, "I think you should have known there was a time limit, and that it was now up." Underhill stated that article due dates were printed in each issue of *Appalachia*, and "that it is supposed to be the business of the members of the Committee to rush things

---

1   Robert L.M. Underhill to Myron Avery letter, 4 October 1933, Avery Collection, Maine State Library Special Collections.

2   Myron Avery to Robert L.M. Underhill, 6 October 1933, Avery Collection, Maine State Library Special Collections.

3   Ibid.

along and not to maneuver for holding them up."[4] He continued, "I'm not trying to do you out of any chance to get publicity for your Maine story, and in fact should be very glad indeed to have it."

After making it clear he had already received all other articles for the next issue and had sent half of them to the printer, Underhill laid out a new set of conditions for Avery to get Jackman's story into the December issue, even given that doing so could create a mess of things when the journal went to press.[5] Underhill would not accept any story that needed much revision or editing, and he would not accept a story that ran too many pages. "No more than 2,200 words," he wrote. "If it's a good story and you want more, then it's June!" He gave Avery one week to deliver the manuscript. Regarding the story on Philbrick's trip, as proposed in Avery's earlier letter, Underhill said if it was story, he'd like to run it in the June issue.

"If he hasn't, or won't write it . . . suggest including his stuff in your note [for the December issue] and enlarging the note to 1000 words. Or we can put another note in June . . . Of course, there is a divergence of interest in all this, as you're primarily after publicity for your trail and I'm after stuff interesting to our readers. I don't mind your getting all the publicity you can, but the provision of it must be secondary. So I hope you can send me really good walking stories."[6]

After telling Avery he could see no reason to go over the piece Avery wrote for *In the Maine Woods* (after all, it was appearing in another magazine), yet promising to run the Guyot article as soon as the maps to accompany it were available, Underhill offered a more personal note to the man who had been so difficult to work with over the past several years.

> *As to your criticism of the "supercilious attitude" in our notes and reviews, I can't help replying that we aren't the only ones! I thought that Allen's [Chamberlain's] letter to me re your guidebook, to which I never replied, several times as complacent as my proposed review. Didn't I hear from somewhere down there that you were going to show*

---

4 Robert L.M. Underhill to Myron Avery, 12 October 1933, Avery Collection, Maine State Library Special Collections.

5 Ibid.

6 Ibid.

*the world for the first time what a really good guidebook was like?*
*Then, when we jump on it, we're told after all that you are a poor*
*little Club that is managing to do wonders with its meager resources.*
*I suppose inconsistent attitudes are O.K., as they are in the law, where*
*you plead (1) that John Doe was 100 miles away and couldn't have*
*struck the plaintiff, and (2) that altho he struck him, it was in self-*
*defence [sic]. Well, enough of these recriminations! They started with*
*my comment on the Vagabond shoe—which I remind you was made*
*to you privately; in reviews I always say your equipment list is the*
*cat's whiskers and ought to be in the hands of every member of the*
*A.M.C. And privately, I repeat that you ought to take out all mention*
*of the Vagabond shoe for "mountaineering," it is a rotten shoe, and*
*that's that.*[7]

In a letter written to Underhill five days later, Avery laid his feelings bare.

*I had thought (until today) that my letter of October 12th, stat-*
*ing that no Maine story would be forthcoming, was mailed the 12th.*
*I was much chagrined to find it on my desk this morning . . . I regret*
*very much my oversight—both because of the delay and further since*
*the arrival would have saved the writing of your long letter of October*
*12th. Please accept my apologies.*[8]

Avery went on to tell Underhill that, as Avery would not be providing
any further material, Underhill would need to confirm whether he intended
to run Avery's article in *In the Maine Woods* with the first and last paragraphs
removed, as well as "any other eliminations that are required" to meet space
limitations. The letter then took a snarky turn. Avery wrote:

*I think it beside the mark to say that I "maneuvered" to gain time*
*for a story by Jackman. As always, I have done everything you asked*
*in this connection and if the result is a blank, please don't throw the*
*responsibility this way. When you told me, with the best Underhillian*

---

7   Ibid.

8   Myron Avery to Robert L.M. Underhill, 17 October 1933, Avery Collection, Maine State
    Library Special Collections.

*courtesy, that anything which I could contribute on the Maine trip wouldn't do, as you requested, I tried to induce Shailer to write it, and failing that, then tried to get a substitute. I must admit that I had my tongue in my cheek all the while, for, without knowing these boys, where you developed the idea that they would turn in what you wanted was beyond me. You were assuming a whole lot. I am sorry that they didn't—it might have told you something.*[9]

*I have seen Philbrick. He may write a story and he may not. To be frank, he has the frequently-met-with outside conception of the A.M.C., which furnishes no incentive to offer anything into Appalachia. I can't venture a prediction on his writing.*

*I suppose 500 words isn't much, but I am badly crowded with office work and, after the middle of next week, shall be away so much the rest of the month that little time is left. Frankly, I am disinclined to do anything more. My main consideration would be to take away your alibi if, perchance some reader might say that opening 185 miles of Trail in Maine should have received some recognition. Perhaps I have already done that. I suggest you call it mutiny and drop me from the board.*

*By the way, your comment about "maneuvers" to hold up the issue for Jackman's story either shows something peculiar about the activities of the Board or unusual remissness on my part. I wrote to ask the dead-line, because I didn't know. What should I?*

*The Board does nothing. Never meets. It is a useless collection of names. I suggest that it be abolished and have the record show the true facts, that R.L.M.U. [Underhill] does all the work, the always creditable issues are solely his work and that to him belongs all praise. Why drag along in parasitic-fashion a non-functioning board? Either the theory or practice has some serious defects.*

*You have been generous in offering some more time to Jackman. I personally appreciate your attitude.*

*By the way, this is the second time you have used what you term "lawyer's arguments" on me. What is their source? Are you by any chance going to Law School these days?*

---

9  Ibid.

*My paragraph about "supercilious" feature of notes, reviews and A.M.C. attitude in the field, was merely passing on to you—for your own reflection—what I hear on the outside. I am in touch with different groups from those which the Boston people know. The information isn't wanted and I shall not waste either my time or yours by dwelling on it. But it is what the "outsiders" think.*

*I will appreciate your looking over my photos and sending back promptly what you do not wish to use.*[10]

The advent of Avery's letter had been building for several years and was perhaps bolstered by his growing list of accomplishments and positions of authority: chairman of ATC, president of PATC. When Avery accused AMC of being a one-man show, "that R.L.M.U. does all the work, the always creditable issues are solely his work and that to him belongs all praise," he could have been writing about himself. He had certainly burned bridges and frayed nerves—within AMC, and up and down the eastern seaboard—by acting similarly. How that sat with various AMC members would be revealed in the future.

When Underhill responded two days later via a two-page, single-spaced letter, he made a diplomatic attempt to restore peace. Straightaway he established that he wanted to avoid further squabbles. "I have been reflecting further on the Maine story business during the last few days and will give you the whole result," he wrote. "This, I hope, finally without any tendency to controversy! We apparently have some issues on the boards, but these (such as the general tone of *Appalachia*) cannot be profitably discussed in letters and had best await more favorable opportunities."[11]

Underhill then agreed "entirely that the opening of 185 miles of trail, particularly thru the Maine wilderness, deserves some mention." This wasn't a new opinion, Underhill wrote. He had thought the Maine story had merit ever since Arthur Comey first told him of it the past summer. Underhill was also enthusiastic about getting Shailer Philbrick to Boston to talk to the

10  Ibid.

11  Robert L.M. Underhill to Myron Avery, 19 October 1933, Avery Collection, Maine State Library Special Collections.

Appalachian Trail Conference and he "still felt the matter was important enough to be dealt with both in a lecture and a talk."[12]

"But I made one mistake, as I should have seen and discovered from what you told me," Underhill wrote. "When you go over a trail as fast and working as hard as you did, no walking trip story in the sense that I wanted can possibly come out of it. The idea of combining such a story with notice of the opening of the trail was a bad and quite unworkable one."[13]

Underhill then presented Avery with three ways forward to get an article about the Maine AT published in *Appalachia*:

1. Run a story as told by someone hiking the trail "in more leisurely fashion," to be written by a third party (not Avery).

2. Run a story of how the trail took shape, in the style of Avery's *In the Maine Woods* article. Underhill made the case against this option for a number of reasons: that the article wouldn't fit *Appalachia*'s editorial style; that the article would fail to hold the reader's interest if it came across as a thank you to the landowners and volunteers who made the trail possible; and that the article had already been published elsewhere.

3. Run a story as "a descriptive article on this portion of the trail, with appreciation of what is to be found there. This is the sort of thing you have done for the more southerly sections, and to my mind, done very well. It now seems to me the way the Maine section ought to be dealt with in *Appalachia*, and I am sorry I didn't realize this sooner." The story would have to run in the June issue, Underhill wrote, because "it is meant to set people walking on the trail."[14]

Underhill concluded his letter by offering his perspective that the AMC board "shall be sorry if you resign from the board (though I'm trying my best to do so myself!). You're not quite right about its uselessness, however. It functions alright. We have only one formal meeting a year, but that's enough for the discussion of general policy, which is what a meeting is for; for the

---

12  Ibid.

13  Ibid.

14  Ibid.

rest, I am in constant touch with the members individually, and some of them do quite a hell of a lot."[15]

Avery responded by complimenting the "mighty fine, frank letter" written in "the best Underhillian form." Further, he stated that "to stay set now in my 'disinclination' not to touch the thing again would show such a lack of cooperation, that I shall certainly send in the 500 words." After promising to send the work by November 1, Avery informed Underhill, "You understand, however, that I am doing this because you specify it, not that the plan arouses my enthusiasm."[16]

Avery then resumed the discussion of featuring a "Maine story" in *Appalachia,* stating unequivocally he would not submit any material for it. "Announce a June article, if you wish, but where is it going to come from?" Avery asked. "I leave it with you" [to decide].[17] One by one, Avery went through his reasons for not submitting further work, crafting each example to lay criticism at Underhill's feet.

"I doubt you had the opportunity to do much more than skim the 'Maine Woods' story," he wrote. "I would have preferred its reaching *Appalachia* readers than *In the Maine Woods.* I recently showed it to the boys here. They liked it very much. It represents the best I could do along the lines you were specifying. So that's out."[18]

Avery then said he would not be able to provide another story in the vein of the Pisgah piece he previously had written for *Appalachia,* as Underhill suggested in option 3, because although that article was one of the best combinations of descriptive and historical interest Avery had put together, "its two slashings [sections cut by Underhill, presumably to make the article meet space constraints] make me dubious of my success in attempting that line again." Further, Avery wrote: "The boys complain that this (my) type or style lacks interest for a general reader; you apparently agree. (I feel there

---

15   Ibid.

16   Myron Avery to Robert L.M. Underhill, 21 October 1933, Avery Collection, Maine State Library Special Collections.

17   Ibid.

18   Ibid.

is definite purpose served by this essentially factual material and my poor attempts to give publicity to the Trail can rise no higher.)"[19]

Underhill's response read: "Shouldn't let it get your goat when I suggested Shailer as the man [to write the walking trip story]; very few people can write such stories, and no criticism is involved. If you will undertake the descriptive article shall be very glad to have it."[20]

Avery responded: "I don't think I needed the injunction about 'getting my goat.' If it had, I wouldn't have tried to get Jackman to give you what you wanted, and would tell you now that since you didn't want anything of mine, I wasn't to be dragged into it now. I've been fair throughout and hope to stay so. If it hadn't been for your idea that these boys could do what you wanted, you would have gotten a 'descriptive' article, such as you now want, in ample season for this issue."[21]

So it was. As far as Underhill and *Appalachia* were concerned, Myron Avery was taking his ball and glove elsewhere. The exchanges with Underhill reveal how Avery's obstinacy was so strong, it obscured his ability to take criticism or to entertain other points of view. As far as he was concerned, his writing never needed revisions. Woe to the editor who requested rewrites or edits. Avery demanded his articles run in their entirety, regardless of whether they fit the publication's editorial agenda or space requirements.

Avery's inability to connect on a human level was also on display. Even when Underhill offered several options for Avery to gain publicity for the newly opened section of the AT in Maine, Avery couldn't see them for the opportunity they were. Instead, he verbally bludgeoned Underhill for what Avery perceived as a lack of judgment and took the role of martyr—as in, "You didn't want an article from me before; now you want one, so I'm not giving it to you."

In a younger person, one might chalk up Avery's responses to immaturity. But at the time of these letters, Avery was 33 years old. Clearly, whatever drove Avery forward also drove key people in his circle away.

---

19  Ibid.

20  Robert L.M. Underhill to Myron Avery, 19 October 1933, Avery Collection, Maine State Library Special Collections.

21  Myron Avery to Robert L.M. Underhill, 21 October 1933, Avery Collection, Maine State Library Special Collections.

Underhill's offer to meet Avery is interesting. Underhill knew that meeting in person would be a better forum for hashing out differences and concerns. He was keenly aware that communicating through letters alone was rife with problems. (Ron Gower would observe that Arthur Comey was far more gracious and amenable to achieving consensus in person.) What would have happened if Avery was willing to sit down with Comey, Underhill, and other perceived nemeses? Comey extended several offers to Avery to meet in Boston. Avery almost always replied that he was unavailable. On the few occasions Avery offered to meet with Comey, Comey replied that he would be out of town. Whether this was true or whether Comey was avoiding Avery will probably never be known.

As for Underhill's suggestion, Avery replied, "Shall be in Boston twice in November." He left it up to Underhill to take it from there.

In one final flourish, Avery signed off his letter to Underhill with this:

> I didn't say I would resign from the Board—unless your interpretation is a suggestion. I said I expected to be dropped for heresy. I would like to be in a position where I could exert pressure to keep you from getting off, however.[22]

This wasn't the final time Underhill would hear from Myron Avery. In a letter from February 1934, Avery's ongoing grudge with the editor of *Appalachia* came to the fore. After announcing he had received notice of "the *Appalachia* meeting next Thursday" but that a week's notice was not enough for him to arrange his schedule to attend, Avery wrote:

> I have sent you our A.T. Publication No. 5 and The Guide to the Appalachian Trail in Maine. (Incidentally, this cost about one-third of the N.E.T.C. Guidebook.) Within a month, the second edition of Guide to Paths in the Blue Ridge will follow the other two of the slaughter. Produced neither under the aegis of the A.M.C. nor of Harvard nor of Boston, these should be good red meat. You will have a

---

22  Myron Avery to Robert L.M. Underhill, 21 October 1933, Avery Collection, Maine State Library Special Collections.

*pleasant evening. And, as with the case of the last edition, I shall count on the pleasure of a preview of your efforts.*[23]

Avery then let Underhill know that his decision to publish the book through ATC—rather than through AMC, which had been AMC's preference—was based in part on "the irksome necessity of subjecting everything to superior wisdom" and the ability to "bring it out in the form we wanted." "This is a satisfaction in itself—even if a secession," Avery declared.[24]

The effect of Avery's missives was not immediately seen, and there is no record of Underhill's response, but by late 1934, the damage was so complete that the two were no longer talking. In a letter dated November 21, 1934, Ron Gower updated Avery on the activities of the Committee on Excursions, of which Gower was now a member, and offered his perspective on the feud.

> *Don't worry about my joining "the opposition," I think it is a shame that such a condition should have arisen. . . . A little forbearance on both sides would undoubtedly have helped. Personal contact, instead of correspondence, generally makes for more permanent relations; one can say things without offence being taken, that look very rough in print. However, I think a great deal of both of you, and I am taking no sides. Shall be very glad to act as an intermediary between you, should there be anything you wish taken up on this end.*"[25]

This was at least the second occasion someone volunteered to act as an intermediary between Myron Avery and his chosen rival. Judge Perkins had offered to do the same when Avery was squabbling with Arthur Comey years before. Despite further bumps in the road, Avery and Comey were able to forge a working relationship, even producing a guidebook together. But the rift with Underhill ran deeper and would never be salvaged. Ultimately, the feud between Avery and the entire organization would become irreconcilable.

---

23  Myron Avery to Robert L.M. Underhill, 2 February 1934, Avery Collection, Maine State Library Special Collections.

24  Ibid.

25  Ronald Gower to Myron Avery, 21 November 1934, Avery Collection, Maine State Library Special Collections.

# CHAPTER 12

## The Struggle to Stay Solvent

MYRON AVERY LED AN AUGUST 1933 TRAIL-BUILDING TRIP FROM Katahdin to Blanchard that included Walter Greene, Dr. J. Frank Schairer of the Carnegie Geophysical Laboratory, Albert H. Jackman, and Dr. Shailer S. Philbrick. Upon his return, Avery drafted a status report for NETC: "With the exception of a 3-mile gap at the head of the East Branch of Pleasant River, we have now a completed, painted and signed trail from Katahdin to Blanchard," he stated, adding, "the measured distance is 119.1 miles." (Avery undoubtedly measured the distance using his cyclometer, an odometer attached to a bike wheel that he was often seen rolling down the trail.)[1]

Avery used his report to drive home a number of points to the NETC leadership. One was the need for publicity. "If we can get some travel over the Trail next year so that the Camp owners will see that they will benefit from it, it will help greatly with maintenance problems," he wrote, noting that their own expedition generated considerable revenue for the sporting camps they visited nightly along the route.

He also praised Walter Greene's efforts to blaze the northern reaches of trail in Maine, particularly the stretch along the Barren–Chairback Range: "It is the greatest single-handed piece of trail work that I know of and I hope that you will see to it that his efforts receive the recognition which they deserve. If he could have had $50 more so as to have hired some of the clearing, it would have saved him tremendous labor and both mental and physical strain. . . . So let us all remember that the Maine Trail is due solely to his efforts."[2]

---

1   Myron Avery to NETC board, 6 September 1933, Avery Collection, Maine State Library Special Collections.

2   Ibid.

Avery continued by making a strong pitch for adding more miles to the AT in Maine before winter. He mentioned that during their work trip, Philbrick proposed building an additional 50 miles of trail in Maine, from the Kennebec River to Mount Bigelow. Philbrick provided Avery with a detailed estimate of $36.50 to get the job done, which Avery suggested should be $45 to include an extra day's work that Philbrick inadvertently omitted from his bid. "It would be most short-sighted to pass up this opportunity," Avery advised, noting that adding 50 miles toward the completion of the Maine trail would create a 170-mile segment even more worthy of publishing a guidebook supplement.

Avery then moved on to the issue of an unexpected snag. One sporting camp owner asked for the AT to be routed away from his cottages—hence the 3-mile gap mentioned at the beginning of the letter. Avery proposed NETC hire Greene to reestablish the connection by rerouting the trail away from the owner's camp at a cost of $15 to $20.

Finally, Avery brought up the subject of trail maintenance for the Maine link. "Like the A.M.C. White Mountain trails and all other trails, some sections will require work. The Conference will have to care for this section in its infancy," Avery reported. He proposed a budget of $50 to $60 total per year, perhaps contributed by NETC, AMC, or both.[3]

But above all, Avery contended, "Our present problem is to get the link known and used." He mentioned efforts to publicize the trail, including: his plan "to turn over a news release to the Maine Publicity Bureau"; upcoming stories in *Appalachia* and *In the Maine Woods*; a forthcoming pitch to the *Christian Science Monitor*; and the possibility of enlisting Raymond Torrey's *New York Post* column as a means of getting the word out. "But to me the listing of an excursion over it will be the biggest help. I am asking if Comey will broach this to A.M.C. powers," Avery wrote—an indication that his own standing with AMC had worsened to the point where he would rather not approach the organization himself.[4]

---

3   Ibid.

4   Ibid.

Two days later, Raymond Torrey sent a check for $45 to Shailer Philbrick and a check for $20 to Walter Greene. The additional 50-plus miles would be added to the Maine Trail in 1933.[5]

On October 1, 1933, Avery received a letter from Philbrick that began:

> *The job is done as you will know from the receipt of my probably intelligible day letter. I have been so busy since my return that I have not been able to write to you sooner. Greene and I finished up the Boarstone [sic] side trail this week and at the end Greene tacked up the last sticker and heaved the paint pail over the eastern cliff with well uttered threats, imprecations and curses in which I joined. The remarks were not altogether complimentary of the Appalachian Trail Conference especially the financial end of it. It is all done and all that is necessary now is to find a bunch of men good enough to travel it.[6]*

Funding for building, maintaining, and publicizing the AT was a constant issue. It would have been a challenge in any era, but with the country still entrenched in the Great Depression, every expenditure was subject to unprecedented levels of review. In December 1933, Avery learned the conditions of securing funds were even tighter than he had imagined. Unbeknownst to Avery, NETC had appropriated $50 toward continuing work on the AT in Maine. The funds would not be made available, however, unless Avery could secure an additional $2 in funding per $1 contributed by NETC. The NETC Steering Committee advised Avery of this precondition during a meeting on December 12. Avery was doubly vexed that he was not told that he would chair the meeting until just before it convened. He felt he had been denied an opportunity to build a compelling case for removing the matching-funds restriction in advance.

On December 28, Avery sent a letter to the members of the NETC Steering Committee, stating "that such a restriction absolutely defeats its purpose and prevents any further immediate advance in Maine." He reiterated a point he had made during the earlier meeting: that another 50 miles of trail could be

---

5   Raymond Torrey to Myron Avery, 8 September 1933, Avery Collection, Maine State Library Special Collections.

6   Shailer Philbrick to Myron Avery, 1 October 1933, Avery Collection, Maine State Library Special Collections.

completed in Maine in the coming year through the promised efforts of Civilian Conservation Corps (CCC) and Maine fire wardens and game wardens. But, the restriction imposed by NETC would prevent it all from happening.

"If the New England Trail Conference wants to advance the Trail in Maine, it will have to remove this restriction; its imposition only makes our efforts more difficult and discouraging. We need help, not handicaps," Avery wrote. He then urged all members to write to Chairman Comey to have the restriction removed.[7]

## Pushing His Agenda

As mentioned in his report from the Maine work trip, Avery felt the best publicity for the newly opened sections of trail in the Pine Tree State would be for AMC to organize and lead a hike.

Avery knew he was not the man to lead the hike. For one, he was traveling constantly to perform his legal duties and to work on other AT-related projects, such as scouting and building trail segments in the South. He was also shrewd enough to know that his support within AMC was waning. His diatribes to Underhill and others ensured they would not support the idea of Avery leading a trip on their behalf.

As previously suggested to Underhill, Avery felt his friend Shailer Philbrick—who had received a grant from the U.S. Geological Survey to document the Maine terrain through which the AT traversed—would make a fine AMC excursion leader and sent a letter to AMC's president, Dean Peabody, suggesting the same.

Peabody responded by thanking Avery for his input but wrote that "after considerable thought I still believe that this trip should be led by an A.M.C. member and I am asking Ronald Gower to assemble costs and dates." As one of the few members who still got along with and corresponded regularly with Avery, Gower was a savvy choice. Gower could tap into Avery's knowledge of the trail in Maine, minimizing Avery's direct involvement with AMC.

Peabody followed up with Avery in late January to revisit the question of excursion leadership. "There seem to have been a good many cooks in

---

7    Myron Avery to NETC Steering Committee, 28 December 1933, Avery Collection, Maine State Library Special Collections.

this Katahdin broth," he begins. Peabody explains that he "spoke to Gower about leading the trip before he ever heard of Philbrick in this connection" and still believed Gower should be in charge. As Peabody saw it, "You and Arthur Comey want a party over the trail and I want an A.M.C. party somewhere in the Maine forest region." Having Gower lead the trip would accomplish both.[8]

But Myron Avery couldn't let the issue end there. As a final appeal to have Philbrick included on the AMC trip, Avery mentioned a letter he received from Philbrick, offering "to help in any way in which Gower calls on him." Avery also reported that he had previously sent letters to AMC—on October 17 and 25, 1933—recommending that Philbrick lead the trip and that, in a return letter, Comey had responded he agreed with the suggestion.[9]

"I was therefore astonished when you told me in December at Schairer's lecture, that the plan was to secure an A.M.C. member," Avery wrote. "I am sorry to have to devote so much space to the incident, but felt that my actions and position should be clearly understood."[10]

In addition to his letter, Avery sent a copy of the newly ATC-published *Guide to the Appalachian Trail in Maine* to Peabody, perhaps as a way to thumb his nose at the AMC.

Peabody refused to dive into the waters. In a letter to Avery dated February 13, 1934, Peabody wrote, "I suspect I owe you many thanks for the copy of the *Guide to the Appalachian Trail in Maine*. It is a valuable addition to my Guide Book Shelf and I thank you."[11]

From this point on, the AMC trip continued to take shape, as evidenced by cordial letters between Avery and Gower before and after the trip. But the discord between Avery and AMC was clear; the rancor was deeply entrenched on both sides.

---

8 Dean Peabody to Myron Avery, 25 January 1934, Avery Collection, Maine State Library Special Collections.

9 Myron Avery to Dean Peabody, 30 January 1934, Avery Collection, Maine State Library Special Collections.

10 Ibid.

11 Dean Peabody to Myron Avery, 13 February 1934, Avery Collection, Maine State Library Special Collections.

# CHAPTER 13

## *Full Steam Ahead*

As 1934 began, Myron Avery's life was overflowing with possibilities, obligations, and squabbles. In a rare reference to his professional life (Avery was disciplined about separating his legal duties from his AT-related ones), he ended a September 1933 letter to Arthur Comey as follows:

> *We have had an important case become most active. It involves a tremendous amount of work and the October 1st [reassignment to New York City] was shelved for a couple of months while I race around and get testimony. It alone is keeping me going day and night. Have been to Jacksonville, New York, Norfolk, since returning; going to New Orleans next week. Then have to make all trips again.*[1]

One wonders if Avery's railings against AMC were partially due to juggling too many responsibilities. Avery's drive to complete tasks and then move on may have been a defense against being constantly overwhelmed. He took on so much responsibility, he was ill equipped to handle the pressure of projects that didn't go according to plan. If protocol called for slowing down or changing course, he tenaciously fought back. If he didn't get his way, he fashioned a work-around.

Avery was particularly irked at AMC for decisions he felt were arbitrary (often using the decisions of the Nomenclature Committee as proof) and for publication guidelines he found too restrictive. (Underhill often told Avery his articles were too long to run in *Appalachia* and needed to be cut in half.)

---

1   Myron Avery to Arthur Comey, 29 September 1933, Avery Collection, Maine State Library Special Collections.

Yet, as he took on more responsibilities to ensure he was in charge, Avery was damaging more than relationships. Philbrick had taken notice and written to Avery the month before.

> You know every so often I realize what a hell of a lot of work and worry you have put into all this stuff. I think you have done one damn fine job and done it well. You can't beat a good Yankee unless you've got a better Yankee. I hope you won't wrack yourself with too much work and that you will live long enough to see the day when you will get the credit for all the labor and ingenuity which you have devoted to the Appalachian Trail.[2]

Philbrick's concerns were warranted, but Avery didn't seem to want to slow down. He had more work to do.

From the beginning of his involvement with the AT, Avery felt that its continued existence depended on four things: building it, maintaining it, promoting it, and protecting it.

Paramount, of course, was building the trail. The effort of scouting, securing, and building the route from New England south was daunting. But Avery doubled down by taking on the 200-plus miles of Maine trail. Doing so put him at odds with AMC's leadership, who had advocated forming Maine-based clubs first and then engaging them in the project.

Avery feared that failing to build the trail through Maine would cost both his reputation and the likelihood of seeing the route completed (as mentioned in his January 1933 letter to Harry Davis). This partially explains his obsession with getting the job done using whatever resources he could patch together.

Completing the AT through Maine required money—something hard to come by during the Depression. State and federal dollars were tight, and Avery's tiny budget couldn't even pay enough to prevent one young man, Lyman Davis, from forsaking trailblazing for a $3-per-day job at a local orchard. Avery worked night and day to find some way to get the trail done, even if he needed to keep his methods secret.

---

2   Shailer Philbrick to Myron Avery, 14 December 1933, Avery Collection, Maine State Library Special Collections.

A September 1932 letter from Avery to Walter Greene revealed that while Avery was negotiating rates with Harry and Lyman Davis, he had more money to work with than he was letting on.

> *More good news. I hold a check for $50 from Maine Forest Service for [cutting the trail over Barren–Chairback]. Keep it <u>dark</u>. It means $100 for all this work. Now here is the story. When the New England Trail Conference would vote (4 to 3) only $50 rather than $100, I realized that $75 was the minimum on which we should hope to accomplish anything [paying Davis and Son]. So I gambled on getting $25 somewhere and wrote [to Davis] of the $75.*[3]

Avery went on to explain that because they now had another $25 to work with, he recommended waiting to see what kind of job Harry and Lyman Davis would do. If they needed to invest another $25 toward doing a better job of clearing the same trail, they could do that, or, ideally, if the Davises did good work, ATC could put the $25 to use somewhere else.[4]

After Davis and son were off the job and Walter Greene took over blazing the 39-mile Barren–Chairback link, it is unclear what happened to the $100. Perhaps Avery sent a few dollars Greene's way. What is clear is that the ATC was often trying to scrape together funding, particularly as it related to opening and promoting the Maine sections of trail, but also to prepare and print guidebooks and supplements for the ever-emerging path in all states.

In March 1934, Avery wrote to Arthur Comey to update him on trail progress and to make his case for getting more money. "Bigelow to Sugarloaf is an assured C.C.C. [Civilian Conservation Corps] project," he told Comey, not only to indicate further progress in Maine but also to share that at least some of it would be covered by federal funds.

> *The real problem is what I told you when I last saw you . . . from somewhere the funds must come in to buy paint, markers, nails and ship it in. . . . Fifty dollars is ample. So until and unless the restriction of raising $100 to match the N.E.T.C. is removed, the whole thing is at*

---

3    Myron Avery to Walter Greene, 9 September 1932, Avery Collection, Maine State Library Special Collections.

4    Ibid.

*a standstill. . . . I had hoped that with your sense of cooperation, you would appreciate the situation and remove the restriction.*[5]

But something else was bothering Avery even more.

*Here is a bit of encouragement that astonishes me. You will recall that, in my hearing [the incident when Avery felt put on the spot by the NETC Steering Committee held the past December], you spoke to [Charles] Blood about the A.M.C. contribution [a commitment to pay the ATC $15]. It has not been paid.*

Avery then told Comey he had called AMC's secretary, Adelaide Meserve, who told him any payment would need to be approved "in Council Meeting" and that "'they' had made a mess of the Maine Guidebook."[6]

"Do you know the meaning of this?" Avery asked Comey. "It looks like we were due for punishment for some error by having the support of the largest outing club withdrawn." After itemizing the funds owed for printing the *Guide to the Appalachian Trail in Maine*, Avery reiterated the need to immediately promote the trail.

*Use of the Maine sector will determine its future and the support of the camp proprietors [whom Avery had promised increased business as a result of routing the trail on or near their properties]. Therefore, from our point of view, the urgent need of getting the Maine book out and distributed. With more money we could have done a better job but I am at a loss to understand this. Perhaps you can enlighten me.*[7]

"The fact is that practically all contributions are in and there isn't even the few dollars for maintenance work. So further work in Maine rests with you," Avery concludes.[8]

---

5    Myron Avery to Arthur Comey, 5 March 1934, Avery Collection, Maine State Library Special Collections.

6    Ibid.

7    Ibid.

8    Ibid.

Incredibly, Avery didn't draw a connection that perhaps the reason Blood was withholding payment of funds was related to Avery's recent behavior toward Underhill and Peabody of AMC.

If Comey knew of the tension between AMC and Avery, he didn't let on. "Any rift with the A.M.C. was news to me," began his response. "I made sure that the matter of the appropriation for the ATC came up at the Council yesterday, and you may be relieved to know that the $15 was voted." Having averted yet another immediate financial crisis, Comey then made a pitch for discussing all other financial matters in person, which Avery promised to do if he was able, before spending a month on the West Coast for Navy-related legal work.[9]

Another example of just how tight budgets were arose in May 1934, when Maine Game Warden Helon Taylor wrote Avery with an update. Taylor had nearly completed building and marking "his section" of the Maine Appalachian Trail, from the fire warden's cabin near the summit of Bigelow to the summit of Sugarloaf, the second highest mountain in Maine: a distance of 15 miles. Taylor would need at least another gallon of paint and some markers, or metal squares bearing the AT insignia, to get the job done.[10]

Avery's response once again was to lobby the NETC chair, Arthur Comey, for money. "Shall I write and tell him to stop?" Avery asked, regarding Taylor's predicament. "Or will the money for paint and markers be forthcoming?" Avery estimated that $57 for materials should be sufficient to "carry us across Maine" and then signed off with, "I am tossing the problem into your lap."[11]

After noting his delight that [the Maine Forest Service supervisor] "Stubbs, Taylor, et al are doing so much . . . as they will take pride in seeing that the trail, once open, will not disappear," Comey got to the question of financing Avery's needs.

"I regret that you did not see fit to look me up on any of your visits to Boston between Dec. 13 and now, as you might have avoided getting yourself

9   Arthur Comey to Myron Avery, 10 April 1934, Avery Collection, Maine State Library Special Collections.

10  Helon Taylor to Myron Avery, 12 May 1934, Avery Collection, Maine State Library Special Collections.

11  Myron Avery to Arthur Comey, 23 May 1934, Avery Collection, Maine State Library Special Collections.

into a jam as to your finances for continuing your Maine AT project," Comey wrote. He told Avery that, to "avoid a stale mate," he was willing to help. He enclosed a check for $6 (a $5 contribution from Comey's own pocket, plus $1 from another member) and then laid out a plan by which NETC would provide Avery with up to $25, based on a dollar-for-dollar match. Comey said he would attempt to secure some funds from the state of Maine, as he believed its participation would help prevent the trail from languishing.[12]

Comey then asked Avery for help "as a member of the A.M.C." who "can help the Club as no one else can at the moment." Largely on the strength of Avery's recommendation, AMC had engaged the Aeronautical Engineering Company to create its 1934 guidebook maps for *The A.M.C. White Mountain Guide*. The company had agreed to deliver maps "within 15 days after proofs were o.k.'d," but it wasn't coming through. The company offered a range of excuses, and AMC suspected the situation was worse than what was being reported. "Larrabee is wild," Comey wrote, referring to the AMC guidebook editor. He asked Avery to look into the situation on behalf of AMC.[13]

"If you would verify the situation and stick the biggest pin in them you have, so that they can ship the maps at the earliest date it would be doing the Club a great service," Comey wrote.[14]

Comey's letter is reminiscent of the missive Underhill wrote to Avery regarding the publication of a Maine AT article in *Appalachia*. In both cases, the author, seeing Avery in a predicament, offered ways to a solution. In both cases, Avery saw the need to implicate the author for his role in creating the condition. (In this case, Avery suspected Comey as being behind the conditional provision for the ATC to receive matching funds.) But, unlike in his letters to Underhill, Avery's response to Comey contains a measure of gratitude.

Avery began his letter to Comey by thanking him: "Your check makes it very apparent that you personally will do all possible to help move matters in Maine." Comey's support may have been a revelation to Avery, as Comey

---

12   Arthur Comey to Myron Avery, 25 May 1934, Avery Collection, Maine State Library Special Collections.

13   Ibid.

14   Ibid.

formerly had argued against moving into Maine until clubs had been formed to support the effort.[15]

More in keeping with Avery's style, he then moved on to exceptions he took to issues Comey had raised.

First, Avery pointed out that almost five months had passed since he requested that the NETC Steering Committee lift the restriction on matching money, and the results of the committee vote hadn't been shared with him. "So, flatly and definitively—as I wrote in December to the Steering Committee—this business of matching funds just is an impossibility. My interest in the Maine work ought to be the only needed guarantee for such a statement." After explaining the many reasons why the state of Maine would not be a likely source of funds (including that the Maine Development Commission "couldn't even help [fund] the A.T. Guide to Maine" and that, after six months, the state still owed him almost $40 for writing a promotional folder on Katahdin—money he, in turn, still owed the printer for creating the maps in the *Guide to the Appalachian Trail in Maine*), Avery concluded: "If anything breaks I will let you know of it. But—to avoid misunderstandings—on a 'matching' basis it is impossible for me to produce any cash."[16]

Second, Avery disputed Comey's assertion that he was in a financial jam relating to finishing the AT work in Maine.

"I am not," Avery declared. "I made perfectly clear that the A.T. funds had been used up and we would have to rest a year or so until we recuperated for further effort. If the N.E.T.C. or anyone else wanted to capitalize [on] the [existing] impetus, we would get results with the aid furnished."[17]

Avery then adopted a remarkably conciliatory tone.

"Both of us are most anxious to move this along," he wrote. "The completed work has produced a momentum which can well carry it through. This is the stuff which counts. I felt—as you well know—that I got unnecessarily

15  Myron Avery to Arthur Comey, 28 May 1934, Avery Collection, Maine State Library Special Collections.

16  Ibid.

17  Ibid.

rough and raw treatment last December [at the NETC Steering Committee meeting] but all that's behind us. Lets [sic] work to carry this along."[18]

Later, he concluded: "We may be at the decisive point where a little push will carry this through. I will continue, of course, to keep you fully informed."[19]

Given the rancorous discourse of the past between these two brilliant, sometimes stubborn men, it is interesting they had finally come to mutually share the view that, above all, they were both dedicated to the realization of the AT.

In early June 1934, Avery wrote a follow-up letter to Comey, suggesting an idea for resolving the issue AMC had in obtaining its guidebook map. Perhaps this was more as a courtesy to Comey than AMC, which he still kept at arm's length as much as practicable.[20] By October 1934, Comey was fully aware of the fallout Avery had caused with AMC. Writing to Avery on Maine State Planning Board letterhead (Comey was one of three listed consultants on the stationary), he began: "I understand you are having some sort of scrap with some of the A.M.C. officers and are not particularly enthusiastic at helping the club out of any difficulties. Seeing things as you do, I doubtless would feel as you do. On the other hand, I believe I am justified in appealing to you as a personal matter."[21]

Comey explained that the Aeronautical Engineering Company still had not come through with maps of good enough quality for AMC to issue with its guides and was not even answering letters inquiring about the project. "I know that you have been in close touch with them and have steered much other work their way besides the present maps. . . . Won't you please look into it for me?"[22]

Myron Avery's relationship with AMC may have been stuck in reverse, but somehow he and Arthur Comey found a way to continue forward.

---

18  Ibid.

19  Ibid.

20  Myron Avery to Arthur Comey, 4 June 1934, Avery Collection, Maine State Library Special Collections.

21  Arthur Comey to Myron Avery, 4 October 1934, Avery Collection, Maine State Library Special Collections.

22  Ibid.

# CHAPTER 14

## Word Gets Out

FROM THE BEGINNING, MYRON AVERY UNDERSTOOD THE SUCCESS OF the AT hinged on four things: building, maintaining, promoting, and protecting it. As the trail inched closer to completion, he focused even more attention on publicity. ("Perhaps the greatest need of the Trail . . . is to tell people that it is there so it can be used," he once reported.)[1] Avery rarely missed a chance to pitch the story of the AT to any willing audience.

In May 1935, the *Old Farmer's Almanac* came calling. For the second year in a row, the publication asked Avery to write an article. His previous year's story about the trail had been so popular that the venerable publication wanted an encore, "something along the same line as last year—more of what you have done or what you plan to do in the future, or whatever you want to write about."[2]

In September, a press release announced that Avery's old friend Ron Gower was leading an AMC-sponsored 120-mile AT hike south from Katahdin. The party would include the former Maine governor Percival P. Baxter, who had visited the region two years before. That Avery was behind the press release is evidenced by the fact that readers were told they could purchase a "supplement to the *Guidebook to the Appalachian Trail in Maine*" by contacting the ATC.[3]

---

1   *Maine Appalachian Trail Club Newsletter*, April 8, 1937. Avery Collection, Maine State Library Special Collections.

2   Robert Haynes (on behalf of *The Old Farmer's Almanac*) to Myron Avery, 14 May 1935, Avery Collection, Maine State Library Special Collections.

3   "Ex-Governor Baxter Joins Appalachian Trail Hikers 120-Mile Trek," Appalachian Mountain Club press release, September 1, 1935, Avery Collection, Maine State Library Special Collections.

On October 15, 1935, a letter written on Harvard University letterhead arrived in Avery's mailbox.

> *You may know that I always believe in giving the devil his due—be that as it may, I certainly congratulate you on the fine progress now being made, and recently made in Maine, on the A.T. Likewise, I always like to rejoice over seeing things come through the only way that I believe can be right in the long run—and this is certainly the case in Maine. Now that enough spirits have been found to organize an intra-state club, and that the state authorities as well as the local owners up and down the line are favorably interested and active—and how!—the trail is going through right so as to stay. The CCC work is particularly fortunate, to back up the vigorous volunteer efforts.*[4]

The letter was signed by Arthur Comey.

Avery immediately responded in kind. "Thank you very much for your fine letter of October 16th [*sic*]. You are frank, as always, and I appreciate it," he began. "No one can fully appreciate, except perhaps, you [who had scouted the western Maine area in the 1920s], and I, how many of our problems have been solved by Forester Sewall, particularly with the landowners in Western Maine."[5] It was at the suggestion of CCC Forester James W. Sewall that the Civilian Conservation Corps adopted the Appalachian Trail in Maine as a project, thus ensuring the completion of the trail and the building of 14 shelters between Grafton Notch and the Kennebec River.

Avery's letter went on to cover some matters they might tackle together. The significance of how the Avery–Comey relationship evolved is monumental. Where once they needed Judge Perkins to intervene in their squabbling, they were now expressing mutual admiration. Of all the stories to be found in the Myron Avery files, this is the most surprising. Given all of the relationships that Avery soured on, or relationships that soured on Avery, the Comey relationship is the only one that rebounded.

---

4   Arthur Comey to Myron Avery, 15 October 1935, Avery Collection, Maine State Library Special Collections.

5   Myron Avery to Arthur Comey, 17 October 1935, Avery Collection, Maine State Library Special Collections.

Another important milestone in 1935 was announced via press release: the establishment of the Maine Appalachian Trail Club (MATC). The trail through Maine was nearing completion; it was time to formally entrust an organization with its ongoing protection and maintenance. Avery pushed to establish and incorporate MATC. But, as with the Potomac Appalachian Trail Club (PATC) and the Appalachian Trail Conference (ATC), Avery made sure the officers and directors were on his side. Just how shrewd this strategy was would be revealed shortly.

At the time of its founding, the only requirements to become a member of MATC were to contribute to the AT in Maine in some way (e.g., trail maintenance, publicity) and then be voted in. No membership fee was required. Prospective members didn't need to reside in Maine. The roster of MATC officers and directors was a who's who of Maine trail builders: Walter Greene (president), Frank Schairer (secretary), Myron Avery (overseer of trails), Albert Jackman (director), and Shailer Philbrick (director).[6]

In practical terms, the makeup of the MATC board helped Avery get the organization off to a solid start. The board was unlikely to question his recommended courses of action, for example. But the reality was Myron Avery was delegating little and running three organizations in addition to performing his full-time Navy job.

The constant pressure was taking a toll on Avery; however, stresses he could not foresee were about to boil over. He was about to choose sides in the future of the AT and throw several organizations into jeopardy.

---

6   "Club Organized to Promote Appalachian Trail in Maine," press release, 1935. Avery Collection, Maine State Library Special Collections.

*Part 3*

# THE DUEL AND ITS AFTERMATH

# CHAPTER 15

## The Skyline Drive Debate

THE DECADE SINCE BENTON MACKAYE PROPOSED THE APPALACHIAN Trail (AT) had held little public conflict. What squabbles occurred were largely due to Myron Avery's impatience and demands, yet even those flare-ups were mostly confined to letters to and from AMC leadership. But a series of events in northern Virginia was about to force the AT community to choose sides in a battle over the very purpose and meaning of the trail. The fallout would test loyalties, inflict lasting wounds, and literally and figuratively affect the course of the trail in the decades to come.

In the 1920s and early 1930s, regional automobile parkways moved from ideas on planners' drawing boards to physical roads on the mountaintops. The greatest accelerant of activity was the number of automobile owners. In 1910, there was one car owner per 200 U.S. residents. In 1915, one in 40 U.S. residents owned cars. But the real explosion in car ownership was just around the corner. From 1920 to 1930, the number of registered car owners in America surged from 8 million to 23 million, a shift driven largely by the availability of Henry Ford's $490 Model T.[1, 2]

The regional parkway movement did not arise from the rapidly growing automobile culture alone. In fact, the first parkways predated cars. Frederick Law Olmsted and Calvert Vaux advocated for the development of "Park-Ways" in the early 1860s as a means for urbanites to "stroll out into the country in search of fresh air, quietness, and recreation." Expanding on the idea of carriage roads they had designed for New York City's Central Park and

---

1   Wayne Curtis, *The Last Great Walk: The True Story of a 1909 Walk from New York to San Francisco and Why it Matters* (Emmaus, PA: Rodale Books, 2014), 143.

2   "The Age of the Automobile," *U.S. History Online Textbook*, ushistory.org/us/46a.asp.

Prospect Park, the influential landscape architects sought to extend the park experience beyond the park gates. Olmsted and Vaux's parkways were distinct from roads designed for commercial enterprise; the parkways would help promote the healthful growth of cities to include "giving access for the purposes of ordinary traffic to all the houses that front upon it, offering a special road for driving and riding without turning commercial vehicles from the right of way, and furnishing ample public walks, with room for seats and with borders of turf in which trees may grow of the most stately character."[3]

The parkway concept grew in New York City, Buffalo, and Boston—all cities that had hired Olmsted. The fundamental principle of these projects was to bring the restorative qualities of nature into the urban environment. Not designed as transportation routes per se, parkways allowed the flow of local traffic while minimizing access and egress. They also separated pedestrians from carriage traffic, while allowing scenic views for both.

Then came the automobile.

The construction of the Bronx River Parkway, begun in 1907, marked an important change in American parkway design. First, it was designed to serve travelers between multiple communities, in contrast to Olmsted and Vaux's designs, which served people within a single city's footprint. Second, it was offered as an example of a financially successful urban renewal project. Both facets would greatly inform future discussions about parkways throughout the country.

As the parkway development historian Matthew Dalbey states: "The Bronx River Parkway initially was a response to the environmental decline of the Bronx River. Not only had the adjacent houses and buildings contributed to pollution problems, but development along the river had led to severe erosion of the riverbank."[4] The development of what eventually would become a 23-mile parkway extending from the Bronx to southern Westchester County retained three important aspects of Olmsted and Vaux's vision:

3   Olmsted, Vaux, & Co., "Report to the Brooklyn Park Commission," *The Papers of Frederick Law Olmsted: Writings on Public Parks, Parkways and Park Systems, Supplementary Series 1*, ed. Charles E. Beveridge and Carolyn F. Hoffman (Baltimore and London: Johns Hopkins University Press, 1997), 135–137.

4   Matthew Dalbey, *Regional Visionaries and Metropolitan Boosters: Decentralization, Regional Planning, and Parkways During the Interwar Years* (Dordrecht, Netherlands: Springer Science + Business Media, 2002), 25.

picturesque views of the Bronx River and a wooded corridor that varied from 200 to 1,200 feet wide; limited vehicle access, with overpasses built to accommodate local traffic; and a 15.5-mile linear park (and, eventually, a 4.6-acre playground) where locals could enjoy time outdoors.[5]

The most important impact of the Bronx River Parkway was that it became the catalyst for the automobile parkway development movement. Because property values adjacent to the parkway increased "many-fold," proponents began touting the economic advantages of building suburban parkways. (A lesser noted impact was how the Bronx River Parkway strayed from the early vision of the parkway articulated by Olmsted and others. "It no longer brought nature into the built environment of the city. The Bronx River Parkway effort attempted to allow the built environment to penetrate the yet-to-be-settled countryside surrounding the city by giving the city automobile owner access to the countryside.")[6]

The parkway movement was now fueled by at least one economic success story and ready to gain enough horsepower to drive it up and over the Blue Ridge Mountains. The question was whether Benton MacKaye and his regionalist friends could mount enough of a fight to stop it.

MacKaye's vision for the AT identified the needs to negate the effects of what would be later known as "urban sprawl," or the city moving out to envelop the countryside and its way of life, and to retain the forests in a pristine state to restore and revive us.

The need for wilderness was always important to MacKaye's vision for the AT and the surrounding communities. While working on his landmark article "An Appalachian Trail: A Project in Regional Planning" in 1920 and 1921, the redistribution of the nation's population, from country to city, also framed his argument for a regional approach.

> *The rural population of the United States, and of the Eastern States adjacent to the Appalachians, has now dipped below the urban. For the whole country it has fallen from 60 per cent of the total in 1900 to 49 per cent in 1920; for the Eastern States it has fallen during this*

---

5   "Bronx River Parkway," *New York City Department of Parks & Recreation,* nycgovparks.org/parks/bronx-river-parkway/history.

6   Matthew Dalbey, *Regional Visionaries and Metropolitan Boosters,* 26.

*period, from 55 per cent to 45 per cent. . . . This is a shrinkage of nearly 18 per cent in 20 years; in the States from Maine to Pennsylvania the shrinkage has been 40 per cent.*[7]

MacKaye's answer was to entice people out of the overcrowded cities, where roads and subways were "moving people each day from places where they would rather not live to places where they would rather not work, and back again."[8]

The answer, MacKaye felt, was in building communities where people could work and play without having to commute at all. Sustainable jobs in forestry and agriculture were the backbone of his economic plan, "a project to develop the opportunities—for recreation, recuperation, and employment—in the region of the Appalachian skyline."

Looking back at MacKaye's regional plan for "An Appalachian Trail," it is important to note, as historian Matthew Dalbey says, that "MacKaye did not advocate removing people from the land in order to create playgrounds for visitors from the cities. He advocated repopulating of the rural environment so that people could make use of the land, live within the context of the land and take part in the three [employment] opportunities [he outlined]."[9]

Further, MacKaye's own experiences had instilled a belief that access to unspoiled natural areas led to a greater understanding of self and community. The ability to leave the frenetic pace of the built environment to explore natural settings had given him a unique perspective, one he felt was critical to the well-being of individuals and communities.

MacKaye's sense of urgency for protecting the mountaintops as a buffer to urbanization and as a place to experience the vital connection with the wilderness would not only become his overwhelming concern but his purpose.

The role of roads in national parks and forests has been a debate since those federal lands were first designated, but the purposes for building auto routes were changing. Roads, and railroads, in forest regions were built

---

7   "An Appalachian Trail: A Project in Regional Planning," *Journal of the American Institute of Architects* 9, no. 10 (October 1921): 327.

8   Benton MacKaye, "New York a National Peril," *Saturday Review of Literature*, August 23, 1930, 68.

9   Matthew Dalbey, *Regional Visionaries and Metropolitan Boosters*, 26.

almost exclusively to support timber harvesting operations. This utilitarian role of roads—a means for moving goods to market—was woven into MacKaye's regional planning perspective. But the automotive revolution had a profound effect on USFS policy. Roads would become the primary means for getting visitors to the forests and to help people explore the natural areas once they got there.

In 1916, the USFS chief, Henry S. Graves (who earlier had hired MacKaye to be a forest examiner in his agency), wrote an article titled, "Road Building in the National Forests." While Graves acknowledged the ongoing importance of roads for efficient timber harvesting, he made it clear that tourism was influencing road-building decisions like never before.

> Each year sees an increasing use of the National Forests by residents of the more densely populated districts, east and west, who wish to escape the heat and discomfort of the city during the summer months. . . . It will be an increasingly important part of the work of the Forest Service to care for and render accessible these playgrounds of the nation.[10]

In a speech to the Pan-American Road Congress the year before, Graves stressed the economic value new road construction would deliver to communities adjacent to national forests.

> In the selection of projects for construction, preference is given to those sections and communities within or adjacent to national forests that are situated away from the main systems of state or county highways and that would remain without a means of transportation were it not for the assistance of the forest service.[11]

Meanwhile, the National Park Service (NPS) was developing its own view of the role of roads. During the 1920s, the NPS director, Stephen Mather, who had been the first person appointed to that role in 1916, continued to

---

10   Henry S. Graves, "Road Building in the National Forests," *The American City* 16, no. 1 (1916): 4.

11   "Pan-American Road Congress Convenes at Oakland: Chief Forester of United States Tells Delegates How Government is Opening National Forests to Motorists," *Motor Age* 28, no. 12 (September 1915): 18.

try to balance the need for roads and the need for wilderness. In his 1923 *Report of the Director of the National Park Service,* Mather stated: "I am firmly against overdevelopment of the parks by too many roads. Proposed roads must be carefully studied as to location, and then only those most important to facilitate easy access to the most scenic sections permitted. We must guard against the intrusion of roads into sections [of National Parks] that should be kept for quiet contemplation and accessible only by horseback or hiking."[12]

Interestingly, in the same report, Mather mentioned a migration toward the national parks, not only of tourists but of new inhabitants to the parks' adjacent communities.

> *This year 271,482 automobiles registered in our parks. They came from every State in the Union, Canada and Mexico . . . [The parks] draw travel as nothing else does. The slogan "See America first"[13] has become a household expression, and this means that the parks and monuments are becoming more and more the vacation grounds of the American traveler. More than 60 per cent of the park visitors come in their own private automobiles. They are the potential settlers, potential investors. Instances are brought to my attention too numerous to mention of cases where park visitors have invested in farms and ranches, orchards, and mines, in their vicinities, or have altogether cut the ties that bound them to the old homes and reestablished themselves as citizens of a new community. This is worth a lot locally, but is also worth a great deal nationally, for it relieves the overpopulated areas of the East and distributes their overplus where it is needed and can do the most good.[14]*

---

12  Stephen Mather, "Report of the Director of the National Park Service to the Secretary of the Interior for the Fiscal Year Ended June 30, 1923 and the Travel Season, 1923" (Washington, DC: Government Printing Office, 1923), 10–11.

13  "See America First" was a marketing campaign developed in the early 1900s to boost tourism in the western United States. Over time, the phrase was picked up by businesses and organizations including the National Park Service to promote park visits by automobile. To learn more about how the "See America First" campaign developed, see Marguerite Shaffer, *See America First: Tourism and National Identity 1880–1940* (Washington, DC: Smithsonian Books, September 2001).

14  Stephen Mather, "Report of the Director of the National Park Service to the Secretary of the Interior for the Fiscal Year Ended June 30, 1923 and the Travel Season, 1923" (Washington, DC: Government Printing Office, 1923), 10–11.

Benton MacKaye may have been pleased that the urban-to-rural shift he proposed in his 1921 article was at least partially underway. But the rapid adoption of automobiles and the subsequent rise in road building were bringing seismic change to the countryside. No project exemplified this more than Skyline Drive, the mountaintop roadway proposed for the Shenandoah Range that would forever change MacKaye's relationship with the trail he envisioned.

After suffering a stroke, which had been preceded by a number of other health issues, Stephen Mather left his office as NPS director in January 1929. His replacement, the longtime assistant director of the National Park Service and superintendent of Yellowstone National Park, Horace Albright, presided over the development of Skyline Drive, which took place with remarkable speed.

The establishment of Shenandoah National Park and Skyline Drive both came about due to an initiative Mather had begun in 1923. In his seventh annual NPS report, he stated:

> *I should like to see additional national parks established east of the Mississippi, but just how this can be accomplished is not clear. There should be a typical section of the Appalachian Range established as a national park with its native flora and fauna conserved and made accessible for public use and its development undertaken by Federal funds. As areas in public ownership in the East are at present limited to a number of forest reserves acquired under the provisions of the Weeks Act authorizing the purchase of lands for the protection of forests and the headwaters of streams, it appears that the only practicable way national park areas can be acquired would be by donation of lands from funds privately donated, as in the case of the Lafayette National Park.*[15]

Mather solicited Secretary of the Interior Hubert Work to spearhead the project. Work quickly organized a committee to evaluate possible additions to the National Park Service in the southern Appalachian Mountains region,

---

15 "Final Report of the Southern Appalachian National Park Commission to the Secretary of the Interior" (Washington, DC: Government Printing Office, 1931), 1.

which would be defined as lands south of the northern border of Maryland. The committee members were Major W.A. Welch of the Palisades Interstate Park Commission of New York (who in one year would be named the first chairman of the ATC); Representative Henry W. Temple of Pennsylvania; Colonel Glenn S. Smith of the U.S. Geological Survey (selected to represent the secretary of the interior on the committee); and two representatives from the Council on National Parks, Forests, and Wildlife, the former AMC president Harlan P. Kelsey and William C. Gregg.[16]

On March 26, 1924, the committee met in Washington, D.C.; elected Rep. Temple as chairman; and adopted the name Southern Appalachian National Park Committee.[17]

Shortly after, the committee received "a large number of requests for examinations of territory" from 23 potential sites. By late July, the committee was in the field, inspecting potential national park sites in Georgia, North Carolina, Tennessee, West Virginia, and Virginia. After the sites were inspected, some as a group and some individually, the committee convened on December 12, 1924, to draft a report and make final recommendations.[18]

The committee had determined that no site under 500 square miles in area should be considered. They also set six additional requirements:

1. Mountain scenery with inspiring perspectives and delightful details.

2. Areas sufficiently extensive and adaptable so that annually millions of visitors might enjoy the benefits of outdoor life and communion with nature without the confusion of overcrowding.

3. A substantial part to contain forests, shrubs, flowers, and mountain streams, with picturesque cascades and waterfalls overhung with foliage, all untouched by the hand of man.

4. Abundant springs and streams available for camps and fishing.

5. Opportunities for protecting and developing the wildlife of the area, and the whole to be a natural museum, preserving the outstanding

---

16  Ibid.

17  Ibid.

18  Ibid., 6.

features of the southern Appalachians as they appeared in the early pioneer days.

6. Accessibility by rail and road.[19]

The committee identified a clear choice to become America's next national park: Great Smoky Mountains. Interestingly, they made the recommendation that the park should be established later. "The Great Smokies have some handicaps which will make the development of them into a national park a matter of delay," the committee wrote. "Their very ruggedness and height make road and other park development a serious undertaking as to time and expense."[20]

A more desirable immediate choice became the "outstanding and logical place for the creation of the first national park in the southern Appalachians": the area that would become known as Shenandoah National Park.[21]

In stating the case for the creation of the park, the committee cited its proximity to the general public (40 million Americans lived within a day's ride), its natural splendor ("many canyons and gorges with beautiful cascading streams" and "splendid primeval forests"), and its historic interest ("mountains looking down on valleys with their many battlefields of Revolutionary and Civil War periods and the birthplaces of many Presidents of the United States").[22]

But the most exciting thing the prospective national park had going for it, the committee wrote, was a human-made feature that could be added to it.

> The greatest single feature, however, is a possible sky-line drive along the mountain top, following a continuous ridge and looking down westerly on the Shenandoah Valley, from 2,500 to 3,500 feet below, and also commanding a view of the Piedmont Plain stretching easterly to the Washington Monument, which landmark of our

---

19  Ibid., 7.

20  Ibid.

21  Ibid., 8.

22  Ibid.

*National Capital may be seen on a clear day. Few scenic drives in the world could surpass it.*[23]

In January 1925, Representative Henry W. Temple and Senator Claude A. Swanson introduced bills into their respective chambers authorizing the secretary of the interior to "determine the boundaries and areas" and to "receive offers of donations of land and monies" in order to achieve the perpetual preservation of Shenandoah National Park, Great Smoky Mountains National Park, Mammoth Cave National Park, and "such other lands in the southern Appalachian Mountains as in [the judgment of the secretary of the interior] should be acquired and administered as national parks."[24]

When President Coolidge signed the bill into law on February 21, 1925, the creation of Skyline Drive and the adjacent Blue Ridge Parkway already had momentum. But the greatest obstacle to those two projects being built would not be local opposition but funding. The newly signed legislation stipulated that the federal government would not provide funds for creating the new parks. If the states wanted to reap the benefits of having a national park, they would have to take ownership of the land and then turn it over to the National Park Service.

To acquire the land to create Great Smoky Mountains National Park, the state legislatures of Tennessee and North Carolina each had appropriated $2 million. By 1930, an additional $1 million in private donations had been gathered, including money chipped in by schoolchildren. In honor of his mother, John D. Rockefeller created the Laura Spelman Rockefeller Memorial Fund and matched the money raised, giving the states more than $10 million total with which to acquire land.

The Commonwealth of Virginia took a different tack. The person in charge of making both Shenandoah National Park and Skyline Drive a reality was Virginia Governor Harry Byrd's former campaign manager, William Carson. Creating the commonwealth's Conservation and Development Commission was one of the newly elected governor's highest priorities, and the bill establishing it passed in just five days. When the bill became law on

---

23  Ibid.

24  Ibid., 9.

March 13, 1926, the newly formed commission was granted the power to "condemn and acquire land and other property for public park purposes."[25]

Neither the governor nor his new commissioner believed in attracting development for development's sake. The charismatic Carson, in particular, was effective at charting a course for the commonwealth that would capitalize on its historical character and natural beauty. As one historian notes, Carson "proposed to develop Virginia by conserving it—using the state's scenic and historic wonders to attract tourists and, indirectly, industry. While not repudiating the idea of industrial development, Carson and the commission did not plunge headlong into the mad scramble to entice new plants into the state with extravagant offers. Rather, Virginia's 'business government' sought a more economical and efficient path to industry."[26]

Although Carson had proclaimed that Shenandoah National Park "could be established in the course of a year," by 1927, he was encountering harsh financial realities. Carson had estimated it would cost the commonwealth $5.5 million to acquire the land to create the 385,000-acre park. By September of that year, he upped the estimate to $8 million. The commission briefly discussed scrapping the idea of a national park in favor of a state park with a toll road through it then ultimately decided to have Carson meet with Secretary Work to inquire about reducing the size of the park.[27]

In October 1927, the assistant director of the National Park Service, Arno B. Cammerer, drafted a report calling for the minimum size of Shenandoah National Park to be amended from its original proposal of 385,000 acres to 327,000 acres. The same report referenced the possible construction of a "skyline" road within the park, recommending that the "discussion of the road only commence once the land had been handed over to the Park Service, and not before." In this way, the federal government would be responsible for surveying and constructing the road.[28]

---

25  "Senate Document Number 6," *Journal of the Senate of the Commonwealth of Virginia* (March 13, 1926): 843–844.

26  John F. Horan Jr., "Will Carson and the Virginia Conservation Commission, 1926–1934," *The Virginia Magazine of History and Biography* 92, no. 4 (October 1984): 395.

27  Ibid., 397–398.

28  Matthew Dalbey, *Regional Visionaries and Metropolitan Boosters*, 101–103.

The acquisition of the land weighed heavily on Carson. Worried that condemnation proceedings with individual landowners could drag on for years, thus placing the creation of the park in doubt, he successfully lobbied the commission, the governor, and the legislature to condemn all the private land within the proposed park through one blanket act. Simply put, when the state raised enough money to purchase the lots at their appraised value, circuit courts would draw up deeds transferring the land. Not surprisingly, the condemnation law headed to the courts. By the fall of 1929, the law had been upheld, and Carson was predicting that "the park would be nearly realized by 1932."[29]

But natural and market conditions would hamper the project yet again. The one-two punch of the lingering Depression and a severe drought slowed progress and diminished enthusiasm of members of the commission other than Carson, who now made Skyline Drive his priority. The road across the mountaintops would no longer be simply a means of spurring tourism; it would immediately create local jobs and "probably mean the saving of many lives from starvation."[30]

Carson began lobbying hard for federal drought relief funds to be put toward building Skyline Drive. In fall 1930, President Hoover, while horseback riding with NPS director Albright in Big Meadows (an open area high above the presidential retreat), suggested the area would be the perfect location for a road. He reportedly told Albright to "talk it over with Mr. Carson."[31] This put even more momentum behind Carson's efforts at both the local and federal levels.

On February 4, 1931, the Skyline Drive project received $250,000 from the Emergency Public Works Act of 1931.[32] But there was an immediate and embarrassing snag. NPS owned the land on which the road would be constructed (it had been conveyed by the Commonwealth of Virginia), but the minimum acreage requirements for the park still hadn't been met.

---

29  John F. Horan Jr., "Will Carson and the Virginia Conservation Commission, 1926–1934," 401.

30  "Records of the National Park Service [NPS], Record Group 79," *National Archives*, archives.gov/research/guide-fed-records/groups/079.html.

31  John F. Horan Jr., "Will Carson and the Virginia Conservation Commission, 1926–1934," 401.

32  "Records of the National Park Service [NPS], Record Group 79," *National Archives*, archives.gov/research/guide-fed-records/groups/079.html.

Carson went back to Congress and asked that the minimum size of the park be reduced to 160,000 acres, which took another full year. Meanwhile, the surveying of Skyline Drive began, even though there wasn't yet a national park to put it in.

## MacKaye and Avery Square Off

If Skyline Drive wasn't yet on the mind of the Potomac Appalachian Trail Club membership at large, at least one person involved was concerned it would be.

Ferdinand Zerkel was a Luray, Virginia, real estate agent, lumber broker, and major local proponent of Shenandoah National Park. Ten days after the Emergency Public Works Act of 1931 was signed, Zerkel sent a letter to the assistant director of the National Park Service, Arno Cammerer, indicating that at least some members of the PATC were upset about the project.

"I have heard that certain officials of the Potomac Appn. Trail Club thought the Skyline Road something to disturb their privacy and otherwise injure the Park from their own viewpoint. Now, Friend 'Cam.,' I am a member of the Club and have some fine friends in it whom I hesitate to lose."[33]

Two days later, Cammerer responded to Zerkel stating that PATC members were friends of the park movement, indicating Cammerer wasn't concerned about them rising up to contest the construction of Skyline Drive. But initially, at least, he was wrong.[34]

The speed at which Skyline Drive was taking shape caught the AT community by surprise. Much of the maneuvering for the road had been done away from the public eye. There had been no hearings nor public debate. The boosters, adeptly led by Commissioner Carson, had used legal maneuverings and political connections to enable the project to get started before there even was a park.

AT proponents were out of the loop for other reasons. In 1925, when Benton MacKaye wrote a letter to the Southern Appalachian National Park Commission member Harlan P. Kelsey, offering his services as a surveyor of the

33 Ferdinand Zerkel to Arno Cammerer, 14 February 1931, Zerkel Papers, Shenandoah National Park Archives.

34 Matthew Dalbey, *Regional Visionaries and Metropolitan Boosters*, 101–103.

AT in the area that was to become Shenandoah National Park, MacKaye was told that the placement of the AT "should come after the park is secured."[35]

Days later, Kelsey wrote another letter to MacKaye, unequivocally stating his preference for where he felt the AT should be placed.

> I am particularly interested in having the trail go along the crest of the Mountains in the Shenandoah National Park area rather than a skyline road which I believe would seriously detract from the ecological value of the Park. More than this I believe that the Park for the most part should be kept entirely wild and restored to its natural conditions as fast as possible.

In a postscript in the same letter, Kelsey shared that his view was only one of many, and that the ultimate decisions on the park would be "a matter of development and administration."[36]

In his response, MacKaye spoke passionately about the affect Skyline Drive would have.

> Your Commission seems to have in its hands the power to determine for this country what the word 'Park' is going to mean—whether the preservation of a bit of the original North America or the making of one more Coney Island. . . . Are Parks going to be offsets to our civilization or adjuncts of it? Unless the first is deliberately worked for the other will inevitably occur. And the choice will have to be made, as you say, early in the game.[37]

The same day Kelsey wrote to MacKaye stating his preference for placing the AT along the mountain crest and keeping the park in as pristine a state a possible, he also wrote to Barrington Moore, the man who had recommended Kelsey to serve on the Southern Appalachian National Park Commission. Kelsey's position on Skyline Drive was consistent with that stated

---

35  Harlan P. Kelsey to Benton MacKaye, 24 March 1925, Papers of the MacKaye Family, Rauner Special Collections Library, Dartmouth College.

36  Harlan P. Kelsey to Benton MacKaye, 27 March 1925, Papers of the MacKaye Family, Rauner Special Collections Library, Dartmouth College.

37  Benton MacKaye to Harlan P. Kelsey, 31 March 1925, Papers of the MacKaye Family, Rauner Special Collections Library, Dartmouth College.

to MacKaye, an indication that he was not simply trying to placate either MacKaye or the trail community at large.

> With the Shenandoah National Park I know that some of my associates want a skyline road. That's good propaganda stuff and it would make a magnificent drive but the Park itself averages about 10 to 12 miles wide and it would split it right in two in the middle. There are two main highways crossing the Park in low gaps and I believe that from these gaps roads could go up to some of those Mountain peaks and that is about all for roads in the Park.[38]

Kelsey continued to express his concern about the construction of Skyline Drive. In April 1931, two months before the Southern Appalachian National Park Committee submitted its final report and disbanded, he raised the issue with the NPS's director, Horace Albright. Even as the route was being staked out, Albright told Kelsey he doubted the road would extend beyond Skyland (a resort that was built in 1895, situated on what would later become the highest point on Skyline Drive) and would probably loop back down to the valley from there. Albright knew this wasn't an accurate portrayal of what was happening with Skyline Drive. The city planner, landscape architect, and road designer Thomas Vint had successfully convinced NPS to pursue only Skyline Drive as a road project and not ancillary roads. So, why did Albright bend the truth to Kelsey? Perhaps he was worried about Kelsey's relationship with the trail community. Kelsey was a former president of AMC and was well connected with that organization, as well as PATC and ATC. Albright probably also was aware that the Southern Appalachian National Park Committee was about to disband, and Kelsey would lose his ability to request updates in an official capacity.[39]

If Albright's intent was to delay discussion, he bought only a few months of time. In early June, the PATC secretary, Harold Anderson, saw

---

38 Harlan P. Kelsey to Barrington Moore, 27 March 1925, National Parks: Shenandoah Central Classified Files 1907–1932, File 0.32; *Records of the National Park Service, Record Group 79*, National Archives at College Park, Maryland.

39 Horace M. Albright to Harlan P. Kelsey, 17 April 1931, Central Classified Files 1907–1942, 1907–1932, File 631.1–901, *Records of the National Park Service, Record Group 79*, National Archives at College Park, Maryland.

surveyor stakes marking a route north from Thornton Gap, Virginia. He told MacKaye, who immediately wrote to Arno Cammerer, the NPS assistant director.

"Does this mean the extension of the policy of motor skyline vs. foot-path skyline in the National Parks?" MacKaye asked. He also asked Cammerer to provide an answer directly to Harold Anderson. Cammerer responded by saying the stakes were only placed as part of a survey and did not necessarily indicate NPS would build the road. Anderson and the rest of the trail community would soon learn otherwise.[40]

In early July 1932, Benton MacKaye met with Myron Avery and Harold Anderson in Washington, D.C., to discuss just how rapidly Skyline Drive was taking shape—in many places over the very path of the AT itself. It is fitting that those three men sat down to plot their response. Ultimately, two of them would take one fork on the philosophical trail, and one would take the other.

The three agreed to go to the ridge top to see the proposed route themselves. Days later, they rendezvoused with a handful of PATC members at Skyland to investigate. The next day, MacKaye stopped in Washington, D.C., to express his displeasure with the state of Skyline Drive in person to Cammerer.

Myron Avery also was unhappy with the proposed road route. He lobbied NPS landscape architects to route the road downslope, on the eastern side of the range, away from the ridgeline where the AT already traversed.

But it was too late. The official groundbreaking for what became the 34-mile section of Skyline Drive, from Swift Run Gap to Thornton Gap, occurred on July 18, 1931, less than one week after MacKaye, Avery, and others had visited the site.

That summer in Shirley, Massachusetts, MacKaye worked on an article about opportunities for nature study along the AT. The reality of a paved road over parts of his envisioned footpath in the wilderness must have weighed on him. Instead of creating islands of refuge from the mechanized world, the trail was becoming a refuge *for* the mechanized world.

MacKaye decided to propose an alternative. In collaboration with Harold Anderson, he drew up a plan for the "Appalachian Intermountain Motorway":

---

40  Benton MacKaye to Arno P. Cammerer, 13 June 1932, Papers of the MacKaye Family, Rauner Special Collections Library, Dartmouth College.

an interstate highway from the Adirondacks to the Great Smoky Mountains that alternatively followed valleys, climbed mountain flanks, and, where necessary, went through mountain passes. This well-considered alternative to the growing skyline road movement would ensure that drivers and hikers would gain majestic views—and that, perhaps, motorists would be inspired to leave their cars and discover the recreational opportunities all around them.[41] MacKaye took his plan to Washington and met with the NPS's Albright and Cammerer several times to promote his plan.[42] But as far as they were concerned, Benton MacKaye had presented an idea with little appeal. NPS was firmly behind Skyline Drive, and potentially other skyline routes like it, because the president, the U.S. Congress, the Commonwealth of Virginia, and the motoring public were behind it.

Skyline Drive was one-third complete and picking up speed. Congress ponied up $1 million in fall 1932 to continue building the route northward in Virginia, from Swift Run Gap to Front Royal. In October, Harold Anderson wrote to MacKaye to say he had recently driven the 34 completed miles of road with Myron Avery and other members of PATC. He told MacKaye the new road was going to be a sensation with motorists and that they would need to "abandon the idea of a Skyline route for the Appalachian Trail [through Shenandoah National Park] because this route has now been preempted by the new road." Anderson then raised an issue that would determine the futures of MacKaye, Avery, Anderson, and the AT.

The ride over Skyline Drive had convinced Anderson that the best solution for rerouting the trail through Shenandoah National Park would be to forsake the ridgeline and proximity to the road entirely and instead run the trail down on the flank.

Anderson asked MacKaye to write to Avery, in an attempt to get Avery to understand what he should already know:

> that the Appalachian Trail should above all things be a wilderness foot-path and that while so far as possible we will want to have a skyline trail, it may be necessary in some sections, such as the Shenandoah

---

41  Larry Anderson, *Benton MacKaye*, 231

42  Benton MacKaye, diary, 18–31 October 1931, Papers of the MacKaye Family, Rauner Special Collections Library, Dartmouth College.

*National Park, to depart from this general idea and that we should as far as possible seek the primitive environment for the Trail, even if we have to sacrifice the skyline route. . . . I cannot help feeling that Myron with all his indefatigable energy and enthusiasm has not fully grasped the idea of the Appalachian Trail. . . . The whole question of road vs. trail is very fundamental. We outdoor folk who love the primitive are accused of selfishness and trying to have preserved inviolate a narrow strip of the little that we have left of the primitive area and preventing the enjoyment (?) by multitudes of the scenery of this area if roads were built therein. It seems to me that it narrows down to the question of whether it is worth while to preserve the primitive.*[43]

Cruising through Shenandoah National Park in an automobile with Myron Avery provided a moment of clarity for Harold Anderson. In his mind, the two potential threats to the trail were: one, skyline roads and other human-made encroachments; and two, Avery's inability to comprehend that these features were incompatible with the sentiment that had inspired the trail in the first place.

By spring 1934, two-thirds of Skyline Drive was either complete or under construction. The scenic byway was enormously popular and hailed as a public works success. The skyline road movement was booming. President Franklin D. Roosevelt approved an extended skyline road all the way to the Great Smoky Mountains, and the Public Works Administration authorized an initial $4 million investment to begin building what would become known as the Blue Ridge Parkway. Soon, proposals appeared for additional skyline roads throughout the east, including along the Massanutten Range to the west of Shenandoah, over the top of the Presidential Range in New Hampshire, and over the tops of the Green Mountains spanning the length of Vermont.

In May, Benton MacKaye attended the Southern Appalachian Trail Conference in Highlands, North Carolina. In a speech to the four member organizations (Smoky Mountains Hiking Club, Carolina Mountain Club, Nantahala Appalachian Trail Club, and Georgia Appalachian Trail Club),

---

43  Harold Anderson to Benton MacKaye, 14 October 1932, Papers of the MacKaye Family, Rauner Special Collections Library, Dartmouth College.

MacKaye responded to the remarks sent by Myron Avery to be shared at the meeting regarding the AT. Avery contended: "Our main problem is to actually create it. Then we may discuss how to use it."[44]

Not surprisingly, MacKaye passionately felt that Avery's view was short-sighted and missing the whole point of the AT. "A wilderness is like a secret," he told the gathering. "The best way to keep it is to *keep* it. Keep the wilderness *wild*. Do not manicure it."[45] MacKaye believed the violation caused by skyline roads was wholesale. Two months before, he had written that a skyline road "violates the wilderness solitude not merely here and there but throughout its whole length."[46]

One month later, the scene repeated itself in reverse at the Sixth Annual Appalachian Trail Conference in Rutland, Vermont. This time, MacKaye sent a message to the conference in the form of a proposal, and Avery appeared in person. MacKaye's proposal called for ATC to stand "unequivocally opposed" to skyline drives as proposed for the "Mountain Ranges of New England" and the Blue Ridge Parkway. Instead, he proposed, ATC should adopt a policy encouraging parkways and highways to be located along the "lower flanks and levels" of the Appalachian ranges.

MacKaye's resolution sparked lengthy debate but ultimately failed for a variety of reasons. The first was the evolving state of the proposed Green Mountain Parkway project. In 1933, the Green Mountain Club (GMC) of Vermont resolved that it was "unalterably opposed to the construction of such a highway," but it since had been forced to change its position.[47] Because the parkway promised to bring federal money and much-needed jobs to the rural state, GMC "leaders recognized that simple opposition was not a good strategy," so, they organized a committee "to design another proposal that would fulfill the goals of the parkway without endangering the mountains

44 Myron Avery, statement for the Southern Appalachian Trail Conference, 22 May 1934, Avery Collection, Maine State Library Special Collections.

45 Benton MacKaye remarks to Southern ATC, May 26 1934, Avery Collection, Maine State Library Special Collections.

46 Benton MacKaye, "Flankline vs. Skyline," *Appalachia* 20 (1934): 104–108.

47 *Long Trail News*, July 1933.

or the Long Trail." With the position unresolved even among its members, GMC couldn't afford to align itself with MacKaye's "unequivocal" stance.[48]

For his part, Avery took a neutral stance on the proposal. This reportedly helped produce the stalemate that doomed MacKaye's proposal.

During the following summer, Avery wrote to Arno Cammerer, who had become the director of NPS in August 1933, with two requests that at least some in the trail community construed as an attempt to placate the anti-road faction, led by MacKaye. In the role of ATC chairman, Avery asked Cammerer to commit to having the federal government reconstruct any sections of trail displaced by further construction on Skyline Drive. In what may have been a surprise to the anti-skyline road crowd, Avery also requested that such sections of trail be routed as far away from Skyline Drive as practicable.

But MacKaye wasn't placated; he was incensed. MacKaye wrote his own letter to Cammerer, accusing the latter of not doing enough to protect the wilderness. Cammerer responded by saying the national parks were the only hope for preserving any wilderness at all. He contended that Forest Service land was subjected to regular timber harvesting, and private lands would always be susceptible to development, but because a parkway had a right of way between 200 and 1,000 feet, it "assures the retention of wilderness conditions in that width, and I daresay, if you and I were living fifty or one hundred years from now we would find these parkways in most places the only wilderness spots left."[49]

MacKaye was incredulous. The director of the National Park Service was contending that a roadside buffer could be called "wilderness." He said as much to Cammerer in a follow-up letter, calling the statement "thoroughly amazing."[50]

Avery was perturbed by MacKaye's letters to Cammerer and let MacKaye know it, saying that such pot stirring "doesn't help what we are trying to accomplish." But there was little "we" left between the father of

---

48 Hannah Silverstein, "No Parking: Vermont Rejects the Green Mountain Parkway," *Vermont History* 63, no. 3 (Summer 1995): 148.

49 Arno Cammerer to Benton MacKaye, 14 September 1934, Papers of the MacKaye Family, Rauner Special Collections Library, Dartmouth College.

50 Benton MacKaye to Arno Cammerer, 21 September 1934, Papers of the MacKaye Family, Rauner Special Collections Library, Dartmouth College.

Benton MacKaye, age 55, in October 1934. Photo: Courtesy of Dartmouth College Library.

the Appalachian Trail and the man who rolled up his sleeves to get it built. MacKaye and Avery's philosophical differences concerning the relationship between the trail and wilderness came to a bruising conclusion at the 1935 Appalachian Trail Conference, in—of all places—Shenandoah National Park.

For the third consecutive important event that would impact the future of ATC and the trail itself, one of the men would not be in attendance. This time, it was MacKaye who was absent. Instead, MacKaye sent a powerfully worded plea and accompanying proposal asking conference members to categorically oppose skyline roads. He reminded attendees that his original proposal for the AT called for it to be a means for gaining the benefits of a wilderness experience and that "the Appalachian Trail is a wilderness trail or it is nothing."

But MacKaye's call again fell short. Avery and his followers believed their top priority was creating and retaining an uninterrupted path from Georgia to Maine. They weren't willing to risk losing what they built in the name of the wilderness ethos alone. When Harold Anderson and a few other MacKaye loyalists offered a revised version of MacKaye's proposal, Avery interceded with an entirely new approach. ATC, Avery argued, should consider projects on their own merits, and federal agencies should be encouraged to relocate and rebuild the trail when such projects interfere with the existing trail.

Avery's proposal passed, but he didn't stop there. He presided over sweeping changes to ATC bylaws that resulted in removing MacKaye followers from positions of power, including a new stipulation that granted voting power on the basis of the number of trail miles maintained by member clubs. This placed the PATC, of which Avery was president, in control of a major voting block and clubs sympathetic to MacKaye (such as AMC and the NY–NJ Trail Conference) at a disadvantage.

MacKaye supporters were irate. Perhaps no one felt the disappointment more than Raymond Torrey, who had been behind the AT idea since the first conference and a consistent promoter of the trail through his *New York Evening Post* articles (the first appearing under the headline "Appalachian Trail: A Great Trail from Maine to Georgia!" in 1922, years before Myron Avery appeared on the scene). In a letter to MacKaye describing the events, a despondent Torrey reported, "We are likely to be outnumbered in any future Appalachian Trail Conference by Avery's ingeniously managed bloc." He also forwarded the notion that although Avery didn't quite control the board of managers, he very nearly did—perhaps a moot point anyway, as Avery didn't consult the board between general meetings.[51]

Toward the end of 1935, several months removed from the fallout of the contentious ATC, Benton MacKaye wrote a letter to Myron Avery. He captured on paper his feelings about their divergent views—the same issues Harold Anderson had identified as problematic in his "post Skyline Drive ride with Avery" note to MacKaye more than three years before. MacKaye must have known he had little chance of getting Avery to adopt his point of view, but he elucidated the differences nonetheless.

After stating that "the purpose of the A.T. Conference, *we all agree*, is to preserve the primeval or wilderness environment," a position Avery may have refuted, MacKaye got to the meat of the matter:

> To preserve the wilderness the trail must of course be a wilderness trail (as to sounds, sights and tread). There are hundreds of non wilderness ways well connected from Maine to Georgia: to make one more is pointless. Here then is the first issue between us. You are for a connected trail—whether or not wilderness. I am for a wilderness trail—whether or not connected.[52]

MacKaye went on to point out that Avery's views on skyline roads didn't seem to be consistent. (This surely irked Avery, as his request to Cammerer to route the trail away from Skyline Drive was made to appease MacKaye and his followers.) MacKaye continued, however: "Your ideas on the trail itself seem wholly consistent and I do not agree with them: you put connected trail first while I put wilderness trail first. You have put great zest and energy into a connected trail from Maine to Georgia, and I have praised you for it, privately to you, as well as publicly. But this very zest for a means (a connected way) has dimmed apparently your vision of an end (a wilderness

51  Raymond Torrey to Benton MacKaye, 6 July 1935, Papers of the MacKaye Family, Rauner Special Collections Library, Dartmouth College.

52  Benton MacKaye to Myron Avery, 20 November 1935, Papers of the MacKaye Family, Rauner Special Collections Library, Dartmouth College.

way)." Then to drive the point home, MacKaye repeated: "Wilderness, not continuity, is the vital point."[53]

One month later, Avery responded with a six-page broadside. In it, he raised questions about MacKaye's commitment to the trail, especially when compared to Avery's. "You speak of 'such time as you can give to the A.T.' I know of no one who should have more. You have a leisurely employment, under no pressures or responsibilities," Avery wrote. Of course, Avery had no basis for making this claim other than his own perception. In fact, as noted, MacKaye spent much of his professional life trying to cobble together an existence, which caused significant stress and illness.[54]

Avery also pointed out that it was Judge Perkins, not MacKaye, who resurrected the trail project in 1927. As far as wilderness was concerned, Avery questioned whether the term even belonged in a discussion about eastern lands and dismissed the idea as a theory put forth by those who had the least to do with creating the trail.

> It is very pleasant to sit quietly at home and talk of primeval wilderness, and to think of a Trail that will make and maintain itself. But to bring such a Trail into being requires hard work, hours of labor under broiling suns and pouring rains, camping out in all kinds of weather, as well as incessant "office work" in connection with guidebooks, maps, markers, publicity, and a thousand and one other details. It is, don't you think, significant that the majority of those who are loudest in their demands and in their abuse of workers, have covered little of the Trail and have done little physical labor on it.[55]

MacKaye had never doubted Avery's commitment; MacKaye had even made a point of acknowledging it. The question was *what* Avery was committed to. But Avery simply couldn't or didn't want to believe that wilderness should be the driving force behind the trail. All he could ever see was the path

---

53  Ibid.

54  Myron Avery to Benton MacKaye, 19 December 1935, Papers of the MacKaye Family, Rauner Special Collections Library, Dartmouth College.

55  Ibid.

in front of him and the potential obstacles in the way. In his mind, MacKaye was now one of those obstacles.

Six weeks later, MacKaye sent a letter to Avery. Rather than wade into the choppy waters of the wilderness debate again, the nearly 57-year-old founder of the Appalachian Trail offered an observation.

> For sometime past I have noticed in you a growing, self-righteous, overbearing attitude and bullying manner in your expression. Your statements to me now—of assumption, distortion, and accusation—constitute a piece of insolence which confirms my former observations, as well as various reports of your conduct which have come to me from individual club members in the North and South. In your present frame of mind, therefore, I feel that further words are futile.[56]

Shortly thereafter, the two men most responsible for creating a 2,000-mile footpath from Georgia to Maine stopped talking to each other and would never speak again.

The schism between MacKaye and Avery was caused by differences in philosophy and style. MacKaye was a man of systems and ideas. Avery was a man of plans and action. MacKaye saw the trail as a place to escape the mechanized world, where the journey was at once physical and metaphysical. Placing and maintaining it in a wilderness state was a precondition. Avery simply wanted to get the trail built. His only prerequisite was that the trail should be uninterrupted, regardless of what compromises he needed to make.

Myron Avery seized control of Benton MacKaye's idea and built a fiefdom—and a legacy—around it. But if Avery took advantage, MacKaye was complicit in the outcome. MacKaye was not given a meaningful leadership position in the ATC from the outset. His many years of semi-nomadic work and long periods of relative isolation in Shirley kept him detached from the day-to-day operation of the ATC and essentially all trail-building activities. If the AT was ever going to get built, it needed a Myron Avery. One may find fault with Avery's approach and outbursts, but it's hard to find fault with the outcome.

---

56  Benton MacKaye to Myron Avery, 4 February 1936, Papers of the MacKaye Family, Rauner Special Collections Library, Dartmouth College.

For his part, Avery had spent years guiding the Appalachian Trail to completion. He was not universally liked, but he was widely respected, particularly due to what he had accomplished along the 2,000-mile path. The people in Avery's closest circle were loyal to him and vice versa. Greene, Philbrick, Schairer, Buck, and others had been integral to the AT effort and had held positions in PATC, MATC, and ATC. When the proposal to make a stand against all skyline highways came up for consideration, Avery had the backing to move forward without the support of those who felt differently—and to strengthen his base.

# CHAPTER 16

## *Carrying the Load*

Myron Avery's workload was bearing down hard on him. The philosophical battle over Skyline Drive had torn the ATC in half. His Navy work was suddenly requiring him to rush all over the country to gain depositions. In between train trips from coast to coast, he barely spent time at home. Between June and November of 1936, he took eight trips to Maine to gather trail data for the latest edition of the *Guide to Hiking the Appalachian Trail in Maine* and to place signs and blazes along the route.

In a July 2000 interview, Avery's son Hal discussed what it was like to grow up with such a driven man for a father.

> *He would work extremely long hours. There were some times when whole weeks would go by, with all of us living in the same house, and I'd never see him. He was gone in the morning before I got up and didn't come back until after I went to bed. We'd sometimes see each other on the weekends, and it was kind of like we were having a reunion. "I haven't seen you for a week," he'd say to me.*[1]

Before 1936, Myron Avery rarely mentioned his government work in AT-related correspondence, even in his letters to confidants. When he did, it was simply to establish his availability for work trips or meetings. By 1936, he started sharing his situation and needs in explicit detail. An August letter to Walter Greene explained just how burned out and exasperated Avery was and how he felt Greene could help ease the burden.

---

1   Robert A. Rubin, "The Short, Brilliant Life of Myron Avery," 24.

When he wasn't hiking or measuring, Myron Avery, center, was often taking notes, as in this photo from a trip to Maine's Baxter State Park, likely taken in 1935. Photo: Courtesy of Avery Collection, Maine State Library.

*My present situation necessitates that I write you very frankly. I am overwhelmed with work of all sorts and much as I dislike to say so, least I hurt your feelings, your methods of doing things contribute materially to my burdens. You have told me so many times that you don't intend to add to my labors—although the result is the opposite of your intentions—that I feel sure that you will, without offense, permit me to point out the details in which I must ask your help. I have been away for 7 days. I return here flooded with work. I have dictated for 7 hours—all vital letters to keep this project going—and still haven't touched the trail data.*

*I appreciate your temperament. I know that is hard for you to do things systematically and when I ask. Also you are troubled by the complex that you can't follow directions but must do as you deem fit—because of what you believe to be local conditions which I can't appreciate. The net result of inserting your own judgment and varying arrangements is to leave some unfinished link. We have a big task; it demands efficiency. You must give more thought to adhering to the details and not leave so many loose ends. You seem to have the thought—well toss it back to me to straighten out—like the finances. How many times have I explained that to you. There is no reason for your mixing that up.*

*Now here is one thing I can't and won't waste more time on. Your letters of July 25 and 30th took an hour out of my time. Why must you select me to impose your scribbling on? You say you write other letters; if they are like what you send me those letters aren't read—and can't be. If they aren't, why do I have to suffer. You are always in a hurry, it seems, hence the scrawl to me. Now if you must hurry, why not omit some of the irrelevant detail such as what you ate or what you slept on and give me something legible. Why not try a pen or sharpen those stubs and only write on one side of the paper. Your postage is being reimbursed but what I want to say is to stop making me the victim of your haste. I am going to quit struggling with those letters.*[2]

Avery spent the next two pages crafting a thirteen-point to-do list for Greene—tasks that needed to be done and instructions on how to achieve all of them most efficiently.

*Now Walter, I hope you will see that I have a tremendous amount to handle and while I don't want you to feel I am criticizing you, you must see that you[r] [sic] way of doing things adds to my burdens and I am crying for help. Don't go writing me any long letter of explanations. Let's just try and think of these details and you do less master-minding.*

---

2    Myron Avery to Walter Greene, 1 August 1936, Avery Collection, Maine State Library Special Collections.

*We have got a big job and we have to handle it on a business-like basis. When you take a job you must see it thru to every detail.*

*There is a strong chance that after I come back from Jacksonville that I will go to the West Coast. So you can see the more why we must change our ways a bit. It is the cost of dealing with a genius and temperament—yourself old fellow.*[3]

In 1935, the AMC member Thelma Bonney Hall encountered Avery (center, with his wheel) and his Potomac Appalachian Trail Club group on Katahdin, where she snapped this picture. "It seems that Myron, tho' a young man, is something of a crank in one way and another," she wrote. "One of his particular hobbys [*sic*] is the length of trails. Everywhere he goes he takes a bicycle wheel for measuring trails. And if a trail is, according to his measure, .01 of a mile longer than the guide book gives it, he lets no grass grow under his feet before he writes to the club and tells them about it. Of course, that doesn't go down very well. Altho', to give the devil his due, he has done some really good work in connection with the Appalachian Trail, still when it turned out that Ronald Gower was the first to take a party through the Maine section after its completion, Mr. Avery was very much put out." Photo: Thelma Bonney Hall, courtesy of AMC Library & Archives.

---

3   Ibid.

If Avery hoped the letter would help Greene suddenly understand the cumulative toll of the latter's disorganized work style and rambling missives, Avery would soon be disappointed. Greene's return letter to Avery included an accounting of some relocations he had made on the Maine AT and a plea for money—both subjects known to infuriate the recipient.

"We have talked so much of the financial situation that it is hardly necessary to write about it," replied an exasperated Avery in a letter just before he departed for the West Coast. He explained that the money for trail work in Maine had run out and that "even if there were worthy projects on hand, they would simply have to go by the board because of the lack of funds.... This is the situation and there is no use fussing or writing me elaborate letters about it." Avery also explained that every relocation of trail caused additional effort and expense, requiring Avery to visit the sections and gather new trail data, which in turn affected his ability to get the trail guide published on time.

Avery signed off by again imploring Greene to see the world through Myron Avery's eyes, to stop being a martyr, and to buck up in the name of the AT.

> *If you have a feeling you are degenerating into a sign-painter, you can perhaps imagine that I am getting a little weary of this endless taking of notes and checking of Guidebook data and maps and all of the clerical details, and the myriad inquiries, complaints and discontent of people we have to deal with. Both of us will have to suffer in silence. Let's not add to each other's load by continually writing and talking about conditions that are well understood and cannot be remedied.*[4]

Not long after he sent his letter, Avery heard back from Walter Greene. This time the news carried far more importance than discussions about sign painting, trail relocations, or finances: Greene was fighting for his life.

---

4    Myron Avery to Walter Greene, 16 September 1936, Avery Collection, Maine State Library Special Collections.

# CHAPTER 17

## Enter the CCC

Maine's Baxter State Park was established in 1933 by the Maine legislature upon accepting the gift of the mountain and surrounding area from former Governor Percival P. Baxter. One year later, a national park conservation camp was established in the park, "for the purpose of improving the Sourdnahunk–Millinocket road and establishing recreational facilities on the southwestern side of Mount Katahdin."[1] A Civilian Conservation Corps (CCC) team arrived on June 1 and spent the next two weeks battling a forest fire that burned "thousands of acres of forest lying south of Katahdin."[2]

Over the next three years, CCC would build or improve portions of the AT in Maine. In 1934 alone, CCC relocated 1 mile of Hunt Trail, which doubled as the AT from Katahdin Stream Campground to Baxter Peak, the northern terminus of the trail; blazed the AT and side trails with white and blue paint, respectively; and built shelters.[3]

"In 1935, CCC established a number of work camps in Maine. Many of these would provide manpower to improve the AT and to build shelters, something Myron Avery had pushed mightily to make happen. In March, James W. "Jim" Sewall, an assistant forester with the Maine Forest Service and the coordinator of the CCC work in Maine, wrote to Avery with a problem. Because the AT in Maine traveled over so much private property, CCC's authority to build trails on these lands without holding formal easements was in question. In ten days, Avery reported back to Sewall that, with the help

---

1   Percival P. Baxter to ATC, 23 January 1934, Avery Collection, Maine State Library Special Collections.

2   *National Park Service Recreational Development Report*, 1934.

3   Ibid.

of Major Welch (general manager of the Palisades Interstate Park Commission), CCC director Robert Fechner, and Forest Service director Ferdinand Silcox, CCC had reached an agreement with the landowners and could proceed. In typical Avery fashion, he provided a list of six projects he felt CCC should tackle first.[4]

Under Sewall's leadership, CCC accomplished an incredible amount of Maine AT work in 1935. He dispatched work crews to the Bigelow Range and the Kingfield–Stratton area near Sugarloaf Mountain to help Game Warden Helon Taylor build uncompleted sections of trail. Sewall also reported to Avery, "The Army would be allowed to let us have 15-man parties for the trail work from each of the base camps concerned."[5]

Procuring the materials and labor to build the bridge, seen here, over Nesowadnehunk Falls in Maine was one of Myron Avery's pet projects. The bridge was built 1935–1936; this photo was likely taken shortly thereafter. Photo: Courtesy of Avery Collection, Maine State Library.

---

4   Myron Avery to James Sewall, 10 April 1935, Avery Collection, Maine State Library Special Collections.

5   James Sewall to Myron Avery, 20 May 1935, Avery Collection, Maine State Library Special Collections.

In June 1935, Helon Taylor reported that CCC crews were working everywhere.

> *There are 12 CCC boys working between the old G.N. lumber camp and Horns Pond . . . they have done excellent work up there. . . . They do about one half mile a day. There are also 14 men camping at the old Poulin camps. I talked with Mr. Ray Viles (forrester [sic] at the Rangeley CCC camp) last Monday. He said he has 10 or 12 men working on Saddleback now. . . . I feel that we are getting ahead fast this year.*[6]

In September, Taylor wrote to Avery with an unexpected trail-usage pattern. "I find that the bear are using the trail quite a lot around Cranberry Peak Pond and the lumbered over sections on each side," he reported. "I found where the cubs had climbed many of the small spruce and fir that I had painted spots on and had chewed the spots or the tree above and below. I think they like our shade of blue."

With Sewall still in charge, the CCC continued to cut new sections of Maine trail and improve existing ones in the spring and fall of 1936. But by September, Avery learned a change was imminent. He wrote to Walter Greene:

> *Our situation with respect to the CCC the next year is not so good. Confidentially, Sewall says that if business conditions improve much more in his line, that he will sever his connection. This will be a real loss. He feels that Dort, the Regional Inspector of the Forest Service at Laconia, is not as interested in the Trail project as his predecessors and that the Forest Commissioner is reflecting his attitude. It may be necessary for us to use considerable exertion here in Washington next year to prevent any lapse in the support, if the political situation remains unchanged. In telling you about this, I want you to keep it confidential and not write any letters or take any action premised on your knowledge of the situation.*[7]

---

6   Helon Taylor to Myron Avery, 7 June 1935, Avery Collection, Maine State Library Special Collections.

7   Myron Avery to Walter Greene, 16 September 1936, Avery Collection, Maine State Library Special Collections.

In March 1937, Avery received the dreaded letter from Sewall, confirming, "Our business has increased very considerably and I feel I can no longer stay in the C.C.C. employ as there is but little pay in it and of course no prospects."[8]

Avery was hit hard by the loss of such an able leader and contributor.

> *I have been pessimistically anticipating your letter of March 5th, so I was somewhat prepared for the shock. . . . I am, of course, glad that your private work has gotten to the point where it fully occupies you, but I must say that I cannot see very much more than our own loss. . . . One of the fine things of this Appalachian Trail work—as with many other contacts—are the people that we come to know and in this case it has been an acquaintance that I greatly value, with a man of whom I have known as long as I knew anything about the Maine woods but never expected that our paths would cross in the manner which they have.*[9]

Before they left Maine in 1937, CCC crews from Millinocket, Greenville, Flagstaff, and Rangeley built a new 27-mile section of trail between Saddleback Mountain and the Andover–South Arm Road in the western part of the state, substantially improved the trail in other places, and reblazed it (with titanium paint!) wherever needed. The crews also built fourteen new lean-tos along the length of the Maine trail. On August 14, 1937, a CCC crew completed the final 2 miles of trail in Maine: a section on the north slope of Spaulding Mountain. What they likely didn't know at the time was they had just closed the last remaining gap in the Appalachian Trail, which was now a continuous path from Mount Oglethorpe, in Georgia, to Katahdin, in Maine.

---

8    James Sewall to Myron Avery, 5 March 1937, Avery Collection, Maine State Library Special Collections.

9    Myron Avery to James Sewall, 12 March 1937, Avery Collection, Maine State Library Special Collections.

# CHAPTER 18

## New Voices for the Wilderness

After the June 1934 Appalachian Trail Conference (ATC) in Vermont, where Benton MacKaye's unequivocal proposal to oppose skyline roads in favor of "flankline" roads was withdrawn from consideration, feelings were still raw on both sides.

Those who believed, as MacKaye did, that "the Appalachian Trail is wilderness trail or it is nothing" felt especially betrayed. The contention by NPS's Arno Cammerer that a 200- to 1,000-foot strip of land on either side of a road constituted wilderness only added to their angst and fear for the future. Despite their many attempts to educate Myron Avery, MacKaye and his fellow wilderness advocates had failed to convince Avery that a trail that shared its footprint with a road did not, and could not, offer the primeval experience that had inspired the idea for the Appalachian Trail.

No one was aware of the failure to enlighten Avery more than the Potomac Appalachian Trail Club (PATC) member Harold Anderson. He had driven a newly opened section of Skyline Drive, in Virginia's Shenandoah National Park, with Avery and had seen the road's effect on the landscape. Recognizing the inevitable fate of the AT in Shenandoah National Park and frustrated with Avery's willingness to simply move the trail to accommodate the road, Anderson wrote a letter to his friend Guy Frizzell, the president of the Smoky Mountains Hiking Club.

Anderson proposed organizing a handful of "four or five persons of some prominence in hiking circles" to defeat the Blue Ridge Parkway, currently proposed for North Carolina and Virginia. If that failed, the group could lobby to move the AT away from the Blue Ridge and onto the Allegheny Range. Ultimately, Anderson hoped the new group could form a "real federation of hiking clubs which is so sadly needed"—as opposed to Avery's perceived dictatorship.

Anderson sent a copy of his letter to MacKaye, who immediately suggested sharing the idea with the wilderness advocate Bob Marshall, whom he and Harvey Broome, a conservationist who played a key role in the establishment of Great Smoky Mountains National Park, would be meeting in Knoxville, Tennessee. On August 12, 1934, MacKaye and Broome shared Anderson's idea to fight skyline road development with Marshall. Marshall liked the idea but had a more ambitious goal in mind. As Broome related the story to Anderson, Marshall's idea was "to take up other projects than the preservation of the Trail" and to advocate for "the protection and preservation of the wilderness wherever it might occur."[1]

Nine weeks later, Benton MacKaye, Bob Marshall, Harvey Broome, and Bernard Frank (a highly regarded forester and conservationist) attended the American Forestry Association conference in Knoxville. The conference included a field trip to inspect a CCC camp outside of Knoxville. During the drive to the camp, Frank pulled the car to a stop, and the four men gathered outside. There, next to an otherwise nondescript stretch of road near Coal Creek, Tennessee, the four discussed, amended, and adopted the founding principles of their new organization. (MacKaye had drafted them in advance and produced them for discussion.) The men also agreed on a name for their new venture: The Wilderness Society.

MacKaye and Harold Anderson—as well as Raymond Torrey, Frank Pace, and others who had been friends and advocates of the AT from the beginning—left ATC. But the very thing that caused their philosophical split, a steadfast dedication to wilderness and its preservation, sprouted an organization to ensure its protection.

---

1    Larry Anderson, *Benton MacKaye*, 273.

# CHAPTER 19

### *A Pioneer Lost*

IN JANUARY 1937, MYRON AVERY TYPED A LETTER TO A COHORT IN Greenville Junction, Maine, to ask about the likelihood of the CCC camps continuing their work in Maine that year. Avery signed off with a status report of his own regarding Walter Greene. "Probably you have not heard that Walter Greene has been very ill. He has been in the hospital for over a month with an intestinal trouble and is in very much run down condition."[1]

This letter is the first known correspondence from Avery that mentions Greene's health. Avery had expressed concern about Greene's mental state on a few occasions—notably, when Greene was recuperating from his 1933 work trips and fretting about his financial situation. Avery previously had mentioned Greene's physical health only in deference to his trail-blazing prowess.

During Greene's prolonged illness, Avery tried to keep his friend, who was still the president of the Maine Appalachian Trail Club (MATC), up-to-date and engaged in trail activities by sending long letters and assigning him minor tasks, such as incorporating the club in Maine. In April 1938, Greene sent a letter to the directors of MATC explaining, "Mr. Avery suggested that in order to put the Maine Appalachian Trail Club on a more definite basis, it would be well to incorporate." Greene enclosed the paperwork and requested that, upon signing and filing the documents with the state, the club hold a meeting in his absence to make the organization's incorporation official. Walter Greene must have been extremely ill; he did not make his annual pilgrimage to the Sebec Lake camp he so loved.

---

1    Myron Avery to Hugh S. MacNeil, 26 January 1937, Avery Collection, Maine State Library Special Collections.

In February 1938, Avery received a letter from Alice Alden of Montclair, New Jersey. Alden had taken a guided hike through parts of Maine on the AT and believed Avery should be apprised of some inaccuracies she found in his booklet about the Maine AT titled, *The Silver Aisle.*

Avery's response was largely critical of Alden.* "The publication was an effort to attract attention to the trail. We might hope that each user will recognize and aid this process rather than only express criticism. The latter is easy," he wrote, adding, "You were indeed fortunate that you were in a position to employ a Guide for a trip through the Maine woods. Few hikers can do so."[2]

He then brought attention and credit to Walter Greene.

> *I am sure that such a veteran of Maine woods travel such as yourself can adequately appreciate the effort and expense of Greene's exploring trips and the terrific labor of packing supplies onto the Chairback–Barren Range and cutting that trail there—a month's labor. I wonder if you know of a similar performance—I don't. Greene is a very sick man today. I would not want to get abroad—thru any factual inaccuracy of my own—any derogatory comment on what he struggled to do with an intensity I have never seen equaled. So let's not worry about giving him over-much credit.*[3]

Myron Avery never gave his approval lightly. Yet, Avery—a man who poured so much energy into questioning the judgment of others, defending his own decision-making, and promoting his role in creating the trail—consistently cited Walter Greene's considerable contributions, helping ensure Greene would get his due.

---

* Alice Alden replied to Avery on March 23, 1938. She assured Avery that he had misinterpreted the intent of her letter, that she had already been on sections of the Maine AT three times, and that she was appreciative of the trail and the effort it took to build it. She also told him that the reason their party hired a guide was that Avery had previously written to her that "it would be very dangerous for us to attempt to go by ourselves, as we had planned, since the trail was not yet marked," a fact that Avery apparently forgot.

2 Myron Avery to Alice Alden, 10 March 1938, Avery Collection, Maine State Library Special Collections.

3 Ibid.

Perhaps Greene's illness made Avery even more willing to share praise, if not less critical. In March 1937, he had told Jim Sewall, who was stepping down as Maine Forestry commissioner: "We are going to miss you tremendously. You know how much you have meant to the Trail project in Maine. Without you, there would not have been any Trail at all. Even after the project was approved, it took all your energy and initiative to get over all the hurdles and keep it going. The horizon looks very dark to me now."[4]

In the same letter to Sewall, Avery held out hope that Greene's health would improve: "Greene is gaining strength slowly and I am hoping that he will be in Maine this summer again. It will be, however, a matter of time before he regains his old energy."[5]

But it wasn't to be.

For the next four years, Greene would reside at Edgewater Rest, a convalescent home in Long Island, New York, while his health continued to decline. Avery and Greene corresponded frequently during the first two years, and Greene wrote a robust annual report for MATC in April 1937 and two letters to The Wilderness Society, in November 1937 and January 1938, voicing the opinion that the organization was impugning the reputation of MATC.

For most of 1938, Avery and Greene didn't communicate. After Greene wrote a mid-November letter, Avery responded in kind, explaining that the reason for not sending trail updates and other news was "due to the information that these things taxed your strength and that you were better off without thinking about these problems because you were bound to devote thought to trying to straighten them out and that was bad for you."[6]

Avery assured Greene that, because the latter had requested updates, "I have sent you everything dealing with Maine and I shall continue to do so."[7] Unlike many of his past missives to Greene that were long on procedure and short on personal news, this letter revealed a different side. First was the admission to Greene that Avery had been hospitalized himself.

---

4   Myron Avery to Jim Sewall, 12 March 1937, Avery Collection, Maine State Library Special Collections.

5   Ibid.

6   Myron Avery to Walter Greene, 29 November 1938, Avery Collection, Maine State Library Special Collections.

7   Ibid.

*Your letter . . . reached me in the hospital. It was mighty good to hear from you. . . . As you will note, you have no monopoly on hospitals and I spent the last two weeks fighting off a threatened attack of pneumonia.*

*Things are badly piled up. I hope you will write to me often. All of your friends down here are more pleased than you will ever know when I tell them that you are coming along in good shape and that that tough old Greene fellow who goes through the woods with his head down will be out on the Trail soon. In fact, we are hoping very much that your condition will permit your attendance at the Trail Conference.*

Avery finished his letter to Greene uncharacteristically, by including some local gossip. Avery informed Greene: "You will be tickled to have me admit to you that you were right when it comes to judging 'stage people.'" As Greene had predicted, a local Mainer's wife turned out to be an English actress, divorced the local to marry another, divorced the second husband, and was returning to her first. "This piece of local gossip will amuse you greatly," Avery wrote.

Avery then shared how one sporting camp along the trail was in desperate circumstances ("No guests, the horses have died . . . the boat was wrecked . . . and it is a problem for them to hang onto the Trail travelers that are a good part of their patronage") and that another camp owner's wife "is in the insane asylum and he has gone all to pieces (alcohol)."[8]

For someone who rarely engaged in small talk, Avery must have felt like he was entering strange territory. He was willing to do so for his friend, who was relying on Avery to retain a connection with Maine that extended beyond the trail community.

In April 1939, Avery sent a letter to the rest home: "I had heard from Mr. Greene quite frequently up until the last four months. Under the circumstances, I am writing to ask if you would be good enough to let me know his present condition." Avery included an addressed, stamped envelope to hasten the reply.[9]

---

8   Ibid.

9   Myron Avery to Edgewater Rest, 20 April 1939, Avery Collection, Maine State Library Special Collections.

The rest home didn't immediately respond, but Walter Greene did.

"It was mighty good to hear from you again," wrote Avery, who also reported on his own medical issues. "I find that the siege of pneumonia took a good deal out of me and when I was in Maine in March, I went into the hospital at Bath to prevent a heavy cold from getting the best of me again."[10]

The endless hours of professional and trail-related work were exacting a toll on Myron Avery, who was then just 40 years old.

In early May, Avery wrote a letter to Lotta McGruder, who worked at Edgewater Rest, the facility where Greene was residing in Long Island. The news Avery received in two letters back from McGruder was not promising.

"I am extremely disturbed over the substance of your two letters," he wrote in response to her. "As you know, I have not heard from Walter for some time but I have suspected the situation, despite all the encouragement he tried to put into his communications." He then told McGruder that "I may have been entirely wrong" in sending Greene small tasks to perform on behalf of MATC and that Avery's intent in doing so was to "make [Greene] feel like he was still doing things and have less of the feeling of uselessness and hopelessness and for us to act as if he was pretty much the same as always."[11]

McGruder wrote back to Avery in early July, which brought Avery some measure of relief, although the news from New York was still dire. Avery reiterated to the caregiver that Greene had made repeated requests—including recent ones—for Avery to forward all literature and correspondence related to the trail in Maine. Avery was at a loss as to what would actually afford Greene the greatest comfort.

> *Since your last letter to me, I have known nothing of his condition. Frequently so much time has gone by without any word from him that I had begun to suspect that he might have died. It has been very difficult, under the circumstances, to know what to write or how to approach the matter.*[12]

---

10 Myron Avery to Walter Greene, 26 April 1938, Avery Collection, Maine State Library Special Collections.

11 Myron Avery to Lotta McGruder, 4 May 1938, Avery Collection, Maine State Library Special Collections.

12 Myron Avery to Lotta McGruder, 2 July 1938, Maine State Library Special Collections.

Avery mentioned he had spoken on the phone with Greene whenever he was in New York, but it was quite obvious that "[Greene] did not want me to come see him in his present condition." Avery also told McGruder, "It would be a very distinct personal favor if I know I can count on you to keep me advised of his condition."[13]

Whatever aspects of Myron Avery we saw pouring off the page in other letters—righteousness, criticism, and cynicism among them—these letters decidedly expose different traits. Here was someone who was concerned, empathetic, and willing to admit mistakes and to express feelings for the man who, at times, had frustrated him but above all had worked so diligently on behalf of Avery and the AT.

One week later, Greene had colon surgery. McGruder wrote to Avery again. The only letter from her that Avery retained was handwritten and heartfelt.

> *Walter is in a very bad condition in spite of the operation, but due to his strong constitution and heart, he lingers on. His mind is clear and he still hopes for recovery and apparently does not suspect the nature of his illness, which is remarkable to me. He hasn't cared to have any visitors, as he is always afraid they might come when he was in great pain and could not see them if they came all the way out here.*
>
> *I am glad you have sent him the literature as it diverts his mind and he still has a deep interest in anything pertaining to the Appalachian Trail. Just to hear from you occasionally and have the comfort and assurance that he is not forgotten by the friends he values is all he asks. It has been like a nightmare and seems as though it will go on forever and ever. I will gladly let you know from time to time how he is getting along—but of course it can only be a question of time and endurance.*[14]

As it turned out, endurance and time were on Greene's side. In September 1938, he sent Avery a one-page update, which prompted the following effusive response.

---

13  Myron Avery to Lotta McGruder, 2 July 1938, Avery Collection, Maine State Library Special Collections.

14  Lotta McGruder to Myron Avery, 22 July 1938, Avery Collection, Maine State Library Special Collections.

*Your good old familiar handwriting was the most welcome thing that I have seen for many a day. I just sat there and stared at the envelope. The same old illegible writing and the gray paper and everything else, but you don't know how good it made me feel—just like old times. . . . I have been more worried about you than you will ever know.*[15]

More than one year later, in November 1939, Greene wrote a two-page letter to Avery, telling the latter how great it was to hear his voice over the phone and, "We must manage to have you come over when you are in town again." Greene said that although he needed "to lie down a good deal," he felt stronger and had gained weight.

Myron Avery, third from left, and crew take in the view from Monument Cliff in Maine's Barren–Chairback Range. A monument plaque honoring Walter Greene is located near this spot. This photo was likely taken on the Potomac Appalachian Trail Club trip in 1935. Photo: Courtesy of Avery Collection, Maine State Library.

15  Myron Avery to Walter Greene, 4 October 1938, Avery Collection, Maine State Library Special Collections.

Walter Greene died in Long Neck, New York, on February 20, 1941—more than two-and-a-half years after Lotta McGruder reported, "It can only be a question of time and endurance." Greene was 69. That he single-handedly blazed 15 miles of virgin trail over Maine's Barren–Chairback range at age 61 was only one of his noteworthy achievements. He also had single-handedly blazed new trails into the Gulf Hagas area and scouted the route of untold miles of the AT through Maine on foot and by canoe. He had won the respect of actors and theatre critics on the world's greatest stages. Perhaps most remarkable, he had won the respect and love of the toughest critic of them all: Myron Avery.

## A Fitting Tribute

Monument Cliff on Third Mountain is a 2,083-foot peak in Maine's Barren–Chairback Range. The mountain may not be high, but the views from the granite slab are breathtaking. In 1933, a trailblazer armed only with hand tools; an unequaled appreciation for the woods, lakes, and mountains of Maine; and an artist's gift for sculpting trail popped out of the spruce trees to take in the scene. It is fitting that he is immortalized here, an unforgettable stop along the trail he built himself. Here, members of MATC installed a brass plaque on the granite slab of the summit in honor of their first president, Walter Greene.

# CHAPTER 20

## *No Room for Compromise*

By 1940, Myron Avery had been involved with the Appalachian Trail (AT) for more than twelve years. He had spearheaded the charge to get the trail built from end-to-end and had succeeded. He had also walked every mile of the trail, obtained funding, started or helped start at least four organizations supporting the trail, written several guidebooks, and been the force behind publicizing and maintaining the path. But those achievements came at a heavy cost. His incessant drive and need to be right had alienated many leaders, including the Appalachian Mountain Club and Benton MacKaye, the man who proposed the AT to begin with. Now Avery would wage a verbal battle with a new foe: the Washington Planograph Company.

Avery had discovered that the new technology known as "planographic printing" (later known by the more familiar term "offset printing") saved hundreds of dollars over the letterpress printing method commonly used until the 1930s. Avery had a history with the Washington Planograph Company, a firm that specialized in the new process. It had printed guidebooks for the Appalachian Trail Conference (ATC), Potomac Appalachian Trail Club (PATC), and Maine Appalachian Trail Club (MATC), beginning with *The Guide to the Appalachian Trail in New England*.

In May 1940, Avery asked representatives of the Washington Planograph Company how much it would cost to make corrections to a few maps whose negatives the company had on file. Upon receiving a quote he thought was unreasonably high, Avery asked the company to refer to their contract.

*I suggest you review the correspondence which constitutes the arrangement for printing the Maine Guidebook and the maps. . . . I should like to know if you will forward the negatives (not the glass)*

*to me at New York so that we may have the corrections made, as the
costs quoted by you are entirely beyond what we are able to spend in
the matter.*[1]

The response from the company's secretary-treasurer indicated Myron
Avery had previously communicated about the issue. "Dear Mr. Avery," the
representative began, before launching into arguably one of the most memo-
rable first paragraphs in business correspondence history.

*After you heaped all the insults that you could find in your vocabu-
lary on this institution, every one of them based on fiction, or some
brainstorm, you now ask that we send you our negatives.*[2]

The bulk of the letter explained that prior communications from Avery
and the ATC's secretary, Marion Park, requested the company hold the
negatives for safe keeping. Before signing off, the company representative
included another critique of Avery's behavior.

*This will serve notice that these negatives will not be held for longer
than 30 days from this date, unless some arrangement is made to have
them held for a longer period, by conference or correspondence with a
background of reasonableness and without insults.*
*There is no objection to you disagreeing with our service or prices,
but there is objection to being insulted about it.*[3]

Avery then launched into a war of words that made his past feud with
Robert Underhill, the former editor of *Appalachia*, seem tame. In a three-
page response, Avery lashed out at the company, starting with a critique of
the secretary-treasurer, Paul Heideke.

*Apparently your correspondence suffers from the same defects as
your telephone conversations. . . . Perhaps you are the owner of the*

---

1    Myron Avery to Washington Planograph Company, 9 May 1940, Avery Collection, Maine
     State Library Special Collections.

2    Washington Planograph Company to Myron Avery, 13 May 1940, Avery Collection, Maine
     State Library Special Collections.

3    Ibid.

*Washington Planograph Company, so that loss of business is no concern to other than yourself, but the other planograph companies in Washington are to be congratulated on having you attempt to do business with customers. It should make good business for other companies if your conversation with me is a fair sample of your business methods.*[4]

Avery was just getting warmed up. Even though he had originally asked to have the negatives of the AT maps in question sent to him, now he told the company it was obligated to hold the original negatives for safe keeping while allowing future use by the Appalachian Trail Conference under the terms of its contract. If the company released the slides back to ATC within 30 days, as proposed in the preceding letter, the company would be held in breach of contract, and ATC would subsequently withhold a portion of the $186 it owed to the Washington Planograph Company.

Avery then threatened to withhold future business from the company, saying:

*We shall be interested to know of any propositions you care to make for adjusting these matters. If you intend to be stubborn and see how much trouble you can make for us, we can, I think, meet the situation.*[5]

Three days later, Heideke wrote back to make his company's position clear. After standing up for the conduct of his employees, Heideke turned to the threat of losing ATC's business.

*I believe that it is a matter of record that you have had some difficulties before with printers and lithographers, however, that is your business, and not mine.*

*No definite inquiry has been given us for reprints, the negatives are here to serve you on a definite order, although no promise was given to you to hold them forever. Maybe the whole printing industry is all wet, in having trade practices, especially where a Mr. Avery is concerned.*

---

4    Ibid.

5    Myron Avery to Washington Planograph Company, 17 May 1940, Avery Collection, Maine State Library Special Collections.

*The Appalachian Trail and its subsidiary requirements is work we were ready to do and we are still ready to do it, provided it is profitable, and that we are not obliged to put up with threats and abuses.*

*If it is not profitable to us, we do not want it, and if we must be abused for wanting a profit, we do not want it. For your information the work up to the present writing has not been so profitable that it would cause me more than a bucket of tears to lose it.*

*I do not intend to quarrel with you any further, and what you are threatening to do or not do is your business, we will turn that corner when we get to it.*

*If our prices and <u>terms</u>, as well as myself are so objectionable to you, then the only thing to do is try someone else, there are plenty of them.*

*It has been a pleasure to deal with your associates, such as Mr. Walker and Miss Stephenson, and others, and it is indeed regrettable that you should have taken a viewpoint that you are always right, cannot be wrong, and that you have the right to heap abuse on those that venture to differ with you.*

*In so far as I can learn, it is not an unforgivable sin to be in error, and if I had the slightest knowledge of being in error, I would gladly admit it.*[6]

Avery responded by suggesting that the Washington Planograph Company got themselves into this mess and that they were responsible for presenting a solution. That said, Avery presented one of his own: "Since future business transactions are apparently not desired by either party and you will have no future use for the negatives, I suggest we pay the balance at this time and you release into our custody the negatives."[7]

Two days later, the saga continued. The Washington Planograph Company sent Avery a response, reiterating that, consistent with industry practices, "the negatives are our property," and signed off with the following:

---

6  Washington Planograph Company to Myron Avery, 20 May 1940, Avery Collection, Maine State Library Special Collections.

7  Myron Avery to Washington Planograph Company, 23 May 1940, Avery Collection, Maine State Library Special Collections.

*You have all the information, and you may have more if required, but there is no disposition on our part to continue correspondence for the only reason that you may display your rancor and hate. This is a democracy not a totalitarian state, and therefore you have a perfect right to disagree with me.*[8]

Avery responded by raising the breach of contract issue again. He felt that, because the Washington Planograph Company "threatened to destroy the negatives for the Maine Guide within a month," the whole dustup was entirely due to the company's conduct. Avery drafted a check to Washington Planograph Company for $146.32, deducting $40 from the money owed, which he guessed was the cost of the negatives.[9]

Taking the high road, Heideke sent a letter of acknowledgement to Avery, thanking him for the payment. He took issue with Avery's assertion that the company was difficult to deal with, saying, "You refer to problems all along, which I am afraid are not existent, but are the result of anger." He concluded by promising Avery that he would not find a better or fairer company to deal with anywhere.[10]

But Myron Avery always needed to have the last word. Eight days later, he sent a letter to Heideke. Avery told Heideke that unless he or someone from his company returned the negatives to eliminate the breach of contract status, the company would not get any more work from the ATC nor affiliate clubs. Further, if the company did return the negatives, any future work would be rewarded on the basis of a successful bid.

It is the last correspondence related to the event.

The interaction between Avery and Heideke is instructive. Heideke's letters included the most pointed criticisms of character Myron Avery would ever receive in writing. Yet instead of considering whether the criticisms were warranted, Avery hurled an ever-escalating barrage of insults and threats.

---

8   Washington Planograph Company to Myron Avery, 25 May 1940, Avery Collection, Maine State Library Special Collections.

9   Myron Avery to Washington Planograph Company, 28 May 1940, Avery Collection, Maine State Library Special Collections.

10  Washington Planograph Company to Myron Avery, 31 May 1940, Avery Collection, Maine State Library Special Collections.

Once again, Avery chose to ignore input, as he had consistently done in the past. Shailer Philbrick had warned that Avery's overworking could prevent him from living long enough to get the credit he deserved. Virginia Gates from *Sun-Up* magazine, Robert Underhill of *Appalachia*, and Arthur Comey of the AMC Guidebook Committee had all urged Avery to adapt his writing style to ensure publication. Following their advice likely would have brought Avery earlier notoriety and perhaps created opportunities to take part in collaborative efforts. Even the decline of Walter Greene and Avery's own health issues (pneumonia, heart problems, and fatigue among them) presented opportunities to reconsider his approach and his relationships. And now, a business associate had stated directly to Avery that the 'viewpoint that you are always right, cannot be wrong, and that you have the right to heap abuse on those that venture to differ with you' had damaged Avery's reputation in the printing industry and far beyond.

## Vials of Wrath

By now, Myron Avery's position within the AT community was secure. He would be forever hailed as the man who turned a vision into a reality. The path that stretched more than 2,000 miles would forever be a testament to that feat. But Avery's means of completing the AT had left a different mark. Those who had felt Avery's wrath were still wary of his approach. And he was on the verge of losing yet another ally.

In October 1940, Jean Stephenson, the editor of ATC's newsletter, *Appalachian Trailway News,* sent a letter to AMC's president, William P. Fowler, on behalf of Myron Avery. The stated reason for the letter was to allow Fowler to review Avery's proposed response to an AT hiker from New York who had posed a few questions regarding AMC's methods of marking the trail. Principal among these was AMC's decision not to include mileage on trail signs along the portions of the AT that AMC was responsible for maintaining.

Stephenson wrote: "I thought it might be advisable to forward you a copy of this article previous to its appearance in the January 1941 issue of *Appalachian Trailway News* in the event there was some further comment or point you would think might be desirable to be made in this connection. We want to avoid any statement to which exception could be taken in the way of its accuracy."[11]

The letter initiated a great bit of activity, both between AMC's Fowler and Myron Avery and behind the scenes at AMC. Fowler immediately responded to Stephenson with a letter that, among other things, refuted the proposed *Appalachian Trailway News* article's insinuation that AMC omitted mileages from trail signs so that hikers would have to buy their guidebooks and maps—a rumor Avery seemed pleased to propagate. Fowler also requested that Stephenson send him a revised copy of the article so he could review the text and respond before it went into publication.

Myron Avery stepped into the fray by launching a two-and-a-half-page, single-spaced barrage that evoked his past sparring matches with AMC. After pointing out how magnanimous ATC was to offer AMC the chance to review and respond to a proposed article, to "avoid any inadvertent misstatement of fact or impression ... (incidentally a courtesy never extended by *Appalachia* to us)," Avery questioned Fowler's motives and tone.

> *I am sure that when you look at your reply again, you will hardly label it a reciprocation of the Editor's gesture.... If the letter of October 21st warranted taking someone to task, as your letter proceeded to do, then I suggest that it is I who should be on the receiving end, not the Editor. But even so, I am very much at a loss to understand how a gesture of this sort could warrant such an acrid reply. I am hard put to reconcile, for Miss Stephenson, my presentation of the polished, urbane, diplomatic Dartmouth, Boston A.M.C. President with that communication. Ants in one's outer garments or being summarily dismissed by the Court a short time before could perhaps set the stage.*[12]

In his response, Fowler called on Avery to cease insinuations that AMC left mileages off signs to sell guidebooks but declined to enumerate the reasons why, at least for the time being. Avery chose to keep stirring the pot instead.

---

11  Jean Stephenson to William P. Fowler, 21 October 1940, Avery Collection, Maine State Library Special Collections.

12  Myron Avery to William Fowler, 28 October 1940, Avery Collection, Maine State Library Special Collections.

*You refer to insinuations. What are these, may I ask? What is there amiss in the suggestions of a good Yankee practice to build up a Guidebook market? Just what is wrong with advertising or a practice which impresses on the traveler the need for a Guidebook? If this is the theory, how is it reprehensible? Is it not most desirable, for the safety and pleasure of the traveler that he have a Guide and maps? . . . This is the first time that I have ever heard the suggestion that it is off-color for a trail-maintaining organization to attempt to stimulate the sale and use of its publications.*[13]

Avery continued, making a point-by-point list of perceived past indiscretions by AMC editors and publications.

"We are indebted to *Appalachia* for numerous destructive and trouble-making notes," he wrote, before listing the many ways he felt ATC had been wronged. But even though "my protest against the malicious articles on the reviews of the Conference's publications resulted in the omission of my name from the editorial board when I was serving by supplying Appalachian Trail notes" and "an opportunity to reply was refused me," Avery claimed he was not upset, concluding, "This history makes all the more plain our desire not to retaliate in kind."[14]

Before holstering his verbal six-shooters, Avery pointed out that Stephenson was "a member of the bar" and "a member of the Appalachian Mountain Club and thoroughly cognizant of its repute in New England and elsewhere." He continued: "I doubt very much she will be disposed to accede to the direction of your letter to submit to you a revised paragraph. After all, of course unintended, your direction comes close to censorship and is a little out of order when one considers what other organizations have received from *Appalachia* notes."[15]

Finally, Avery reiterated his hope that, upon further reflection, Fowler would see ATC's intent was "to deal with a matter of general interest"— that is, why AMC chose not to include trail mileages on its signs—and "our

---

13  Myron Avery to William Fowler, letter, 28 October 1940, Avery Collection, Maine State Library Special Collections.

14  Ibid.

15  Ibid.

concern, out of courtesy to the Appalachian Mountain Club is to avoid statements which could be questioned after publication."[16]

Reactions to Avery's letter were varied. Howard M. Goff, the chairman of the Guidebook Committee, wrote to Fowler to express his views on the initial letter's criticisms. After detailing the many reasons he felt AMC guidebooks were sufficient to "serve the important needs of any person traveling the A.T. system," he addressed the subject of Avery's demeanor.

> For quite a few years the feeling of our Club, or I might say that part of our Club which includes the Guide Book Committee, Committee on Trails, Huts, etc., has been anything but cordial to Mr. Myron Avery, and perhaps the source of this condition goes back to the time when Mr. Morse was Chairman of the Guide Book Committee and certain warm arguments developed around the publication of our Katahdin Guide. This coolness is not due to any prejudice or feeling against the Appalachian or N.E. Trail Conferences but is really a personal matter. This is of course unfortunate, and the strange part of it is that Mr. Avery in person seems a friendly, likeable, and cooperative person. I have met him and in fact he has called on me here at the office, and we had a very interesting and frank conversation concerning our organizations and the work which each does with respect to trails, camps, signs, etc. The so-called strained relations seem to be carried along by correspondence alone, and I'm inclined to believe the true cause will be found in the individual himself, and that our favor could more readily be courted if he were willing to admit that some of us had a not too antiquated conception of our duties and accomplishments in certain sections of the northern Appalachian mountains. You know as well as I that the omission of distances from our signs is customary, but certainly not because of any intention that this will force the traveler to buy a copy of the Guide Book in order . . . to judge distances in a more accurate manner. This statement has been directed to us before, and I would like to see something done so that it will not again be repeated. This I believe is another one of Mr. Avery's caustic remarks

---

16  Ibid.

*which certainly is not conducive to recovery of the former good feeling*
*which existed between our associations.* [17]

Goff then recommended that he and Fowler meet in person to discuss the finer points of Avery's letter before responding to Stephenson.

On November 1, 1940, Fowler wrote a follow-up letter to Avery. After asserting that Avery was right in suggesting Fowler's initial letter was "not intended to be as acrid as it may appear . . . since the only intent was to call attention to an error in the article" (until there was time to do further research), Fowler got to the crux of the sign issue.

The reason for omitting trail distances on signs, Fowler explained, was because the distances did not "furnish a true criterion of the difficulty of a given stretch of trail, as matters of elevation, roughness or smoothness of footing, and the like all enter into the reckoning.

"You appear to have picked up a rumor that [the omission of trail distances] was done to promote sales of the Guide Book, but you should be well aware how easy it is for unfounded rumors of this nature to be spread," Fowler continued. He therefore asked Avery to give "serious consideration to correcting" the article.[18]

If Fowler and Goff were frustrated by Avery's letter and threats, their reactions were tepid compared to that of Avery's old friend Ron Gower, who then held the position of recording secretary within AMC. Gower, who had once promised Avery he would not choose sides, sent a fiery, three-page internal memo to Fowler.

> *May I make the following observations which have occurred to me*
> *as the result of thinking this matter over. . . . I rather question if anyone*
> *actually wrote such a letter to the Conference; instead, I am sure that*
> *the whole business is a device for drawing you out and putting you on*
> *record on a number of controversial items, this method having been*
> *used instead of the more direct one of questioning you about them,*
> *which might have led you to argue their propriety.*

---

17   Howard M. Goff to William Fowler, 30 October 1940, Appalachian Mountain Club Archives.

18   William Fowler to Myron Avery, 1 November 1940, Appalachian Mountain Club Archives.

*Perhaps I am unduly suspicious, but having had dealings with these folks ever since Avery took over the high command of the AT, and having been one of them for a number of years, I have had opportunity to observe how things are "rigged", and how adroitly he accomplishes his purpose Their threat to publish, with or without your views, this article, which seems to place the Club in an unfavorable light, indicates their true feeling and aim in this.... One has only to examine the probable meaning of the following excerpts. . . . "I have understood that the omission of distances from these signs was quite intentional and deliberate. The theory is that the users of the trail will be forced to buy the guidebook," and "We did suggest the desirability of milling the AT on these board signs for the through route; apparently the suggestion did not meet with favor."*

*Further on [in the proposed article] . . . we come across the self-sacrificing phrase, "It was felt that it was most desirable and essential to omit from the new through New England Guide that any detailed description for these areas (those covered by our Guide and the GMC [Green Mountain Club] Long Trail Guide) to avoid <u>any thought</u> (the underscoring is mine) of competing guidebooks." Shades of Machiavelli! Do you recall the letter which Avery wrote to Mr. Blood in which he earnestly recommended that we abandon the publishing of our Katahdin Guide (which had then been published for 20 years continuously) because the AT[C] was going to issue a vastly better chapter on the Katahdin area and because they had a monopoly on the authoritative sources of information regarding the region? This was only back in the fall of 1937, and now Avery smites his chest and cries out against such an unholy practice.[19]*

Gower recommended that Fowler not respond to Avery with "anything which would sound like a defensive explanation" and that it might be better to explain that other matters prevented Fowler from "giving all these weighty matters of theirs the profound investigation which their importance warrants."

---

19  Ronald Gower to William Fowler, 12 November 1940, Appalachian Mountain Club Archives.

Gower then directly addressed what he believed was the greatest problem of all, Avery himself.

> *The underlying situation, of which this is only a surface indication, points to the necessity of a thorough housecleaning in the high command of the AT[C]. . . . The AT[C] is a fine thing, and doubtless the rank and file of the outfit are splendid folks—but the high command needs overhauling. They will never command the respect and cooperation of other organizations as long as they go about with such a large and obvious chip on their shoulder, and the friction is not altogether on the outside either, I am reliably informed.*
>
> *Coming down to personalities, Avery made a good driver to force through the completion of the AT. Now that phase is over, it needs a smooth operating diplomatic head who will make people want to work with and for him in order that the vast gains may be permanently consolidated. You ask anyone who has had any close dealings with Avery over any period, and you will, in the great majority of times, uncover an enemy of his. Such men as Comey, Underhill, Peabody, MacMillan, Cabot and Nicholson, are not one-sided, narrow-minded, prejudiced people—ask them, and they are only a few of the many who have felt the outpouring of Avery's vials of wrath. Ask Christine Reid and Ruth Hardy, if you think he pulls his punches just because they are women.*[20]

While the internal AMC discussion about Myron Avery went on, Howard Goff wrote his own letter to the ATC chairman. Goff thanked Avery for sending the proposed *Appalachian Trailway News* article, saying some of the information in it would help inform updates to the supplement of the AMC guide to be published in the spring. He then characterized the assertion that AMC left mileages off signs "so that people will be required to purchase a Guide Book in order to help them find their way around" as a "misconception of the truth." He also invited Avery to drop by for a visit on one of Avery's frequent trips to Boston.[21]

---

20   Ronald Gower to William Fowler, 12 November 1940, Appalachian Mountain Club Archives.

21   Howard Goff to Myron Avery, 13 November 1940, Appalachian Mountain Club Archives.

A few days later, Avery responded to Goff by letter. "I can allay any apprehension by stating that I propose to substitute in to Mr. Fowler's explanation for that which I understood for so many years to be the situation," Avery wrote before also informing Goff that, for reasons of space, the matter would wait until the April 1940 issue of *Appalachian Trailway News* to appear in print. Then Avery revisits a theme he seemingly can't let go of: his history with the AMC publication committees.

> *Although it is a matter in which neither you nor Mr. Fowler has any responsibility, I cannot refrain from commenting upon the anxiety of the club to avoid the appearance of any statement which could be interpreted, by any stretch of the imagination, to be unfavorable in view of the very violent attacks made upon our guidebooks in the columns of* Appalachia *and the very real detriment resulting therefrom. The matter went to the extent of our being denied the opportunity to reply to statements not only unfounded in fact but totally misleading. It is, you may understand, because of this situation that, since I have ventured into a field where it might be suggested that I was indulging in some sort of recrimination, I shall be very sure to have my comment to the approval of Mr. Fowler—if he does not carry his brief too far.*[22]

The matter simmered down until March 1941, when Avery sent a copy of the article to appear in *Appalachian Trailway News* to Fowler, which Fowler, in turn, sent to Gower for review. Gower's response to Fowler offers another window into the longtime Avery associate's evolved point of view.

> *I have studied Avery's article closely. I am more than ever convinced that it is his way of putting on pressure to have things done the way he would like them. He smarts under the realization that the AMC does not jump at the crack of his whip, but rather becomes increasingly stubborn. All his years of high pressure, innuendo, false impressions, misleading publicity and vituperation which have been heaped upon the heads of all who thought differently from him and*

---

22  Myron Avery to Howard Goff, 16 November 1940, Appalachian Mountain Club Archives.

*had the courage to say so, have failed to change the ideas and practices of the AMC and he bitterly resents this.*

*I would not reply to his letter, since he has left it that you need not—in fact he sounds as though he really didn't expect you to. Corresponding with him leads to controversy which always ends in a dispute, controversial recrimination and bitterness. He must have been a spoiled child—surely he has grown up to be a mighty poor sport. He must exert control over all he touches or he becomes angry. If he can't have his own way he becomes revengeful, always watching out for a chance to undermine and stab in the back.*

*His obvious intention is to force the AMC "into line" by threatening to publish these critical things. Let him go ahead and find out how little it benefits his ideas. Just ignore him—it's actually becoming fashionable! The number of people who take him seriously is continuously diminishing.*

*We see things one way—he and his high command see them another. We do not always try to make him conform to our way, yet he seems always to be trying to compel us to follow him. Don't let him get away with it. Time will tell who is right.*

*Many people think with me that neither the AT nor any other project warrants the enduring of such dictatorship as Avery imposes, and there has grown up a considerable body of more or less organized "rebellion" headed by one W. Sterling Edwards of Maryland.*[23]

Gower went on to explain that Sterling Edwards, a hiker from Virginia, independently published a "Report of the AT" several times a year, which was "devoted to impartial criticism of the AT."

He wrote: "In this rare journal, one finds brave folk who speak their minds about the 'perpetual Chairman of the AT Conference' and the AT *Trailway News* as being just so much controlled aggrandizement of Avery and his tools."

After stating he had heard rumors that Avery was using the AT as a vehicle for attaining "some as yet undisclosed objective," such as heading the U.S. Forest Service or the National Park Service, Gower proclaimed:

---

23  Ronald Gower to William Fowler, 18 March 1940, Appalachian Mountain Club Archives.

*I do not believe the above is so. I think that basking in the warmth of so much adulation, publicity and fan-mail has stimulated his reactions to demanding continually more of the same. This same mental quirk would naturally lead him to give short shrift to some unknown trail worker who might honestly and constructively differ with the "big boss." It definitely seems that one has to be a yes-man in order to remain in his graces. I can point to many who have disagreed—and walked the plank!*

*Before I write so much on this topic, I should realize that perhaps you are not as keenly interested in the subject as I am. Should you care to have "chapter and verse" quoted, I am sure it will be interesting reading. I have just finished reading over some 20 carbons of letters which Edwards has written to some of his readers. They disclose how brittle the AT set-up really is.*

*May I reassure you that I am perfectly sane about all other matters! If you will stir me up on this—your blood will be on your own head!*[24]

Predictably, Myron Avery could not see past what he perceived as slights on both his intelligence and methodology. Avery held on to the belief that he knew what was right, both for him and for the future of the trail. His consistent conclusion was that the only way he could make sure everything came together was to do it himself. The result was a 2,000-mile monument to his resolve and stubbornness, built at a tremendous personal toll.

---

24  Ibid.

# CHAPTER 21

## *End of the Trail*

*I have been working night and day and am racing*
*everywhere, so be charitable of me.*

—Myron Avery, in a letter to Walter Greene[1]

BY 1951, MYRON AVERY WAS DYING. ONLY IN HIS EARLY FIFTIES,
Avery's body and mind were suffering from physical and mental stress. He
had given everything he had to his two passions in life: the Appalachian Trail
and his other full-time job as a maritime lawyer. He was exhausted. He had
experienced episodes of exhaustion, including hospitalization for pneumonia. But this time, he would not recover.

In early January 1951, he wrote to his current guidebook publisher: "I
received your comment on the New England Guide Book at the hospital,
where I am in the process of being overhauled and having 'new parts' installed."[2]

Just over a year later, Avery wrote a letter to the Maine Appalachian Trail
Club (MATC) to discuss its spring meeting time and location, revealing
more about his health.

> *I regret to say that I shall not be able to be in Maine or to partici-*
> *pate in any meeting in the spring of 1952. I experienced, in the fall of*
> *1951, intestinal difficulties as a result of which I have been confined,*
> *since January 1, to the hospital and a sanitarium. The prognosis is*
> *that my treatment and recuperation will extend over a considerable*

---

1   Myron Avery to Walter Greene, 1 October 1933, Avery Collection, Maine State Library
    Special Collections.
2   Myron Avery to Bronson W. Griscom, 7 January 1951, Avery Collection, Maine State
    Library Special Collections.

*period, even if a possible operation is deferred or finally eliminated. Consequently, I have been obliged to suspend all activities, professional as well as recreational.*[3]

By March 1952, Avery had entirely stepped aside from both the legal profession (he had been discharged from the Navy in 1947) and his work related to the AT. He confided to his friend Roy Fairfield that he was looking forward to a new challenge involving the area where he was born and raised.[4]

*Now, that I am a gentleman of leisure—a man with no occupation—I have high hopes of picking up my long-intended research on the history of Eastern Maine. It is curious that all the work in that connection has been done by the Canadians. Unfortunately, too, I am commencing too late, for some of the most qualified researchers on the Nova Scotia side have departed from this earthly scene.*[5]

The next day Avery wrote a letter to the owners of West Carry Pond Camps in Maine's Bigelow region, Mr. and Mrs. Elwyn Storey, who had earlier sent an update from the North Woods. Avery's reply was more personal than most of his correspondence and showed a yearning for simpler times.

*Changes in the Maine woods are occurring with unbelievable speed. . . . We just cannot seem to keep up with all the developments. . . . I have been reading, with amazement, the stories of the extent of snow and flying out the lumber crews from the country north of Katahdin. It seems to me that things must be changing for, in the old days, the crew stayed in all winter and no one bothered much about the snow.*

*I have not done very well of late. . . . My troubles seem to have come down on me all at once. My present trouble is intestinal difficulty, which I think would be cured if I could persuade the physicians*

3    Myron Avery to MATC, 16 February 1952, Avery Collection, Maine State Library Special Collections.

4    Robert A. Rubin, "The Short, Brilliant Life of Myron Avery," 27.

5    Myron Avery to Roy P. Fairfield, 27 March 1952, Avery Collection, Maine State Library Special Collections.

*to install a new copper-lined stomach. The special diet was anything but a pleasure, particularly when I would think of how baked tongue a la West Carry Pond Camps would taste in preference to what they were serving for food.*[6]

Myron Avery died on July 26, 1952. He was on a trip to Nova Scotia with his son to trace his family's ancestry. Upon climbing up a cemetery hill, he collapsed and almost immediately expired. The man who had spent so much time in the hills and so little time with his family would pass in a place where both were close at hand.

The *Appalachian Trailway News* editor Jean Stephenson, who had ably helped Myron Avery keep ATC moving ever forward, ran a beautiful tribute to her boss and friend in the publication, indicating it was not the work on the AT that had taken the greatest toll on the man with the relentless drive.

Noting that not many people were aware Avery had a lifelong affiliation with the Navy, had served in both World Wars, was a maritime lawyer, and had been awarded the Legion of Merit, Stephenson wrote:

> *To his Navy work he gave himself unstintingly; it was this that drew too deeply on even his iron constitution. He was definitely a "war casualty" even though he died on a peaceful lawn instead of a field of battle.*
>
> *Indeed, even after the war ended, his work for the Navy continued to be related to legal matters—international law, jurisdiction over armed forces, base agreements, settling airplane accidents, and so forth. For much of this period, he ran the legal office by himself, at a time when its work increased fourfold.*[7]

Writing a one-page tribute to Myron Avery must have been a daunting task. Upon referencing a few of his greater accomplishments, Stephenson acknowledges, "Mention has been made of but a few of his many activities," and, "his passing leaves a great void."

---

6   Myron Avery to Mr. and Mrs. Elwyn Storey, 28 March 1952, Avery Collection, Maine State Library Special Collections.

7   "Myron H. Avery," *Appalachian Trailway News* 13, no. 3 (September 1952).

Potomac Appalachian Trail Club members stand at the summit of Katahdin, marking the end of their hike north from Blanchard, Maine, in 1935. Myron Avery is on the far left. Photo: Courtesy of Avery Collection, Maine State Library.

But the measure of a person is less about what they have done and more of what they have left for others. Stephenson addressed this most beautifully in her final paragraph.

> *It has been said that every achievement is but the lengthened shadow of one man. As Myron Avery, facing into the sunset, follows the trail over the hills into the land from which there is no return, we can see the long shadow of his erect and vigorous figure stretching back over mountain and woodland until it changes imperceptibly into a footpath from Maine to Georgia and Georgia to Maine, a path where all may find once again the one-ness of Man with Nature and feel with him joy because the Trail is there and share his peace because the Trail is good.*[8]

The same issue of *Appalachian Trailway News* includes the final "Report of the Chairman Myron H. Avery," which Avery delivered in person to the

---

8   *Appalachian Trailway News* 13, no. 3 (September 1952).

twelfth Appalachian Trail Conference on May 30, 1952, less than two months before his death.

In the report, Avery declined to dwell on his two-decade history with the AT. Instead, he wished to look toward the future of the trail and its meaning.

> *The Appalachian Trail does derive much of its strength and appeal from its uninterrupted and practically endless character. This is an attribute which must be preserved. I view the existence of this pathway and the opportunity to travel it, day after day without interruption, as a distinct aspect of our American life. . . . Mainly, it develops the ability to care for one's self in travel through forests, which is of extraordinary benefit.*[9]

Avery then turned his attention to what he identified as the greatest threats to the AT: "permanent interruption in the through trail route," and the development of ridge tops and other areas "hitherto considered inaccessible." He called for public protection of the trail corridor to preserve "opportunity to travel the forests of the eastern United States as our forefathers knew them."

Myron Avery's last words to ATC, which would be his last to many of the attendees, were the recitation of "the once much-quoted definition of the Appalachian Trail."[10]

> *"Remote for detachment, narrow for chosen company, winding for leisure, lonely for contemplation, it beckons not merely north and south but upward to the body, mind and soul of man."*
>
> *And so, in closing this report of two decades of stewardship, I leave you with this objective for your labors, travel and pleasure along the Appalachian Trail.*[11]

---

9   Robert A. Rubin, "The Short, Brilliant Life of Myron H. Avery," 41.

10   The quote is often attributed to Myron Avery, as he used it without attribution in a 1934 article in the publication *In the Maine Woods*, but it was, in fact, penned by Harold Allen, an early AT trail planner and volunteer.

11   Robert A. Rubin, "The Short, Brilliant Life of Myron H. Avery," 41.

# CHAPTER 22

## *A Serene Passing*

In May 1975, a journalist named Constance Stallings stepped into a "low ceilinged, center-hall colonial with [a] wide-plank floor" in Shirley, Massachusetts. She was greeted with a firm handshake by a man with neatly combed white hair who was dressed in a scotch-plaid robe. Stallings was on assignment for *Backpacker* magazine. She was there to interview Benton MacKaye about the AT, but he had a different trail on his mind.[1]

MacKaye had just heard about plans for the Pacific Northwest Trail, a proposed long-distance trail that would extend from the Rocky Mountains in Montana to the Pacific Ocean in Washington. He peppered the reporter with questions.

> *Will the trail begin at the point in Glacier National Park where the waters divide and drain three ways? What towns will the trail pass on its way across Washington State? What is the route for getting around Puget Sound to the Olympic Peninsula?*[2]

The reporter didn't have much to share, except that she knew a bill for the creation of the trail had been introduced in the Senate.

"By which Senators?" MacKaye asked. "Henry Jackson and Warren Magnuson of Washington? Good!"

After settling into conversation for a while, MacKaye came around to the subject of the AT. He was well aware the trail was more popular than ever.

---

1    Constance L. Stallings, "Benton MacKaye's Last Interview," *Backpacker* 4, no. 2, (April 1976): 55.

2    Ibid.

Benton MacKaye reads under a grapevine in Shirley, Massachusetts, circa the 1950s. Photo: Courtesy of Dartmouth College Library.

"What I hope," he said, "is that it won't turn into a racetrack. I for one would give the prize to the person that took the longest time." [3]

Upon his retirement in 1945, Benton MacKaye had returned to the house in Shirley Center that would be his touchstone for more than 80 years. The surrounding woods and fields had opened his mind to a life that embraced long-distance trails, regional planning, earth science, conservation, and wilderness preservation. At 96 years old, he was still excited by the promise of a new National Scenic Trail. His parting words to the reporter were, "Don't forget that I want to know about the Pacific Northwest Trail!"[4]

On December 11, 1975, MacKaye died in his home. After two days of increasing discomfort, he simply slipped away. His grave is marked not by a traditional headstone but a lichen-covered granite boulder etched with the name "MacKaye." But the greatest memorial to Benton MacKaye is more than 2,000 miles long and is visited by millions of people every year—a place that exists in large part because one man realized: "A period recourse into the wilds is not a retreat into secret silent sanctums to escape a wicked world, it is to take breath amid effort to forge a better world."

---

3   Ibid.

4   Ibid.

# EPILOGUE

Myron Avery's papers are housed in the Maine Authors' Room in the state's Cultural Building, in Augusta. Avery was a nearly incomprehensibly prolific writer. His papers include thousands of letters written and received during the heady days and years of building the AT. Tucked into his correspondence from 1935 is a quote by the architect Daniel Burnham, the designer of such enduring landmarks as the Flatiron Building in New York City and Union Station in Washington, D.C., as well as the director of the 1893 World's Columbian Exposition in Chicago and co-author of that city's 1909 master plan.

Stirred by Burnham's quote, Avery typed it on a blank sheet of paper and kept it at hand precisely when he was leading his philosophical battle around Skyline Drive, setting the wheels in motion to ensure his leadership would not be challenged.

> *Make no little plans; they have no magic to stir a man's blood and probably themselves will not be realized. Make big plans; aim high in hope and work; remembering that a noble, logical diagram once recorded will never die, but long after we are gone will be a living thing, asserting itself with ever-growing insistency. Remember that our sons and grandsons are going to do things that would stagger us. Let your watchword be order and your beacon beauty.[1]*

---

1 The Burnham quote has an interesting history. It first appeared on a holiday card sent by Burnham's architectural partner, Willis Polk, six months after Burnham's death. The quote is largely pieced together from a speech Burnham made in London in 1910. While many historians believe the quotation accurately conveys Burnham's philosophy and literary style, there is no record of him stating it as presented.

Myron Avery's high aim in hope and work—the Appalachian Trail—would indeed become a living thing and would grow to become the most recognized hiking path in the world. He lived long enough to see the vision realized, to walk every step of the way, and to encourage others to do the same.

Benton MacKaye's path through life could hardly have been more dissimilar. His was the well-considered, long view. While Avery was a man of action, MacKaye was a man of order. While Avery dashed off handfuls of letters every day, MacKaye spent months—even years—drafting meticulously researched reports and books. MacKaye loved analyzing systems and weighing the pros and cons of tweaking them. In fact, he enjoyed it so much that he was prone to isolation and lack of follow-through. At times MacKaye struggled to find constituencies for his concepts. Yet, the writings he left behind show us how prescient he was. For example, in the early 1900s, MacKaye predicted that an industry would be created for the purpose of selling things and that this industry would employ hundreds of men and women who would commute to work in giant office buildings. His life's experience gave him valuable insights about the need to sustainably manage forests and the need to set aside and protect wilderness. The restorative power of living and working in proximity to wild lands informed Benton MacKaye's life from a young age until the day he died. His willingness to stay true to that ideal, regardless of consequences, arguably says more about MacKaye than any words he ever wrote.

Perhaps it is appropriate that the accomplishment Benton MacKaye is best known for was merely one piece of a more complex vision. That the piece most easy to people to visualize was the one people rallied behind. That it took someone else to guide the vision from concept to completion. That, unlike his father's Spectatorium, this vision wasn't half completed, then torn down. That it may not have followed the precise blueprint of the architect, but that millions of people would go on to enjoy it.

# APPENDIX A

## An Appalachian Trail: A Project in Regional Planning

THE ARTICLE BELOW, PUBLISHED IN JOURNAL OF THE AMERICAN *Institute of Architects* in October 1921, launched the concept of the Appalachian Trail into the public consciousness.

### An Appalachian Trail:
### A Project in Regional Planning
### By Benton MacKaye

Something has been going on in this country during the past few strenuous years which, in the din of war and general upheaval, has been somewhat lost from the public mind. It is the slow quiet development of a special type of community—the recreation camp. It is something neither urban nor rural. It escapes the hecticness of the one, the loneliness of the other. And it escapes also the common curse of both—the high powered tension of the economic scramble. All communities face an "economic" problem, but in different ways. The camp faces it through cooperation and mutual helpfulness, the others through competition and mutual fleecing.

We civilized ones also, whether urban or rural, are potentially as helpless as canaries in a cage. The ability to cope with nature directly—unshielded by the weakening wall of civilization—is one of the admitted needs of modern times. It is the goal of the "scouting" movement. Not that we want to return to the plights of our Paleolithic ancestors. We want the strength of progress without its puniness. We want its conveniences without its fopperies. The ability to sleep and cook in the open is a good step forward. But "scouting" should not stop there. This is but a faint step from our canary bird existence. It should strike much deeper than this. We should seek the ability not only to cook food but to raise food with less aid—and less hindrance—from the complexities of commerce. And this is becoming daily of increasing practical importance. Scouting, then, has its vital connection with the problem of living.

## A New Approach to the Problem of Living

The problem of living is at bottom an economic one. And this alone is bad enough, even in a period of so-called "normalcy." But living has been considerably complicated of late in various ways—by war, by questions of personal liberty, and by "menaces" of one kind or another. There have been created bitter antagonisms. We are undergoing also the bad combination of high prices and unemployment. This situation is world wide—the result of a world-wide war.

It is no purpose of this little article to indulge in coping with any of these big questions. The nearest we come to such effrontery is to suggest more comfortable seats and more fresh air for those who have to consider them. A great professor once said that "optimism is oxygen." Are we getting all the "oxygen" we might for the big tasks before us?

"Let us wait," we are told, "til we solve this cussed labor problem. Then we'll have the leisure to do great things."

But suppose that while we wait the chance for doing them is passed?

It goes without saying we should work upon the labor problem. Not just the matter of "capital and labor" but the *real* labor problem—how to reduce the day's drudgery. The toil and chore of life should, as labor saving devices increase, form a diminishing proportion of the average day and year. Leisure and higher pursuits will thereby come to form an increasing proportion of our lives.

But will leisure mean something "higher"? Here is a question indeed. The coming of leisure in itself will create its own problem. As the problem of labor "solves", that of leisure arises. There seems to be no escape from problems. We have neglected to improve the leisure which should be ours as a result of replacing stone and bronze with iron and steam. Very likely we have been cheated out of the bulk of this leisure. The efficiency of modern industry has been placed at 25 per cent of its reasonable possibilities. This may be too low or too high.

But the leisure that we do succeed in getting—is this developed to an efficiency much higher?

The customary approach to the problem of living relates to work rather than play. Can we increase the efficiency of our *working* time? Can we solve the problem of labor? If so we can widen the opportunities of our leisure. The new approach reverses this mental process. Can we increase the efficiency of our *spare* time? Can we develop opportunities for leisure as an aid in solving the problem of labor?

### An Undeveloped Power—Our Spare Time

How much spare time have we, and how much power does it represent?

The great body of working people—the industrial workers, the farmers, and the housewives—have no allotted spare time or "vacations." The business clerk usually gets two weeks' leave, with pay, each year. The U.S. Government clerk gets thirty days. The business man is likely to give himself two weeks or a month. Farmers can get off for a week or more at a time by doubling up on one another's chores. Housewives might do likewise.

As to the industrial worker—in mine or factory—his average "vacation" is all too long. For it is "leave of absence without pay." According to recent official figures the average industrial worker in the United States, during normal times, is employed in industry about four fifths of the time—say 42 weeks in the year. The other ten weeks he is employed in seeking employment.

The proportionate time for true leisure of the average adult American appears, then, to be meagre indeed. But a goodly portion have (or take) about two weeks in the year. The industrial worker during the estimated ten weeks between jobs must of course go on eating and living. His savings may enable him to do this without undue worry. He could, if he felt he could spare the time from job hunting, and if suitable facilities were provided, take two weeks of his ten on a real vacation. In one way or another, therefore, the average adult in this country could devote each year a period of about two weeks in doing the things of his own choice.

Here is an enormous undeveloped power—the spare time of our population. Suppose just one percent of it were focused on one particular job, such as increasing the facilities for the outdoor community life. This would be more than a million people, representing over two million weeks a year. It would be equivalent to 40,000 persons steadily on the job.

### A Strategic Camping Base—The Appalachian Skyline

Where might this imposing force lay out its camping ground?

Camping grounds, of course, require wild lands. These in America are fortunately still available. They are in every main region of the country. They are the undeveloped or under-developed areas. Except in the Central States the wild lands now remaining are for the most part along the mountain ranges—the Sierras, the Cascades, and Rocky Mountains of the West and the Appalachian Mountains of the East.

Extensive national playgrounds have been reserved in various parts of the country for use by the people for camping and kindred purposes. Most of these are in the West where Uncle Sam's public lands were located. They are in the Yosemite, the Yellowstone, and many other National Parks—covering about six million acres in all. Splendid work has been accomplished in fitting these Parks for use. The National Forests, covering about 130 million acres—chiefly in the West—are also equipped for public recreation purposes.

A great public service has been started in these Parks and Forests in the field of outdoor life. They have been called "playgrounds of the people." This they are for the Western people—and those in the East who can afford time and funds for an extended trip in a Pullman car. But camping grounds to be of the most use to the people should be as near as possible to the center of the population. And this is in the East.

It fortunately happens that we have throughout the most densely populated portion of the United States a fairly continuous belt of under-developed lands. These are contained in the several ranges which form the Appalachian chain of mountains. Several National Forests have been purchased in this belt. These mountains, in several ways rivaling the western scenery, are within a day's ride from centers containing more than half the population of the United States. The region spans the climates of New England and the cotton belt; it contains the crops and the people of the North and of the South.

The skyline along the top of the main divides and ridges of the Appalachians would overlook a mighty part of the nation's activities. The rugged lands of this skyline would form a camping base strategic in the country's work and play.

Let us assume the existence of a giant standing high on the skyline along these mountain ridges, his head just scraping the floating clouds. What would he see from this skyline as he strode along its length from north to south?

Starting out from Mt. Washington, the highest point in the northeast, his horizon takes in one of the original happy hunting grounds of America—the "Northwoods," a country of pointed firs extending from the lakes and rivers of northern Maine to those of the Adirondacks. Stepping across the Green Mountains and the Berkshires to the Catskills he gets his first views of the crowded east—a chain of smoky bee-hive cities extending from Boston to Washington and containing a third of the population of the Appalachian drained area. Bridging the Delaware Water Gap and the Susquehanna on the picturesque Allegheny folds across Pennsylvania he notes more smoky columns—the big plants between Scranton and Pittsburgh that get out the basic stuff of modern industry—iron and coal. In relieving contrast he steps across the Potomac near Harpers Ferry and pushes through into the wooded wilderness of the Southern Appalachians where he finds preserved much of the primal aspects of the days of Daniel Boone. Here he finds, over on the Monongahela side, the black coal of bituminous and the white coal of water power. He proceeds along the great divide of the upper Ohio and sees flowing to waste, sometimes in terrifying floods, waters capable of generating untold hydroelectric energy and of bringing navigation to many a lower stream. He looks over the Natural Bridge and out across the battle fields around Appomattox. He finds himself finally in the midst of the great Carolina hardwood belt. Resting now on top of Mt. Mitchell, highest point east of the Rockies, he counts up on his big long fingers the opportunities which yet await development along the skyline he has passed.

First he notes the opportunities for recreation. Throughout the Southern Appalachians, throughout the Northwoods, and even through the Alleghenies that wind their way among the smoky industrial towns of Pennsylvania, he recollects vast areas of secluded forests, pastoral lands, and water courses, which, with proper facilities and protection, could be made to serve as the breath of a real life for the toilers in the bee-hive cities along the Atlantic seaboard and elsewhere.

Second, he notes the possibilities for health and recuperation. The oxygen in the mountain air along the Appalachian skyline is a natural resource (and a national resource) that radiates to the heavens its enormous health-giving powers with only a fraction of a percent utilized for human rehabilitation. Here is a resource that could save thousands of lives. The sufferers from tuberculosis, anemia, and insanity go through the whole strata of human society. Most of them are helpless, even those economically well off. They occur in the cities and right in the skyline belt. For the farmers, and especially the wives of farmers, are by no means escaping the grinding-down process of our modern life.

Most sanitariums now established are perfectly useless to those afflicted with mental disease—the most terrible, usually, of any disease. Many of these sufferers could be cured. But not merely by "treatment." They need comprehensive provision made for them. They need acres not medicine. Thousands of acres of this mountain land should be devoted to them with whole communities planned and equipped for their cure.

Next after the opportunities for recreation and recuperation our giant counts off, as a third big resource, the opportunities in the Appalachian belt for employment on the land. This brings up a need that is becoming urgent—the redistribution of our population, which grows more and more top heavy.

The rural population of the United States, and of the Eastern States adjacent to the Appalachians, has now dipped below the urban. For the whole country it has fallen from 60 per cent of the total in 1900 to 49 per cent in 1920; for the Eastern States it has fallen during this period, from 55 per cent to 45 per cent. Meantime the per capita area of improved farm land has dropped, in the Eastern States, from 3.35 acres to 2.43 acres. This is a shrinkage of nearly 18 percent in 20 years; in the States from Maine to Pennsylvania the shrinkage has been 40 per cent.

There are in the Appalachian belt probably 25 million acres of grazing and agricultural land awaiting development. Here is room for a whole new rural population. Here is an opportunity—if only the way can be found—for that counter migration from city to country that has so long been prayed for. But our giant in pondering on this resource is discerning enough to know that its utilization is going to depend upon some new deal in our agricultural system. This he knows if he ever stooped down and gazed in the sunken eyes of either the Carolina "cracker" or the Green Mountain "hayseed."

Forest land as well as agricultural might prove an opportunity for steady employment in the open. But this again depends upon a new deal. Forestry must replace timber devastation and its consequent hap-hazard employment. And this giant knows if he has looked into the rugged face of the homeless "don't care a damn" lumberjack of the Northwoods.

Such are the outlooks—such the opportunities—seen by a discerning spirit from the Appalachian skyline.

### Possibilities in the New Approach

Let's put up now to the wise and trained observer the particular question before us. What are the possibilities in the new approach to the problem of living? Would the development of the outdoor community life—as an offset and relief from the various shackles of commercial civilization—be practicable and worth while? From the experience of observations and thoughts along the sky-line here is a possible answer:

There are several possible gains from such an approach.

First there would be the "oxygen" that makes for a sensible optimism. Two weeks spent in the real open—right now, this year and next— would be a little real living for thousands of people which they would be sure of getting before they died. They would get a little fun as they went along regardless of problems being "solved." This would not damage the problems and it would help the folks.

Next there would be perspective. Life for two weeks on the mountain top would show up many things about life during the other fifty weeks down below. The latter could be viewed as a whole—away from its heat, sweat, and irritations. There would be a chance to catch a breath, to study the dynamic forces of nature and the possibilities of shifting to them the burdens now carried on the backs of men. The reposeful study of these forces should provide a broad gauged enlightened approach to the problems of industry. Industry would come to be seen in its true perspective—as a means in life and not an end in itself. The actual partaking of the recreative and non-industrial life—systematically by the people and not spasmodically by a few—should emphasize the distinction between it and the industrial life. It should stimulate the quest for enlarging the one and reducing the other. It should put new zest in the labor movement. Life and study of this kind should emphasize the need of going to the roots of industrial questions and avoiding superficial thinking and rash action. The problems of the farmer, the coal miner, and the lumberjack could be studied intimately and with minimum partiality. Such an approach should bring the poise that goes with understanding.

Finally, there would be new clews to constructive solutions. The organization of the cooperative camping life would tend to draw people out of the cities. Coming as visitors they would be loathe to return. They would become desirous of settling down in the country—to work in the open as well as *play*. The various camps would require food. Why not raise the food, as well as consume it, on the cooperative plan? Food and farm camps should come about as a natural sequence. Timber is also required. Permanent small scale operations could be encouraged in the various Appalachian National Forests. The government now claims this is part of its forest policy. The camping life would stimulate forestry as well as better agriculture. Employment in both would tend to become enlarged.

How far these tendencies would go the wisest observer of course can not tell. They would have to be worked out step by step. But the tendencies at least would be established. They would be cutting channels leading to constructive achievement in the problem of living: they would be cutting across those now leading to destructive blindness.

### A Project for Development
It looks then, as if it might be worth while to devote some energy at least to working out a better utilization of our spare time. The spare time for

one per cent of our population would be equivalent, as above reckoned, to the continuous activity of some 40,000 persons. If these people were on the skyline, and kept their eyes open, they would see the things that the giant could see. Indeed, this force of 40,000 would be a giant in itself. It could walk the skyline and develop its varied opportunities. And this is the job that we propose: a project to develop the opportunities—for recreation, recuperation, and employment—in the region of the Appalachian skyline.

The project is one for a series of recreational communities throughout the Appalachian chain of mountains from New England to Georgia, these to be connected by a walking trail. Its purpose is to establish a base for a more extensive and systematic development of outdoor community life. It is a project in housing and community architecture.

No scheme is proposed in this particular article for organizing or financing this project. Organizing is a matter of detail to be carefully worked out. Financing depends upon local public interest in the various localities affected.

### Features of Project

There are four chief features of the Appalachian project:

1. *The Trail*—

The beginnings of an Appalachian trail already exist. They have been established for several years—in various localities along the line. Specially good work in trail building has been accomplished by the Appalachian Mountain Club in the White Mountains of New Hampshire and by the Green Mountain Club in Vermont. The latter association has built the "Long Trail" for 210 miles through the Green Mountains—four fifths of the distance from the Massachusetts line to the Canadian. Here is a project that will be logically extended. What the Green Mountains are to Vermont the Appalachians are to the eastern United States. What is suggested, therefore, is a "long trail" over the full length of the Appalachian skyline, from the highest peak in the north to the highest peak in the south—from Mt. Washington to Mt. Mitchell.

The trail should be divided into sections, each consisting preferably of the portion lying in a given State, or subdivision thereof. Each section should be in the immediate charge of a local group of people. Difficulties might arise over the use of private property—especially that amid agricultural lands on the crossovers between ranges. It might sometimes be necessary to obtain a State franchise for the use of rights of way. These matters could readily be adjusted, provided there is sufficient local interest in the project as a whole. The various sections should be under some form of general federated control, but no suggestions regarding this form are made in this article.

Not all of the trail within a section could, of course, be built at once. It would be a matter of several years. As far as possible the work undertaken for any one season should complete some definite usable link— as up or across one peak. Once completed it should be immediately opened for local use and not wait until the completion of other portions. Each portion built should, of course, be rigorously maintained and not allowed to revert to disuse. A trail is as serviceable as its poorest link.

The trail could be made, at each stage of its construction, of immediate strategic value in preventing and fighting forest fires. Lookout stations could be located at intervals along the way. A forest fire service could be organized in each section which should tie in with the services of the Federal and State governments. The trail would become immediately a battle line against fire.

A suggestion for the location of the trail and its main branches is shown in the accompanying map.

2. *Shelter Camps*—

These are the usual accompaniments of the trails which have been built in the White and Green Mountains. They are the trail's equipment for use. They should be located at convenient distances so as to allow a comfortable day's walk between each. They should be equipped always for sleeping and certain of them for serving meals—after the fashion of the Swiss chalets. Strict regulation is essential to provide that equipment is used and not abused. As far as possible the blazing and constructing of the trail and building of camps should be done by volunteer workers. For volunteer "work" is really "play." The spirit of cooperation, as usual in such enterprises, should be stimulated throughout. The enterprise should, of course, be conducted without profit. The trail must be well guarded against—the yegg-man, and against the profiteer.

3. *Community Camps—*

These would grow naturally out of the shelter camps and inns. Each would consist of a little community on or near the trail (perhaps on a neighboring lake) where people could live in private domiciles. Such a community might occupy a substantial area—perhaps a hundred acres or more. This should be bought and owned as part of the project. No separate lots should be sold therefrom. Each camp should be a self-owning community and not a real estate venture. The use of the separate domiciles, like all other features, should be available without profit.

These community camps should be carefully planned in advance. They should not be allowed to become too populous and thereby defeat the very purpose for which they are created. Greater numbers should be accommodated by *more* communities not *larger* ones. There is room, without crowding, in the Appalachian region for a very large camping population. The location of these community camps would form a main part of the regional planning and architecture.

These communities would be used for various kinds of non-industrial activity. They might eventually be organized for special purposes—for recreation, for recuperation, and for study. Summer schools or seasonal field courses could be established and scientific travel courses organized and accommodated in the different communities along the trail. The community camp should become something more than a mere "playground"; it should stimulate every possible line of outdoor non-industrial endeavor.

4. *Food and Farm Camps—*

These might not be organized at first. They would come as a later development. The farm camp is the natural supplement of the community camp. Here in the same spirit of cooperation and well ordered action the food and crops consumed in the outdoor living would as far as practicable be sown and harvested.

Food and farm camps could be established as special communities in adjoining valleys. Or they might be combined with the community camps by the inclusion of surrounding farm lands. Their development would provide a tangible opportunity for working out by actual experiment a fundamental matter in the problem of living. It would provide one definite avenue of experiment in getting "back to the land." It would provide an opportunity for those anxious to settle down in the country; it would open up a possible source for new, and needed, employment. Communities of this type are illustrated by the Hudson Guild Farm in New Jersey.

Fuelwood, logs, and lumber are other basic needs of the camps and communities along the trail. These also might be grown and forested as part of the camp activity, rather than bought in the lumber market. The nucleus of such an enterprise has already been started at Camp Tamiment, Pennsylvania, on a lake not far from the proposed route of the Appalachian trail. This camp has been established by a labor group in New York City. They have erected a sawmill on their tract of 2000 acres and have built the bungalows of their community from their own timber.

Farm camps might ultimately be supplemented by permanent forest camps through the acquisition (or lease) of wood and timber tracts. These of course should be handled under a system of forestry so as to have a continuously growing crop of material. The object sought might be accomplished through long term timber sale contracts with the Federal Government on some of the Appalachian National Forests. Here would be another opportunity for permanent, steady, healthy employment in the open.

### Elements of Dramatic Appeal

The results achievable in the camp and scouting life are common knowledge to all who have passed the tenderfoot stage therein. The camp community is a sanctuary and a refuge from the scramble of every-day worldly commercial life. It is in essence a retreat from profit. Cooperation replaces antagonism, trust replaces suspicion, emulation replaces competition. An Appalachian trail, with its camps, communities, and spheres of influence along the skyline, should, with reasonably good management, accomplish these achievements. And they possess within them the elements of a deep dramatic appeal.

Indeed the lure of the scouting life can be made the most formidable enemy of the lure of militarism (a thing with which this country is menaced along with all others). It comes the nearest perhaps, of things thus far protected, to supplying what Professor James once called a "moral equivalent of war." It appeals to the primal instincts of a fighting heroism, of volunteer service and of work in a common cause.

These instincts are pent up forces in every human and they demand their outlet. This is the avowed object of the boy scout or girl scout movement, but it should not be limited to juveniles.

The building and protection of an Appalachian trail, with its various communities, interests, and possibilities, would form at least one outlet. Here is a job for 40,000 souls. This trail could be made to be, in a very literal sense, a battle line against fire and flood—and even against disease. Such battles—against the common enemies of man—still lack, it is true, the "punch" of man vs. man. There is but one reason—publicity. Militarism has been made colorful in a world of drab. But the care of the country side, which the scouting life instills, is vital in any real protection of "home and country." Already basic it can be made spectacular. Here is something to be dramatized.

# APPENDIX B

*The AT Work Trips of Myron Avery*

Frank Schairer and Albert Jackman cross the West Branch of the Penobscot River on their 1933 Maine AT scouting trip. Photo: Courtesy of Avery Collection, Maine State Library.

The following data, compiled by archivists for the state of Maine, presents the known work trips Myron Avery took to create the Appalachian Trail. Dates were compiled from correspondence between Avery and other interested parties, including officers of clubs, state and federal officials, and trip participants. The chart appears below in its original form from the Maine State Archives, with data edited only where necessary for clarity.

| Year | Section | Date | Work done/source |
|------|---------|------|------------------|
| 1933 | Katahdin to Blanchard, Maine | August 19–30, 1933 (12 working days, 2 work days lost due to rain) | Measured trail, placed markers. [Schairer, Jackman, Philbrick, and Greene joined Avery.] *Letter to Torrey, Comey, etc.* |
| 1934 | Blanchard to Bigelow Village, Maine | September 1–4, 1934 | *September 7, 1934, letter to R.M. Stubbs (MFS).* |
| 1936 | Pierce Pond to Blanchard | September 1–2, 1936 | Placed markers, checked data. |
| 1936 | Arnold Trail (Ledge House to junction with Dead River Route on Mt. Bigelow) | July 26, 1936 | Placed markers, checked data. |
| 1936 | Arnold Trail (Ledge House to Pierce Pond) | August 30, 1936 | Placed markers, checked data. |
| 1936 | Bigelow Village to Mt. Saddleback summit | October 31–November 1, 1936 | Measured trail, placed markers. *November 6, 1936, letter to J.W. Sewall* |
| 1935 | Summit of Mt. Saddleback to ME Highway 4 | November 9 and November 11, 1935 | Obtained trail data. *November 14, 1935, letter to J.W. Sewall.* |
| 1936 | ME Highway 4 to ME Highway 17 | July 27, 1936 | Measured trail, placed markers. *August 3, 1936, letter to J.W. Sewall.* |
| 1936 | ME Highway 5 to Andover B Hill Road | July 24, 1936 | Measured trail, placed markers. *August 3, 1936, letter to J.W. Sewall.* |
| 1936 | Andover B Hill Road to Grafton Notch | July 25, 1936 | Measured trail, placed markers. *August 3, 1936, letter to J.W. Sewall.* |

| Year | Section | Date | Work done/source |
|------|---------|------|------------------|
| 1936 | Relocation on Baldpate; to West Peak from Grafton Notch Forest Service Campground | August 28, 1936 | Placed markers, checked data. |
| 1935 | Grafton Notch (ME Highway 26) to South Bank, Androscoggin River (Gorham, New Hampshire) | August 10–11, 1935 | Placed markers over the 28-mile section. *August 16, 1935, letter to C.W. Blood.* |
| 1932 | South Bank, Androscoggin River (Gorham, New Hampshire) to AMC Madison Spring Hut (via Aqueduct Path and Osgood Trail) | September 15–16, 1932 | Marked trail from Pinkham Notch to Madison Spring Hut; markers put over entire section. *September 20, 1932, letter to R.C. Larrabee.* |
| 1930 | Madison Spring Hut to Crawford Notch (over the "Adamses," Jefferson and Clay). | July, 1930 | On A.M.C. Northern Range Walk with Myron Glaser. |
| 1932 | Crawford Notch to Franconia Notch | September 17–19, 1932 | Measured trail, placed markers. *September 20, 1932, letter to R.C. Larrabee.* |
| 1932 | Franconia Notch to Lyme-Dorchester Road | August 5–7, 1932 | Measured trail, placed markers. *August 9, 1932, letter to D.P. Hatch.* |
| 1932 | Lyme-Dorchester Road to Sherburne Pass | July 16–18, 1932 | Measured trail, placed markers. *July 20, 1932, letter to Willis Ross and A.C. Comey.* |

| Year | Section | Date | Work done/source |
|------|---------|------|------------------|
| 1934 | Sherburne Pass to Black Brook (Grout Job) on Arlington-East Arlington Road (70 miles) | June 22–24, 1934 | Notes of observations on trail condition. *July 9, 1934, letter to W.M. Fay, etc.* |
| 1934 | Black Brook (Grout Job) on Arlington-East Arlington Road to Bennington-Brattleboro Road (17 miles) | July 1, 1934 | [C.H. Warner of Fall River, MA, drove Avery to trail and picked him up at other end of 17-mile stretch.] *July 9, 1934, letter to W.M. Fay, etc.* |
| 1934 | Bennington-Brattleboro Road to Blackington, Massachusetts (17 miles) | July 29, 1934 | *July 9, 1934, letter to A.C. Comey.* |
| 1932 | Blackington, Massachusetts, to Jacob's Ladder Highway | May 21–22, 1934 | Measured trail. Accompanied by John B. Dickson. *May 27, 1932, letter to A.C. Comey.* |
| 1931 | Jacob's Ladder Highway to road at north base of Jug End (plus walked to June Mountain) | November, 1931 | Measured trail, placed markers. Accompanied by H.P. Sisk and W.P. Eaton. *December 1, 1931, letter to Partenheimer. December 4, 1931, letter to "Judge" Perkins.* |
| 1931 | Road at north base of Jug End to Bear Mountain (walked out via Alander Road) | November 8, 1931 | Measured trail. Accompanied by N.K. Anderson, Buck, Williamson, and Waite. *November 11, 1931, letter to H.P. Sisk.* |
| 1932 | Road at north base of Jug End to Lion's Head Road, Connecticut | December, 1932 | Remeasured trail. *January 3, 1933, letter to N.K. Anderson.* |

| Year | Section | Date | Work done/source |
|------|---------|------|------------------|
| 1932 | Lion's Head Road, Connecticut, to Prospect Mountain | February 6, 1932 | *N.K. Anderson (of Sherman, CT) record of trips.* |
| 1931 | Prospect Mountain to ridge above Cream Hill Pond | November 7, 1931 | *N.K. Anderson record of trips.* |
| 1933 | Webatuck to Kent, Connecticut, via NE trail over Mount Algo. Cornwall Hollow to base of ridge north of Cream Hill Pond. | November 12–13, 1933 | *N.K. Anderson record of trips,* plus *September 23, 1933, letter from N.K. Anderson.* |
| 1933 | Cornwall Hollow Road to Lion's Head Road (omitting from River Road to Barnam's in Amesville, 2.9 miles and .6 miles from junction of Willard's Trail and Connecticut Highway 199 to Undermountain Road, sections previously traveled on foot on November 7, 1931, and February 6, 1932) | December 23, 1933 | Hiked partly alone and partly with Ned Anderson. *N.K. Anderson's record of trips and trail data dated December 27, 1933. December, 27, 1933, letter to E.L. Heermance.* |
| 1934 | Connecticut Highway 199 (junction Indian Trail) to Clark's Hill over relocated trail | January 13, 1934 | *N.K. Anderson's record of trips.* |
| 1931 | Cornwall Hollow to Kent Falls, Connecticut | July 19, 1931 | Accompanied by Ned K. Anderson. *N.K. Anderson's record of trips.* |

| Year | Section | Date | Work done/source |
|------|---------|------|------------------|
| 1931 | Kent Falls, Connecticut, to Bear Mountain, New York | May 8–10, 1931 | Accompanied by Ned K. Anderson. *May 11, 1931, letter to Murray H. Stevens.* |
| 1930 | Bear Mountain Bridge, New York, to Arden, New York | October, 1930 | *October 9, 1930, letter to Major W.A. Welch.* |
| 1930 | Arden, New York, to Mount Peter Road, New York | October, 1930 | *October 24, 1930, letter to Major W.A. Welch.* *October 24, 1930, letter to "Judge" Perkins.* *December 1, 1930, letter to R.H. Torrey.* *December 4, 1930, letter to Murray Stevens.* |
| 1930 | Mount Peter Road (above Greenwood Lake) to Culvers Gap. (First day with Ridsdale Ellis to Vernon; continued solo to Unionville, then the next day to Culvers Gap.) | November 22–23, 1930 | *December 1, 1930, letter to R.H. Torrey.* [Avery returned in April 1933 to cover the 200 to 300 yards just south of highway on Mount Peter Road that was omitted on this trip.] |
| 1930 | Culvers Gap to Dunnfield Creek, New Jersey | December 13–14, 1930 | *December 17, 1930, letter to Major W.A. Welch.* [Hiked to Catfish Pond on first day with Arman; hiked second day to Dunnfield Creek with Torrey, Scheutz, and Ellis.] |
| 1932 | Road at mouth of Dunnfield Creek to Fox Gap, New Jersey | May 28, 1932 | Driven to Fox Gap by Mrs. Moore from Easton; met B.M.C. party (Zimmerman) at Dunnfield Creek. |
| 1932 | Fox Gap to Wind Gap, New Jersey | September, 1932 | Accompanied by Bingham and D.E. Husk. *July 27, 1932, letter from D.E. Husk.* |

| Year | Section | Date | Work done/source |
|------|---------|------|------------------|
| 1932 | Wind Gap to Smith Gap | August, 1932 | Hiked as far east from Smith Gap as transmission line with Bingham; returned May 29, 1932, and hiked from Wind Gap to the transmission line with R. Torrey and Louis Anderson. |
| 1933 | Smith Gap to Little Gap | July 23, 1933 | Accompanied by D.E. Husk. |
| 1932 | Little Gap to Lehigh Gap | 1932 | Accompanied by D.E. Husk and "former third officer of Ward Line." |
| 1931 | Beginning B.M.C. Trail in Lehigh Gap to Schuylkill Gap (on Bake Oven Knob B.M.E.C.C. trip) | October 10–11, 1931 | *October 15, 1931, letter to H.F. Rentschler.* |
| 1931 | Schuylkill Gap to Fredericksburg-Pine Grove Road | March, 1931 | *March 31, 1931, letter to Arthur Perkins.* |
| 1934 | Fredericksburg-Pine Grove Road to U.S. Route 11. | 1931 | Accompanied by Black and Runkle from Swatara Gap to Manada Gap. Returned May 28, 1932, to cover uncompleted mileage in Swatara Gap (on preceding day, went from U.S. Route 11 across Pennsylvania RR bridge to P.A.T.C. Trail at overview.) |
| 1934 | Manada Gap to U.S. Route 11 | July 8, 1934 | *July 10, 1934, letter to R. Torrey.* |

| Year | Section | Date | Work done/source |
|------|---------|------|------------------|
| 1931 | Overview, Pennsylvania to Lambs Gap | Winter, 1931 | Measured trail and painted blazes. Accompanied by J.M. Huffman (former Director of Pennsylvania Bureau of Parks) and F.R. Allaman of Harrisburg. |
| 1930 | Lambs Gap to Pennsylvania Highway 34 | Various occasions, 1930–1931 | Blazed and measured trail, marked trail (painted blazes). *December 23, 1930, letter to Norris.* [Also in April 1932, at time of Club trip on North Mountain, Avery returned to this section (from Brandtsville to Lambs Gap) to paint blazes and place mileage signs (numerals).] |
| 1931 | Gardner Trail on Piney Mountain to High Mountain Road | 1931 | Accompanied by Norris and Schairer. Measured and marked trail. |
| 1931 | Re-traveled from Pennsylvania Highway 34 to Pine Grove Furnace. (Had previously covered from Pine Grove Furnace to Hunters Run.) | September 30, 1931 | Checked trail data and marked trail. |

| Year | Section | Date | Work done/source |
|------|---------|------|------------------|
| 1930 | High Mountain Road to Penn-Mar State Park. | October 24–25, 1930 | Accompanied by J.F. Schairer, Bradley, Norris, etc. Obtained trail data and marked trail. *October 29, 1930, letter to Illick.* (Returned to cover from highway north of Corl's Ridge to Caledonia State Park as relocated by Norris.) |
| 1931– 1932 | Maryland (Penn-Mar to Harpers Ferry) | 1931–1932 | Obtained trail data and marked trail over many trips. (See second edition, *Guide to Paths in the Blue Ridge.*) |
| 1927– 1931 | Harpers Ferry to Rockfish Gap | 1927–1931 | Obtained trail data and marked trail over many trips. *July 28, 1930, letter to "Judge" Perkins.* (See second edition, *Guide to Paths in the Blue Ridge.*) |
| 1930 | Natural Bridge National Forest (from Sherando via Bald Mountain to Mons). | June 20–23, 1930 | Measured trail. *July 16, 1930, letter to Fitzgerald, Allen, and Garrett.* (See second edition, *Guide to Paths in the Blue Ridge.*) Returned on October 4, 1930, with Schairer, on October 4, 1932, with E.M. Wood, and December 6, 1932, with R.S. Freer to complete section. |

| Year | Section | Date | Work done/source |
|---|---|---|---|
| 1933 | Mons to Lee Highway (Cloverdale) | April 1, 1933 | Measured trail, wrote trail data for second edition, *Guide to Paths in the Blue Ridge*. Accompanied by Willis (of N.B.A.T.) for whole trip and from Fincastle Road with Dick and David. |
| 1933 | Lee Highway (Cloverdale) to Mason Cove | April 2, 1933 | Measured trail, wrote trail data for second edition, *Guide to Paths in the Blue Ridge*. Accompanied by Dick, McGinnis, Pownell, etc. of P.A.T.C. |
| 1933 | Mason Cove to U.S. Route 121 | April 29–30, 1933 | Measured trail, wrote trail data for second edition, *Guide to Paths in the Blue Ridge*. Accompanied by Robinson, Dick, McGinnis, and Pownell. |
| 1933 | U.S. Route 121 to Virginia Highway 23 | June 24–25, 1933 | Measured trail, wrote trail data for second edition, *Guide to Paths in the Blue Ridge*. Accompanied by Pownell, Dick, McGinnis, and Gates. |
| 1931 | Virginia Highway 23 over Rocky Knob to Ridge Road | December 31, 1931 | Measured and marked trail, wrote trail data for second edition, *Guide to Paths in the Blue Ridge*. Accompanied by S.L. Cole. |

| Year | Section | Date | Work done/source |
|------|---------|------|------------------|
| 1933 | Ridge Road to U.S. Route 58 | July 1, 1933 | Measured and marked trail, wrote trail data for second edition, *Guide to Paths in the Blue Ridge*. Accompanied by Charles Matthews. |
| 1933 | U.S. Route 58 to Galax, Virginia | February, 1933 | Measured and marked trail, wrote trail data for second edition, *Guide to Paths in the Blue Ridge*. Accompanied by E.M. Wood. |
| 1932 | Galax to Tennessee Highway 34 | May, 1932 | Measured and marked trail, wrote trail data for second edition, *Guide to Paths in the Blue Ridge*. Accompanied by C.S. Jackson (1 day) and Steve Comer (½ day). *May 13, 1932, letter to C.S. Jackson.* |
| 1932 | Tennessee Highway 34 to Mt. Guyot (except section from Nochilucky River to Devils Fork Gap) | August and September, 1932 | Measured trail *(some data printed in April and July 1933 P.A.T.C. newsletters.)* Accompanied by E.M. Wood. |
| 1933 | Nochilucky River to Devils Fork Gap | August 5–6, 1933 | Measured trail, obtained data. Accompanied by Marcus Book and Roger V. Morrow. |
| 1930 | Mt. Guyot to Newfound Gap | August, 1930 | Accompanied by P.M. Fink and W.S. Diehl. See *Appalachia* December 1930, pages 198–199. |

| Year | Section | Date | Work done/source |
|---|---|---|---|
| 1935 | Newfound Gap to Deals Gap (39.5 miles) | July 4–6, 1935 | Measured trail and obtained data. Accompanied by C.C. Campbell, A. Guy Frizzell, A.G. Roth, A.H. Jackman, and O.W. Crowder. *July 12, 1935, letter to Superintendent Eakin, Great Smoky Mountains National Park.* |
| 1933 | Newfound Gap to trail from North Carolina Highway 10 to Wesser Bald | May 27–29, 1933 | Measured trail and obtained data. Accompanied by Roth, Campbell, and Frizzell. |
| 1931 | Trail to Wesser Bald and North Carolina Highway 10 to Mount Oglethorpe | June 3–10, 1931 | Accompanied by Warner Hall and other members of the Georgia A.M.C. for 5 days, hiked solo for 3 days. *June 20, 1931, letter to regional forester Kircher.* See "Along the Appalachian Trail in the Georgia Blue Ridge," *Appalachia*, December 1931, pages 491–495. |
| 1937 | North Carolina–Tennessee. Relocation—0.5 mile west of Newfound Gap to junction with old AT. | July 2, 1937 | Measured relocation. |
| 1937 | North Carolina–Tennessee. Newfound Gap to Big Pigeon River. | July 3–5, 1937 | Checked trail data. Installed mile markers (except miles 15 to 19). |

| Year | Section | Date | Work done/source |
|------|---------|------|------------------|
| 1937 | North Carolina. Big Pigeon River (west bank) to Max Patch Road (partly over new trail). Big Pigeon to Snowbird; Browns Gap to summit west. | July 5, 1937 | Checked trail data. Installed mile markers. |
| 1937 | North Carolina. Rich Mountain west to junction of Round Top Trail with old AT. | July 6, 1937 | Obtained trail data. |
| 1937 | Massachusetts. Kitchen Brook Lean-to over Mount Greylock to Blackington. (11 miles.) | July 17, 1937 | Obtained trail data on relocation. |
| 1937 | Massachusetts. From point 3.3 miles from Tyringham to Massachusetts Highway 17 (6.7 miles.) | July 18, 1937 | Obtained trail data on relocation. |
| 1938 | Connecticut. From foot of St. Johns Ledges (section 2, N. to S.) via River Road to Cathedral Pines | June 27, 1938 | Obtained trail data. |
| 1938 | Cathedral Pines to Bunker Hill Road (Connecticut Highway 4 to Connecticut Highway 43) | July 12, 1938 | Obtained trail data. |

| Year | Section | Date | Work done/source |
|------|---------|------|------------------|
| 1938 | Relocation from West Yelping Hill Road to Cream Hill Pond Ridge | July 12, 1938 | Obtained trail data. |
| 1938 | North Carolina. Hot Springs to Lemon Gap (Max Patch Road). | July 2, 1938 | Obtained trail data (south to north). |
| 1938 | North Carolina. Max Patch to Waterville. (Completion of covering new trail partly covered July 5, 1937.) | July 3, 1938 | Obtained trail data. |
| 1938 | North Carolina–Georgia. Wallace Gap to North Carolina/Georgia line. | July 4–5, 1938 | Obtained trail data (both directions). |
| 1938 | Maine. Relocation from 3 mile marker (from Maine Highway 4) to Sabbath Day Pond Lean-to. | July 23, 1938 | Obtained trail data. Accompanied by W.H. Sawyer and Gordon Hunt. |
| 1938 | Maine. Section 21, Maine Highway 5 to Andover B Hill Road. | July 23–24, 1938 | Obtained trail data. Accompanied by W.H. Sawyer. |

# APPENDIX C

*Key Milestones in the Development of the Appalachian Trail*

Information compiled from *Guide to the Appalachian Trail in Maine, Publication No. 4*, Fourth Edition (with 1947, 1949, and 1950 Supplements). Compiled by Myron H. Avery. The Appalachian Trail Conference, Washington, D.C., 1942.

1921      Benton MacKaye proposes the Appalachian Trail (AT) in the article "An Appalachian Trail: A Project in Regional Planning" in the *Journal of the American Institute of Architects.*

1922      The first part of the AT is constructed in the Bear Mountain section of the Palisades Interstate Park by clubs affiliated with what would later become the New York–New Jersey Trail Conference.

1922–25      Interest in the undertaking spreads to New England and Pennsylvania, but enthusiasm fades before much actual work is done.

1926      Arthur "Judge" Perkins, a retired lawyer from Hartford, Connecticut, undertakes the job of translating the concept of an endless trail into an actual one. He engages groups in "cutting the footpath through the wilderness which had been discussed for the past five years."

1926–37      The AT is established as a continuous footpath from Georgia to Maine.

1936      The Maine section of the AT is nearly completed. Between 1933 and 1936, 265 miles are built. A 2-mile gap remains between Sugarloaf and Spaulding mountains.

1937      The Eighth Appalachian Trail Conference is held in Great Smoky Mountains National Park. Conference member Edward B. Ballard proposes the concept of an "Appalachian Trailway" protective zone on either side of the AT "to assure the perpetuation and protection of the Appalachian Trail."

1938    The National Park Service (NPS) and the United States Forest
        Service (USFS) sign an agreement to promote the Appalachian
        Trailway. The states through which the trail passes enter into a
        similar form of agreement with the ATC and NPS.

The following description appeared in the first *Guide to the Appalachian Trail in Maine*, written by Myron H. Avery.

### The AT in Maine

The Maine section of the Appalachian Trail was the last unit, both to be undertaken and to be completed. By reason of the fact that the Trail route here leads through an utter wilderness and the absence of any of the outing or mountaineering clubs which have sponsored the construction of other sections of the Trail, it was, at one time, thought it would be necessary to abandon the original project of having the Trail begin or terminate—according to one's point of view—at Katahdin and establish the northern terminus at Mt. Washington in the White Mountains of New Hampshire. However, before abandoning, as a part of the Trail route, this unequaled area of Maine wilderness, a very comprehensive study of a possible Trail route was undertaken. In 1933, after a two-year survey of existing routes, a feasible location was developed, utilizing existing tote-roads and trails and constructing the necessary connecting links. . . . The route selected includes the finest of Maine's mountains, lakes, streams and forest. A unique feature is the location of the Trail so as to provide accommodations, at the end of a moderate day's journey, at attractively situated sporting camps. In addition, a chain of lean-tos is being developed along the route of the Trail.

#### 1933
Walter D. Greene "almost single-handed" opened the route over the Barren–Chairback Range and marked the Trail from Blanchard to Pleasant River.

*1933*

Walter Greene, Myron Avery, J.F. Schairer, S.S. Philbrick and A.H. Jackman mark 77 miles of trail from Katahdin to Pleasant River.

*1933*

S.S. Philbrick, Elwood Lord, Chief Fire Warden Ralph Sterling, George Martin, Viles Wing and Herbert Blackwell mark trail from Blanchard to Bigelow.

*1933*

J.M. Harris and sons cut trail from Troutdale to Joe's Hole.

*1933*

Helon Taylor cuts Bigelow Range Trail.

*1934*

Helon Taylor cuts trail from Bigelow to Sugarloaf.

*1934*

Walter Greene cuts side trails to Joe Mary Mountain and Gulf Hagas.

*1934*

W.H. Sawyer and Bates Outing Club scout trail between Grafton Notch and Saddleback Mountain.

*1935*

CCC Forester James W. Sewall suggests that the AT in Maine be adopted as a project by the CCC and gains the support of the US Forest Service to do so. Over the next three years, crews from Millinocket, Greenville, Flagstaff and Rangeley materially improve the trail in most locations. The crews also build a new 27-mile section between Saddleback Mountain and the Andover–South Arm Road and build fourteen new lean-tos along the length of the Maine Trail.

### 1937

On August 14, 1937, the CCC completed the final two miles of Appalachian Trail in Maine (and from Maine to Georgia) on the north slope of Spaulding Mountain.

### 1938

The Bridgton CCC camp builds four lean-tos (Spaulding Mountain, Jerome Brook, East Carry Pond and Pierce Pond). The Greenville CCC camp builds a lean-to on the east slope of Moxie Bald Mountain.

### 1939

U.S. Forest Service crews and Jefferson CCC camp clear the trail from Maine Highway 16 to the New Hampshire state line—sections heavily damaged by the hurricane of September 1938.

### 1940

Bridgton CCC crew cleans up 1938 hurricane damage between Mount Bigelow and the Kennebec River.

# BIBLIOGRAPHY

## Books

Anderson, Larry. *Benton MacKaye: Conservationist, Planner, and Creator of the Appalachian Trail*. Baltimore: Johns Hopkins University Press, 2002.

Beveridge, Charles E., and Carolyn F. Hoffman, eds., *The Papers of Frederick Law Olmsted: Writings on Public Parks, Parkways, and Park Systems, Supplementary Series*, Volume I. Baltimore and London: Johns Hopkins University Press, 1997.

Curtis, Wayne. *The Last Great Walk: The True Story of a 1909 Walk from New York to San Francisco and Why it Matters*. Emmaus, Pennsylvania: Rodale Books, 2014.

Dalbey, Matthew. *Regional Visionaries and Metropolitan Boosters: Decentralization, Regional Planning, and Parkways During the Interwar Years*. Dordrecht, Netherlands: Springer Science + Business Media, 2002.

Easterling, Keller. *Organization Space: Landscapes, Highways, and Houses in America*. Cambridge: Massachusetts Institute of Technology, 1999.

Harvard University Alumni, *The Harvard Forest 1907–1934. A Memorial to its First Director Richard Thornton Fisher*. Cornwall, NY: The Cornwall Press, Inc., 1935.

Kilbourne, Frederick W. *Chronicles of the White Mountains*. Boston: Houghton Mifflin Company, 1916.

Lawson, Russell M. *Passaconaway's Realm: Captain John Evans and the Exploration of Mount Washington*. Hanover and London: University Press of New England, 2002.

Leonard, John William, ed. *Woman's Who's Who of America: A Biographical Dictionary of Contemporary Women of the United States and Canada 1914–1915*. New York: The American Commonwealth Company, 1914.

MacKaye, Benton. *Expedition Nine: A Return to a Region.* Washington, D.C.: The Wilderness Society, 1969.

MacKaye, James. *The Economy of Happiness.* Boston: Little, Brown & Co., 1906.

*Maine Data Book, 1930.* Augusta: State of Maine, 1931.

Pinchot, Gifford. *Breaking New Ground.* Washington, D.C.: Island Press, 1998.

Sarnacki, Aislinn. *Family Friendly Hikes in Maine.* Camden: Down East Books, 2017.

Scheuering, Rachel White. *Shapers of the Great Debate on Conservation: A Biographical Dictionary,* vol. 4, *Shapers of the Great American Debates,* ed. Peter B. Levy. Westport, Connecticut: Greenwood Press, 2004.

Shaffer, Marguerite. "Negotiating National Identity: Western Tourism and 'See America First.'" In *Reopening the American West,* ed. Hal K. Rothman. Tucson: University of Arizona Press, 1998.

Steffens, Lincoln. *Autobiography of Lincoln Steffens.* New York: Harcourt, Brace and Company, 1931.

## Periodicals and Public Records

Abbott, M.F. "The Latest in Alaska: Controller Bay and Its Control of the Alaska Situation," *Collier's Weekly,* May 6, 1911, 19.

Anderson, Larry. "A Classic of the Green Mountains: Benton MacKaye's 1900 Hike Inspires Appalachian Trail," *hut2hut* (blog), October 6, 2015, hut2hut.info/a-classic-of-the-green-mountains/.

Chamberlain, Allen. "Reports of the Councilors for the Autumn of 1907: Exploration and Forestry," *Appalachia* 12 (July 1909): 81–85.

Ganoe, John T. "Some Constitutional and Political Aspects of the Ballinger–Pinchot Controversy," *The Pacific Historical Review* 3, no. 3 (September 1934): 323.

Graves, Henry S. "Road Building in the National Forests," *The American City* 16, no. 1 (1916): 4.

Horan, John F. Jr., "Will Carson and the Virginia Conservation Commission, 1926–1934," *The Virginia Magazine of History and Biography* 92, no. 4 (October 1984): 395.

Lippmann, Walter. "All the MacKayes," *The International* 3, no. 2 (January 1911): 29.

MacKaye, Benton. "An Appalachian Trail: A Project in Regional Planning," *Journal of the American Institute of Architects* 9, no. 10 (October 1921): 326.

MacKaye, Benton. "Flankline vs. Skyline," *Appalachia* 20 (1934): 104–108.

MacKaye, Benton. "Memorandum on Regional Planning" (1921), 19–25. Papers of the MacKaye Family, Rauner Special Collections Library, Dartmouth College.

MacKaye, Benton. "New York a National Peril," *Saturday Review of Literature*, August 23, 1930, 68.

MacKaye, Benton. "Our White Mountain Trip: Its Organization and Methods," logbook of Camp Moosilauke (Wentworth, NH: 1904).

MacKaye, Percy. "Steele MacKaye, Dynamic Artist of the American Theatre; an Outline of His Life Work," *The Drama: A Quarterly Review of Dramatic Literature*, no. 4 (November 1911): 138–161.

Mather, Stephen. "Report of the Director of the National Park Service to the Secretary of the Interior for the Fiscal Year Ended June 30, 1923 and the Travel Season, 1923," (Washington, DC: Government Printing Office, 1923) 10–11.

Pinchot, Gifford. *The Use of the National Forest Reserves: Regulations and Instructions* (Washington, DC: U. S. Department of Agriculture, Forest Service, 1905), 10.

Pinchot, Gifford. *Hetch Hetchy Dam Site: Hearings on H.R. 6281, Day 1, Before the Committee on the Public Lands, House of Representatives*, 63rd Cong. 1 (25–28 June 1913; 7 July 1913).

Riley, Andrew. "Timber, Shotgun, Boot, and Ski: Traditional Meets Modern at Gorman Chairback Lodge and Cabins," *Appalachia* 62, no. 2 (Summer/Fall, 2012): 56–71.

Rubin, Robert A. "The Short, Brilliant Life of Myron Avery," special issue, *Appalachian Trailway News, Trail Years: A History of the Appalachian Trail Conference*, (July 2000).

Stallings, Constance S. "Benton MacKaye's Last Interview," *Backpacker* 4, no. 2, (April 1976): 55.

Stein, Clarence S. *Report of the Commission of Housing and Regional Planning to Governor Alfred E. Smith and to the Legislature of the State of New York* (Albany, NY: J. B. Lyon Company Printers, 1925).

Silverstein, Hannah. "No Parking: Vermont Rejects the Green Mountain Parkway," *Vermont History* 63, no. 3. (Summer 1995): 148.

Small, Albion W., review of *The Economy of Happiness*, by James MacKaye. *The American Journal of Sociology* 12, no. 4 (January 1907): 567.

Taft, President William Howard. *Chugach National Forest Lands in Alaska: Message from the President of the United States Transmitting in Response to a Senate Resolution of June 27, 1911, All Papers and Information Relating to the Elimination from the Chugach National Forest of Certain Lands Fronting Upon Controller Bay in Alaska*, 62nd Cong., 1d Sess., S. Doc. No. 77, (Washington, DC: U.S. Senate, July 26, 1911), 14.

Williams, Gerald W., Ph.D., *The USDA Forest Service—The First Century* (Washington, DC: U.S. Department of Agriculture, 2005), 17, 14.

Zerkel, Ferdinand, to Arno Cammerer, 14 February 1931, Zerkel Papers, Shenandoah National Park Archives.

### Periodicals and Public Records (works without author)

*Appalachia* 1, no. 1. (June 1876).

*Appalachia* 14, no. 1. (December 1916).

"Ascent of Mt. Carrigain." *The Portland Transcript*. (September 13, 1873).

"Ex-Governor Baxter Joins Appalachian Trail Hikers 120-Mile Trek," Appalachian Mountain Club press release, September 1, 1935, Avery Collection, Maine State Library Special Collections.

"Final Report of the Southern Appalachian National Park Commission to the Secretary of the Interior," (Washington, DC: Government Printing Office, 1931), 1.

House Reports, vol. 6129, Report 178, 62nd Cong., 2d sess., December 4, 1911–August 26, 1912 (Washington, DC: Government Printing Office, 1912), 2.

"Mrs. MacKaye Gone, Threatened Suicide," *The New York Times* (April 19, 1921).

"Myron H. Avery," *Appalachian Trailway News* 13, no. 3 (September 1952).

*National Park Service Recreational Development Report*, 1934.

"Pan-American Road Congress Convenes at Oakland: Chief Forester of United States Tells Delegates How Government is Opening National Forests to Motorists," *Motor Age* 28, no. 12 (September 1915): 18.

"Records of the National Park Service [NPS], Record Group 79," *National Archives*, archives.gov/research/guide-fed-records/groups/079.html.

"Senate Document Number 6," *Journal of the Senate of the Commonwealth of Virginia* (March 13, 1926): 843–844.

"State Library to Publish Pamphlet on Mt. Katahdin," *Bangor Commercial*, August 20, 1926. Avery Collection, Maine State Library Special Collections.

"Synopsis of the Ballinger–Pinchot Affair," Louis D. Brandeis School of Law Library, louisville.edu/law/library/special-collections/the-louis-d.-brandeis-collection/synopsis-of-the-ballinger-pinchot-affair.

"Tearing Down the Spectatorium," *Chicago Tribune* (October 7, 1893).

*The American Forestry Bulletin—No. 3, The Weeks Bill*, H.R. 11798, 61st Cong., 1d Sess., (July 23, 1909), 2–3.

"The Appalachian Forests Putting the New Law Into Operation," *American Forestry* 17 (March 1911): 290–293.

"The Passage of the Appalachian Bill," *American Forestry* 17 (March 1911): 164–170.

## Internet Sources

"AMC and the Weeks Act," last modified February 9, 2011, outdoors.org/articles/amc-outdoors/allen-chamberlain-weeks-act/.

"Arthur Coleman Comey," *The Cultural Landscape Foundation*, tclf.org/pioneer/arthur-coleman-comey.

"Bronx River Parkway," *New York City Department of Parks & Recreation,* nycgovparks.org/parks/bronx-river-parkway/history.

"CPI Inflation Calculator," *U.S. Bureau of Labor Statistics,* data.bls.gov/cgi-bin/cpicalc.pl?cost1=75.00&year1=193301&year2=201701.

"Gifford Pinchot," Forest History Society, foresthistory.org/ASPNET/People/Pinchot/Pinchot.aspx.

Mangrum, Richard A. "Steele MacKaye: Inventor–Innovator" (master's thesis, University of North Texas, December 1970), 20, digital.library.unt.edu/ark:/67531/metadc131337/.

Pasha, Ronald. "Myron Avery, Lubec, and the Appalachian Trail," *Lubec Historical Society,* lubec.mainememory.net/page/1197/display.html.

Pinchot, Gifford. "Forestry as a Profession: Opportunities for College Graduates in Forestry as a Life Work," *The Crimson,* March 3, 1900, thecrimson.com/article/1900/3/3/forestry-as-a-profession-pmr-gifford/.

"The Age of the Automobile," *U.S. History Online Textbook,* ushistory.org/us/46a.asp.

## Letters, Diaries, and Other Handwritten Materials

The Papers of the MacKaye Family are housed in the Rauner Special Collections Library at Dartmouth College. Myron Avery's correspondence is housed in the Avery Collection at the Maine State Library Special Collections. Both were significant sources for this book. A few materials were also found at the George J. Mitchell Department of Special Collections & Archives, Bowdoin College. The footnotes cite specific source materials.

# INDEX

# ABOUT THE AUTHOR

Maine-based author, speaker, and photographer Jeffrey Ryan has a contagious passion for exploring the outdoors, particularly on foot. Jeff has hiked thousands of miles, including his first "trip of a lifetime," a six-month hike on the Pacific Crest Trail. In 1985, he began section-hiking the Appalachian Trail with a childhood friend (a journey that took nearly three decades to complete and inspired his first book, *Appalachian Odyssey: A 28-Year Hike on America's Trail*, Down East Books, 2016). His AT experiences inspired him to learn about the dynamic relationship between Benton MacKaye and Myron Avery that culminated in the creation and completion of this legendary trail.

# APPALACHIAN MOUNTAIN CLUB

At AMC, connecting you to the freedom and exhilaration of the outdoors is our calling. We help people of all ages and abilities to explore and develop a deep appreciation of the natural world.

AMC helps you get outdoors on your own, with family and friends, and through activities close to home and beyond. With chapters from Maine to Washington, D.C., including groups in Boston, New York City, and Philadelphia, you can enjoy activities like hiking, paddling, cycling, and skiing, and learn new outdoor skills. We offer advice, guidebooks, maps, and unique lodges and huts to inspire your next outing. You will also have the opportunity to support conservation advocacy and research, youth programming, and caring for 1,800 miles of trails.

**We invite you to join us in the outdoors.**

## YOUR CONNECTION TO THE OUTDOORS

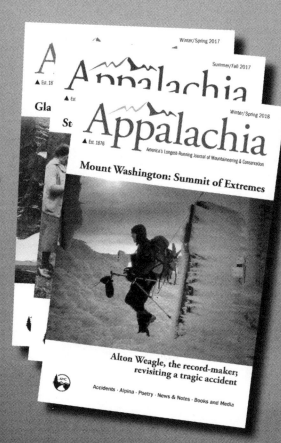

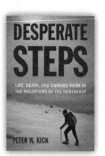